Political Science Research Methods
Exploring America at a Crossroads

Political Science Research Methods
Exploring America at a Crossroads

Cal Clark
Auburn University, USA

Augsburg College
Lindell Library
Minneapolis, MN 55454

NEW JERSEY · LONDON · SINGAPORE · BEIJING · SHANGHAI · HONG KONG · TAIPEI · CHENNAI

Published by

World Scientific Publishing Co. Pte. Ltd.
5 Toh Tuck Link, Singapore 596224
USA office: 27 Warren Street, Suite 401-402, Hackensack, NJ 07601
UK office: 57 Shelton Street, Covent Garden, London WC2H 9HE

Library of Congress Cataloging-in-Publication Data
Clark, Cal, 1945–

   pages cm
   ISBN 978-9814460439 (hardcover : alk. paper)
   1. United States--Politics and government--Research. 2. Political science--Research
Methodology. 3. Social sciences--Research--Methodology. I. Title.
   JA88.U6C535 2013
   320.973072--dc23

                                                2013000715

British Library Cataloguing-in-Publication Data
A catalogue record for this book is available from the British Library.

Credit for Cover
Photo of US Senator Barack Obama at Change We Need Presidential Rally October 30, 2008, at Verizon Wireless Virginia Beach Amphitheater in Virginia Beach, VA

Credit: Spirit of America/Shutterstock

Photo of Former Massachusetts Governor Mitt Romney at a town hall meeting on June 4, 2010 in Mesa, Arizona

Credit: Christopher Halloran/Shutterstock

Copyright © 2014 by World Scientific Publishing Co. Pte. Ltd.

All rights reserved. This book, or parts thereof, may not be reproduced in any form or by any means, electronic or mechanical, including photocopying, recording or any information storage and retrieval system now known or to be invented, without written permission from the Publisher.

For photocopying of material in this volume, please pay a copying fee through the Copyright Clearance Center, Inc., 222 Rosewood Drive, Danvers, MA 01923, USA. In this case permission to photocopy is not required from the publisher.

In-house Editor: Monica Lesmana

Typeset by Stallion Press
Email: enquiries@stallionpress.com

To the many students in my research methods classes over the years who have evidently derived some laughs and pleasures from them despite all the numbers.

About the Author

Cal Clark is an Emeritus Alumni Professor of Political Science and Director of the MPA Program at Auburn University in the United States who received his Ph.D. from the University of Illinois. He has the authored and edited over 20 books and over 250 journal articles and book chapters. His books include the co-authored *Taiwan's Political Economy* (2012) and *Comparative Development Patterns in Asia* (1997); the edited *The Changing Dynamics of the Relations among China, Taiwan, and the United States* (2011); and the co-edited *Beyond the Developmental State* (1998) and *Institutions and Gender Empowerment in the Global Economy* (World Scientific, 2008). In 2012, he received the Student Government Association's award for the Outstanding Graduate Faculty member at Auburn University.

Preface

The principal goal of this text is to provide clear and elementary descriptions of the major statistical techniques used in political and social science research. The book is built on two basic assumptions. First, I believe it is possible to explain social science statistics in a simple and straightforward manner so that students with a minimal background in mathematics can understand even fairly advanced techniques, such as multiple or even logistic regression. Second, I have found in teaching research methods courses that undergraduate and even graduate students have less trouble in understanding specific techniques than in interpreting what statistical results mean substantively. Consequently, the book stresses the interpretation of research findings. In essence, the book argues that political science research is like piecing a jigsaw puzzle together. Pieces of information — statistical and nonstatistical — must be assembled and interpreted both logically and creatively.

The text is organized in a manner which, so far as I am aware, is unique. This is that it uses the various techniques being discussed to analyze the current state of the United States as it seemingly stands at a crossroads in both its political orientations and socioeconomic nature. Thus, to make the statistical interpretation more meaningful and easier to understand, the results throughout the book are integrated by their focus upon two central questions related to the theme of *America at a Crossroads*: Are Americans conservative or liberal in their political beliefs? How do economic and social outcomes in America compare to those in other developed democracies?

I have many debts that I am very happy and grateful to acknowledge. First, Monica Lesmana, my editor at World Scientific, has been extremely supportive and encouraging during the development of this project. Second, the many students in my methods classes who over the years have shared both their satisfactions and frustrations with me deserve a significant part of the credit and none of the blame for whatever the reader finds good, bad, or ugly in the following pages. Third, I would specifically like to thank Ms. Christy Tanner, who took a graduate seminar in research methods from me, served as my Teaching Assistant in an undergraduate methods course, and reviewed this entire text for me. Last but far from least, I want to thank my wife Janet (a Professor of political science, too) for all her support and understanding, both intellectual and personal, during my work on this project.

Contents

About the Author   vii
Preface   ix
Foreword for Faculty   xvii

Chapter 1.   Research as Puzzle Solving   1
     1.1   America at a Crossroads: Two Jigsaws   1
     1.2   Plan of the Book   11
     Exercises   12

Chapter 2.   Introducing Our Data   15
     2.1   Frequency Distributions: Are Americans Conservative or Liberal?   15
     2.2   Data Arrays and Graphs: How Does the U.S. Compare to Other Developed Nations?   28
     Exercises   39

Part I. Designing Research Projects   41

Chapter 3.   The Logic of Inquiry and Research Design   43
     3.1   Concepts and Indicators in Quantitative Research   44
     3.2   Reliability and Validity   48

	3.3	Characteristics of Empirical Theory	53
	3.4	Constructing Explanatory Theories	57
	3.5	Deriving Two Simple Theories	64
	Exercises		67
Chapter 4.	Approaches to the Study of Politics		69
	4.1	Types of Political Analysis	70
	4.2	Changing Fashions or Paradigms in Political Studies	72
	4.3	Alternative Strategies for Showing a Relationship	81
	Exercises		94
Chapter 5.	The Relationship of Qualitative Approaches to Quantitative Analysis		95
	5.1	Qualitative Approaches to Political Studies	96
	5.2	Content Analysis: Attaching Numbers to Qualitative Materials	106
	Exercises		118

Part II. The Foundations for Statistical Analysis   119

Chapter 6.	Some More Complex Issues in Interpreting Data		121
	6.1	The Dangers of Distortion	121
	6.2	Why Simple Percentages Are Not Always So Simple	132
	6.3	Different Scales or Levels of Measurement	137
	Exercises		142
Chapter 7.	Summary Statistics for an Entire Distribution: Moving Beyond Data Arrays and Graphs		145

	7.1	Measures of Central Tendency	146
	7.2	Measures of Variability	153
	7.3	Types of Distributions	158
		Exercises	166

Chapter 8. An Introduction to Inferential Statistics — 169

	8.1	Sampling	171
	8.2	The Sampling Distribution	181
	8.3	Two Applications of the Sampling Distribution	188
		Exercises	195

Part III. Discovering Relationships for Nominal and Ordinal Data — 197

Chapter 9. Crosstabulation: Why Do Americans Vote Democratic or Republican? — 199

	9.1	Crosstabulation Tables: The Basics	200
	9.2	Testing the Socioeconomic Model of Voting	209
		Exercises	217

Chapter 10. Multivariate Tables: More Nuanced Explanations for Conservative Attitudes and Behavior — 219

	10.1	Multivariate Tables: The Technique	220
	10.2	Revealing and Replicating Relationships	223
	10.3	Removing and Reducing Relationships	228
	10.4	An Overview of the Effects of Multivariate Tables	233
		Exercises	236

Part IV. Discovering Relationships for Interval Data 239

Chapter 11. Regression Analysis: International Patterns and Benchmarks for American Performance 241

    11.1 Scatterplots and Regression Analysis: The Basics 243
    11.2 A Closer Look at the Conservative and Liberal Hypotheses Regarding Government Size and National Performance 252
    11.3 Using Regression Analysis for Benchmarking 258
    11.4 Assumptions of Regression Analysis 261
    Exercises 268

Chapter 12. Multiple Regression and Path Analysis: More Complex Models of the Policy Process 271

    12.1 The Basics in Multiple Regression Analysis 272
    12.2 Using Multiple Regression to Test the Conservative and Liberal Hypotheses About the Effects of Government Activism 276
    12.3 Assumptions of Multiple Regression 281
    12.4 Path Analysis and Causal Modeling 285
    Exercises 298

Chapter 13. Logistic Regression: Developing More Complete Models of Partisanship 301

    13.1 Crosstabs, Simple Regression, and Logit as Alternatives for Explaining a Dichotomous Variable 302
    13.2 Logistic Regression: The Basic Results . . . 309
    13.3 More Complex Logit Results: Creating Models of How Issues Shape Voting 317
    Exercises 328

Conclusion   329

Chapter 14. The Joy and Challenge of the Jigsaw Puzzles
in Political Research   331

     14.1   How Our Quantitative Research Relates
to the Paradigms in Political Studies   332
     14.2   Expanding the Response to the Research
Questions Motivating Quantitative
Analysis 335
     14.3   The Joy and Challenge of the Jigsaw Puzzles
in Political Research 338
     Exercises 340

Index   341

Foreword for Faculty

The organization of this textbook reflects three basic principles. First, a central goal is to give students the ability to understand the statistical analysis used by political scientists. The book seeks to do this by first describing a technique, such as bar graphs or regression analysis, in some detail and then providing several substantive illustrations of how results produced by the technique are analyzed and interpreted. Second, to make the statistical interpretation more meaningful and easier to understand, the results throughout the book are integrated by their focus upon two central questions related to the theme of *America at a Crossroads*: Are Americans conservative or liberal in their political beliefs? How do economic and social outcomes in America compare to those in other developed democracies? Finally, the book recognizes that courses on Political Science Research Methods are taught in a variety of ways. Thus, it has been explicitly designed to be compatible with two different approaches:

1. Those that emphasize a basic understanding of the research process and how to present the distribution of a single variable and measure the association between two items; and
2. those that cover more advanced techniques, such as multiple regression or logistic regression.

DIFFERENT STRATEGIES FOR USING THESE MATERIALS

A course on research methods in Political Science can be taught in a variety of ways; and this text has been designed to be compatible with several approaches. The principal goal of the text is to show students how to understand and interpret quantitative research in Political Science, including crosstabulation and regression but not the more advanced multivariate analyses. This presumably forms the core of most research methods classes. Part I in Figure 1 summarizes the chapters that present these materials. Chapters 1 and 2 introduce students to the text's major themes, research questions, and data sets; and Chapters 3 and 4 describe concepts and theories in political science and differing approaches to doing research. Three chapters then provide a foundation for more advanced statistical analysis. Chapter 6 raises some more complex issues in interpreting data; the first part of Chapter 7 discusses measures of central tendency; and Chapter 8 is an introduction to inferential statistics. Finally, Chapter 9 describes crosstabulation; and Chapter 11 covers simple regression.

I. Basic Overview of the Research Process and Statistical Analysis

Chapter 1, Introduction, ENTIRE
Chapter 2, Data, ENTIRE
Chapter 3, Concepts and Theories, ENTIRE
Chapter 4, Approaches, ENTIRE
Chapter 6, Data Complexity, ENTIRE
Chapter 7, Summary Statistics, CENTRAL TENDENCY
Chapter 8, Inductive Statistics, ENTIRE
Chapter 9, Crosstabs, ENTIRE
Chapter 11, Regression, ENTIRE

II. Advanced Statistics

Chapter 10, Multivariate Tables, ENTIRE
Chapter 12, Multiple Regression, ENTIRE
Chapter 13, Logistic Regression, ENTIRE

III. Supplement to Basic Materials

Chapter 5, Qualitative Analysis, ENTIRE
Chapter 7, Summary Statistics, VARIABILITY & DISTRIBUTIONS
Chapter 14, Conclusion, ENTIRE

Figure 1: How the text materials fit into different instructional emphases.

This "core" can be covered in well less than a semester. Thus, as summarized in Parts II and III of Figure 1, several options are provided for adding other topics about research methods. One option in Part II of the table is to include more sophisticated statistical analysis. Chapter 10 covers multivariate tables; Chapter 12 multiple regression; and Chapter 13 logistic regression. Finally, Part III of Figure 1 includes supplements to the basic or core materials that may or may not be included in the course depending upon which, if any, of the other options are used. These include Chapter 5 on qualitative analysis, the second and third parts of Chapter 7 on measures of variability and different types of distributions, and the concluding Chapter 14.

Each of the chapters in the main text includes a set of "Exercises" at the end. These ask the students to apply the topics covered in the chapter to new situations. They may be asked, for example, to look up data on a web site and interpret what the statistics mean or to apply concepts introduced in the chapter to new materials and situations. Assigning these exercises, hence, should reinforce and promote greater understanding of the text materials by having students use them analytically.

Chapter 1

Research as Puzzle Solving

In essence, political science research consists of asking and answering questions about our social and political world. The research process rests both on asking interesting questions and on finding convincing answers to them. Political science research, therefore, is like piecing a jigsaw puzzle together. Pieces of information — statistical and non-statistical — must be assembled and interpreted both logically and creatively. It is a challenging and surprisingly open-ended process, but it also can be quite interesting and intriguing. This text is organized around exploring two such puzzles concerning the theme *America at a Crossroads*. Focusing on two central questions or problems throughout the book should make it much easier to understand how the various parts of the research process fit together.

1.1 AMERICA AT A CROSSROADS: TWO JIGSAWS

In the early 21st century, the United States seemingly stands at a crossroads in both its politics and its socioeconomic development. Politically, the Democratic and Republican parties are almost evenly balanced in popular support. The two major parties, moreover, have become increasingly polarized ideologically over the last generation. Thus, a decisive shift in one direction or another would almost certainly have profound political consequences.

Economically, America is in the middle of a basic transformation from an industrial to an information-age society that holds great promise for some but great threat to others. Moreover, each downturn in the business cycle over the last two decades seems to be worse than the preceding one, culminating in the Great Recession of 2008–2012, making the threat of ongoing economic change even more dire. Thus, the question of whether we are ascending toward greater prosperity or starting to slip down the slope of economic decline is assuming greater urgency and poignancy.

1.1.1 The Political Crossroads

The crossroads in the political realm represents what might be called a delayed realignment. Historically, American politics has evolved through a series of party systems that lasted 30 to 40 years each. In each new system, the parties, dominant party, or the social coalitions underlying the parties changed considerably from the preceding one.[1] The twentieth century, for example, went through three political eras. Republicans dominated the first third, Democrats the second, and neither the third. Thus, since Richard Nixon won the presidency in 1968, many have waited for a **critical realignment** that would move the U.S. into a new era. The partisan balance has certainly flip-flopped over the last 40 years, but no stable party control of the government has emerged. During the 1970s and 1980s, Republicans won the Presidency and Democrats the Congress most of the time; and this pattern was reversed in the 1990s. More recently, the Republicans did control both the executive and legislature for much of George W. Bush's administration. Their majority was short-lived, though, as Democrats won Congressional majorities in the 2006 elections; and Barack Obama was elected President in 2008.[2] Yet, this Democratic domination was even more transitory than the Republican one; and the instability in the party balance continued. In 2010, the Republicans captured a solid majority in the House of Representatives and came

---

[1] Walter Dean Burnham, *Critical Elections and the Mainsprings of American Politics* (New York: W.W. Norton, 1970).
[2] John Heilemann and Mark Halperin, *Game Change: Obama and the Clintons, McCain and Palin, and the Race of a Lifetime* (New York: HarperCollins, 2010).

close to winning the Senate in a major victory for the party, while in 2012 President Obama was re-elected; and the House and the Senate remained under different party majorities.

The views of the American electorate will almost certainly play a major role in determining where our government and political parties are headed. In particular, the question of whether we are conservative or liberal in our political attitudes would appear critical given the ideological polarization between the generally liberal Democrats and conservative Republicans. Thus, we need to understand the major dimensions of public opinion.

For the last several decades, political science research has found that two different major dimensions or types of issues exist in American politics which have been called **economic and cultural issues**.[3] More recently, especially after the tragedy of September 11th, **national security** has emerged as an important separate issue dimension as well. Table 1.1 summarizes the stereotype of how conservatives and liberals divide on these issues. The first issue dimension has its roots in the Great Depression and focuses upon the "politics of rich and

Table 1.1: Ideological divisions in contemporary America.

Issue	Conservatives	Liberals
I. Government Role	**Anti-Government**	**Activist Government**
	Personal Freedom	Social Equity
	Market Economics	Regulatory Protection
	Corruption and Inefficiency	Social Benefits
	Social Dependency	Human Capital
II. Security Issues	War on Terror	Human Rights
	Anti-Communism	Human Rights
	More Defense Spending	Anti-Defense
	More Support for Domestic Police Power	Protection vs. Police Abuses
III. Cultural Issues	Traditional Values	Personal Freedom

---

[3] Gary Miller and Norman Schofield, "Activists and Partisan Realignment in the United States", *American Political Science Review*, Volume 97 (May 2003), pp. 245–260; Byron E. Shafer and William J.M. Claggett, *The Two Majorities: The Issue Context of Modern American Politics* (Baltimore: Johns Hopkins University Press, 1995).

poor".[4] On this dimension, conservatives generally advocate smaller government and reduced public spending in order to free resources for private utilization which is justified both in terms of individual liberty and in terms of the efficiency of *laissez-faire* economics. In contrast, liberals advocate expanded government responsibility both to promote the economy and, usually more importantly, to help those on the margins of society. The second area of national security and public safety form an important exception to this normal cleavage about the role of government, though, since conservatives generally support and liberals tend to be suspicious of governmental activism in this area.

The third set of issues is rooted in the social upheaval of the 1960s and 1970s when the traditional values of American society came under increasing challenge by insurgent political and social groups trumpeting a new morality.[5] Here, conservatives and liberals actually exchange positions on the desirability of freedom and, at least by implication, of governmental activism. Conservatives, fearing that we are *Slouching Towards Gomorrah*,[6] stress traditional values and maintaining order, while liberals are more supportive of secularism and individual liberty.

Evaluating how the public hews to these two major ideological lines, hence, involves charting American public opinion on a wide variety of political issues. This should raise several vital questions. First and probably most obviously, what is the distribution of Americans' ideological allegiances? Are they conservative on most issues? Or liberal? Or, are they moderate in the sense of rejecting both the strong conservative or strong liberal stances? Or, do they hold a mix of liberal and conservative views? The answers to these questions should prove quite suggestive about the partisan direction in which we are likely to move in the near future. For example, a conservative public should be the precursor of a new Republican era, while a liberal one would suggest that the Democrats are getting ready to regain their lost dominance.

---

[4] Kevin Phillips, *The Politics of Rich and Poor: Wealth and the American Electorate in The Reagan Aftermath* (New York: Random House, 1990).
[5] David Frum, *How We Got Here: The 1970s, the Decade that Brought You Modern Life (for Better or Worse)* (New York: Basic Books, 2000).
[6] Robert H. Bork, *Slouching Towards Gomorrah: Modern Liberalism and American Decline* (New York: ReganBooks, 1996).

If Americans are essentially moderate, the advantage should go to the party that can move toward the middle of the ideological spectrum without alienating its base constituencies. Finally, if Americans are committed conservatives in some areas and staunch liberals in others, political success may rest in coming up with a new policy package or public philosophy that better reflects Americans' beliefs than the two existing alternatives.

In addition, not just the relative conservatism or liberalism of U.S. citizens is important here, but also how Americans' ideological positions are related to their other attitudes, characteristics, and behaviors. Most basically, is ideology central to partisanship in the United States, as everyone assumes? That is, do conservatives vote strongly Republican and liberals strongly Democratic? This brings us to a second important question of how political attitudes are related to peoples' demographic or socioeconomic characteristics. That is, what types of Americans are liberals or conservatives? Are, as we generally assume, more affluent and more religious people mostly conservative, while the poorer and more secular are mostly liberal? These questions really seek to discover the causes and consequences of ideological beliefs in the United States. This provides substantial information beyond a single snapshot of how conservative or liberal Americans are at any one time which is valuable, if not essential, for understanding the dynamics of American politics.

This short discussion will, I hope, have convinced you that exploring Americans' ideology and relating it to the positions of our major political parties should produce a large, yet manageable jigsaw. There are lots of pieces that need to be taken out of the box and assembled before we have the final picture that answers these questions. Still, the shape of the picture and the color of the pieces in its various parts should be fairly clear since all the research questions that have been posed have fairly clear-cut answers. More importantly, once we have assembled these pieces, we should have a good understanding of a major force in American politics.

1.1.2 The Economic Crossroads

The crossroads in the economic realm refers to more than the normal ups and downs of the business cycle or even the abnormal downturn

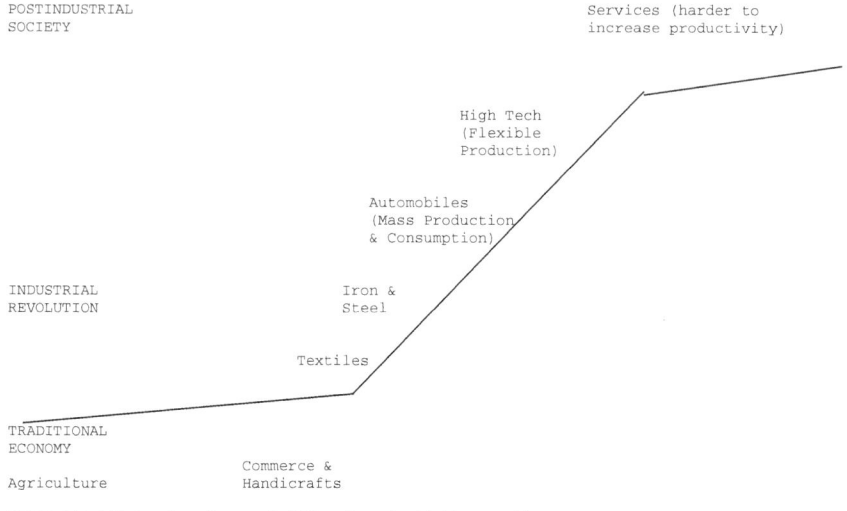

Figure 1.1: Changes in leading economic activity and the "S-curve" of productivity and GNP growth

of the Great Recession. Rather, we are somewhere in the middle of a fundamental transformation in the American economy and society from the industrial age to the information age,[7] which is being driven by the growing international economic competition called globalization.[8] Figure 1.1 presents an overview of this long sequence of economic development from agriculture to light industry to heavy and high tech industry to a service-based economy.[9] This is called an S-curve because, at least to an economist, it looks like an S. The slope of the curve represents the rate of economic growth and productivity. The figure shows that while growth is fairly low in traditional economies, it "takes

---

[7]This fundamental economic transformation was popularized by Alan Toffler and Heidi Toffler, *The Third Wave* (New York: Morrow, 1980). For an updated discussion, see Lester C. Thurow, *Building Wealth: The New Rules for Individuals, Companies, and Nations in a Knowledge-Based Economy* (New York: HarperCollins, 1999).

[8]Thomas Friedman, *The Lexus and the Olive Tree* (New York: Farrar, Strauss, Giroux, 1999).

[9]This model is based on W.W. Rostow, *The Stages of Economic Growth: A Non-Communist Manifesto* (Cambridge: Cambridge University Press, 1960).

off"[10] at the beginning of industrialization and accelerates as more productive industries develop.

This model of industrial sequencing suggests that development is neither smooth nor beneficial to all. First, new industries supplant old ones in what Joseph Schumpeter has called a process of "creative destruction".[11] While the creation of new industries generally brings higher productivity and greater prosperity, the destruction of old ones can devastate communities and people with particular skills. Second, the advantages of the most advanced industrial nations will eventually be undercut as they move beyond the high tech industry to a post-industrial society where the economy is dominated by the service sector whose productivity gains come more slowly than in industry.

Consequently, it is not surprising that the last few rounds of the business cycle have unleashed conflicting hopes and fears about our material well-being in something of a manic-depressive pattern. The recession of the early 1990s generated fears that the "American Century"[12] was being replaced by *Declining Fortunes*;[13] the rapid growth of the late 1990s brought theories of a recession-proof "new economy";[14] the recession of 2001, along with the horrible tragedy of September 11th, created a new funk; and by the middle of the decade the economy had resumed its growth but had yet to stimulate a new round of optimism, in large part because many people still had fears about job security.[15] Much more ominously, the Great Recession of 2008–2012 raised very substantial fears about the nation's stability.

---

[10] Ibid.

[11] Joseph A. Schumpeter, *Capitalism, Socialism, and Democracy*, 3rd Edn. (New York: Harper & Row, 1950).

[12] This phrase originated with Henry Luce of *Time* in 1941. See Robert Reich, *Tales of a New America: The Anxious Liberal's Guide to the Future* (New York: Vintage Books, 1987), pp. 53–54.

[13] This phrase is taken from Katherine S. Newman, *Declining Fortunes: The Withering of the American Dream* (New York: HarperCollins, 1993).

[14] Robert D. Atkinson and Randolph H. Court, *The New Economy Index* (Washington, D.C.: Progressive Policy Institute, 1998), Section I.

[15] For example, in August 2005, only 36% of Americans felt that economic conditions were good or excellent. See, Gallup Organization, "The State of the Nation", available at www.gallup.com.

Furthermore, the United States faces a fundamental problem in that no other country has preceded it down the path of the transformation to an information-age economy. Thus, we can only guess or rely upon a crystal ball to anticipate whether growing prosperity, economic decline, or something in between is on the horizon.

The future of the U.S.'s economic well-being almost certainly has political implications as well because the state of the economy affects people's political perceptions and voting behavior. Here, though, the most important political distinction is not between liberals and conservatives but between the incumbent party, which holds the presidency, and the out or challenging party. Substantial historical and statistical research shows that when times are good, incumbents have a strong advantage in being re-elected. In contrast, economic hard times make the citizenry much more eager to "throw the rascals out". Thus, what might be called the **economic model** of voting relates the state of the economy to whether the incumbent administration has an electoral advantage or disadvantage.[16]

This pattern can certainly be seen in Table 1.2 which summarizes the presidential elections since 1950. When Americans were faced with either economic problems or severe foreign or domestic threats to peace, they retired the party of the presidential incumbent by voting for brand X. In contrast, in times of peace and prosperity, they almost inevitably rewarded the incumbent President or his Vice-President. The 2000 election stands out in these data as a sharp exception to this trend. Despite peace and prosperity which should have favored incumbent Bill Clinton's Vice-President Al Gore, George W. Bush avenged his father's 1992 defeat by Clinton. Four years later, the situation was more ambiguous. Early in his presidency, George Bush had gained almost unprecedented popularity for his response to the September 11th attacks. By 2004, however, there were growing questions about the War in Iraq and disillusionment with the economic situation at home,

---

[16]Robert S. Erikson, "Economic Conditions and the Presidential Vote", *American Political Science Review*, Volume 83 (June 1989), pp. 567–573; Douglas A. Hibbs, Jr., *The American Political Economy: Macroeconomics and Electoral Politics* (Cambridge: Harvard University Press, 1987), especially Chapter 5.

Table 1.2: Summary of presidential elections since 1950.

Year	Election environment	Election outcome
1952	Foreign fears	Eisenhower (R) ends 20 years of Democratic presidencies
1956	Prosperity and peace	Eisenhower re-elected
1960	Minor recession	Kennedy (D) wins
1964	Good economy	Johnson (D) landslide
1968	Growing social chaos	Nixon (R) wins
1972	Good economy	Nixon landslide
1976	Watergate and misery index	Carter (D) wins
1980	Stagflation = big misery index	Reagan (R) wins
1984	Peace and prosperity	Reagan landslide
1988	Peace and prosperity	Bush (R) wins
1992	Recession just ending	Clinton (D) wins
1996	Peace and prosperity	Clinton re-elected
2000	Peace and prosperity	Bush (R) avenges his father
2004	Bush strongly supported for War on Terrorism, but growing unease about Iraq; Recovery from 2001 recession, but many worried about economy	Close election, with Bush re-elected
2008	Beginning of Great Recession and worries over Afghan and Iraq Wars	Obama (D) wins by comfortable margin
2012	Great Recession and disillusionment with Afghanistan, but major battle over role of government	Obama narrowly re-elected

Note: R represents Republicans. D represents Democrats.

resulting in another close election. The 2008 presidential elections certainly reconfirmed the general pattern in Table 1.2. The Great Recession was taking off; and there was considerable dissatisfaction with the Wars in Iraq and Afghanistan. Consequently, the solid victory of Democrat Barack Obama reflected popular discontent with the incumbent Republican brand.[17] Four years later saw a replay of 2004 with the roles of the parties reversed, as the Democratic incumbent Barack Obama beat the Republican challenger Mitt Romney despite very significant voter disenchantment with the *status quo*.

---

[17] Heilemann and Halperin, *op.cit.*

With little basis for economic projections, either statistical or otherwise, finding a jigsaw with all the pieces is a much harder task. Here, we shall compare the social and economic conditions in the U.S. with those that exist in other advanced industrial nations. The guiding, though far from scientific, assumption is that it is not very likely that the whole world is entering an era of economic implosion. Thus, if the United States compares favorably to other developed countries at present, there is a good chance that it is making the transition to an information-age society better than most of its competitors and will probably continue to prosper. Conversely, if it is a laggard among similar nations, the dangers of economic decline would be much greater as others would be better poised to dominate the leading global economic sectors.

Several chapters in this book examine three different types of socioeconomic and political indicators for 21 advanced industrial democracies. First, we shall examine economic indicators to see whether America's economy is performing better or worse than other nations at comparable levels of development. Second, social outcomes in terms of the health, education, and welfare of the citizens will be considered to see how well-off, at least in relative terms, Americans are. Finally, some data will also be presented on the size of government in these nations to see whether there are significant differences between the performance of large and small governments. Thus, this jigsaw will be created from the pieces produced by the answers to two broad questions. First, how well-off are Americans compared to the residents of other advanced industrial nations? Second, if conditions in the U.S. are significantly better or worse than in most other nations, how much of this difference can be explained by the role of government?

1.1.3 Uncertainty at the Crossroads

In both murder mysteries and most political science research reports, the final solutions or results are not revealed until the end. Here, it may be helpful to give the reader a preview of what our excursion through the world of statistical techniques will discover. In terms of American public opinion, four points stand out:

(1) Americans are quite evenly divided in terms of partisanship and voting.

(2) Americans possess a complex combination of conservative and liberal beliefs.
(3) Ideology has a very strong impact on partisanship and voting in the U.S.
(4) Perhaps surprisingly, though, ideology is only weakly linked to socioeconomic status or to traditional roles and values, although there does seem to be a marked tendency for traditional values to be the more important determinant of ideology and voting.

Taken together, these findings strongly imply that the direction which we will take from our current political crossroads remains contested and uncertain.

The results are just as complex in the statistical analysis of differences among industrial nations:

(1) Compared to other developed nations, the United States is marked by small government, good economic performance, but lagging social outcomes.
(2) More generally, the differences among wealthy countries support *both* the conservative contention that big government hurts economic performance and the liberal argument that big government promotes better social outcomes.

In sum, America has a conservative government in terms of being relatively small compared to the overall economy. This small government, though, evidently produces good results in some areas and bad results in others. Consequently, both conservatives and liberals can point to factors supporting their philosophical arguments, again leaving us up in the air about what path to follow.

1.2 PLAN OF THE BOOK

This text assumes that the best way to get students involved in the research process is to introduce them quickly to simple data that are easy to understand and are presented in formats that are often seen in the mass media. Consequently, the book begins by giving the reader an overview of the data that will be used in trying to piece together our two jigsaws in Chapter 2. Once we have established a good foundation in understanding the variables that will be used in the two analyses, Part I on "Designing Research Projects" describes how political scientists develop the theories that structure their research and how research can be used to test scholarly theories in Chapters 3 to 5. Part II on "The Foundations for Statistical Analysis" then discusses a variety of technical matters that are necessary to understand more advanced statistical results in Chapters 6 to 8. We are now ready to examine the more advanced statistical techniques that measure the existence and strength of possible relationships among our variables, allowing us to answer questions such as: Are more affluent people more likely than other Americans to be conservatives or liberals? Do countries with large welfare states have better or worse economic and/or social records than those that do not? Part III on "Discovering Relationships for Nominal and Ordinal Data" shows how to present such analyses of the public opinion data in Chapters 9 and 10. Part IV on "Discovering Relationships for Interval Data" then discusses how to present statistical analyses for the data on developed democracies, as well as an advanced statistical approach that can be applied to public opinion data. Finally, the Conclusion explores broader themes about "The Joy and the Challenge of the Jigsaw Puzzles in Political Research".

EXERCISES

1. What does the text mean when it says the United States is at a political crossroads? What are the different directions in which it might go? How have the political events since the 2008 elections affected these alternatives? Discuss what you think would be desirable policies on one issue (e.g., taxes, immigration, Afghanistan, etc.). Do you think that the Democratic or Republican Party would be more likely to enact your preferred policies?
2. Select one Democratic and one Republican U.S. Senator. Describe their positions on any two political issues. Are these stances conservative or liberal? Are these results consistent with the stereotype that Democrats are liberal and Republicans are conservative?
3. In 2009 and 2010, the Tea Party became fairly prominent in U.S. politics. How would you describe the Tea Party in terms of the

three types of issues discussed in the text? Does it differ from the Republican Party?
4. What did Joseph Schumpeter mean when he said that economic development brings "creative destruction"? How can this be applied to the current transformation of the U.S. from an industrial to an information-age economy? In particular, how is the changing situation of blue-collar industrial workers reflected in the competition between Democrats and Republicans? What does each party promise this constituency? How successful have they been in fulfilling their promises?
5. After Democratic victories in the 2006 and 2008 elections, the Republicans enjoyed a major resurgence in 2010. How do you explain this dramatic reversal in political fortunes? Use this explanation to add the 2010 elections to Table 1.2.

Chapter
2

Introducing Our Data

The two puzzles examined in this book focus on whether Americans are conservative or liberal in their political attitudes and how the developed democracies differ in terms of their economic and social performance. **Public opinion polls** of individual citizens provide the best data for reaching conclusions about the first, while **aggregate data** on the social and economic performance of the developed democracies allow us to evaluate the second. This chapter provides some simple introductory data on the ideology of Americans and the performance of the industrial nations in a format that is easy to understand and often used in the mass media. Once we understand what these numbers mean and represent, they will be used to illustrate the various facets of the research process that are discussed in Sections 2.1 and 2.2.

2.1 FREQUENCY DISTRIBUTIONS: ARE AMERICANS CONSERVATIVE OR LIBERAL?

Political scientists often investigate how conservative or liberal Americans are by using the results of **public opinion surveys**. For example, we talk about Congresswoman Smith being ahead by 55% to 40% in her latest campaign, or about how three-quarters of Americans favor the death penalty. These figures come from **frequency distributions**, which represent a concise method for reporting how many people take different positions on a specific political attitude. This section first describes how to construct a frequency count and then shows how frequency tables can be used to assess the substantive question of whether Americans are liberals or conservatives.

These examples are primarily based on a data set of 2,102 interviews that constitute the National Election Study (NES) for the 2008 election.[1] The 2008 NES survey is one (the latest for presidential elections) in a series of polls that have been conducted by the University of Michigan for every national election dating back to the early 1950s. These are widely considered to be the premier source of data on elections and public opinion in the U.S. by the political science research community.[2]

The 2008 NES differs from its predecessors in one important respect. Prior to 2008, the samples were drawn to be directly representative of all Americans. The study of the latest presidential election, in contrast, greatly oversampled African-Americans and Latinos to permit more detailed analysis of these politically important groups. This means that the responses of different survey participants must be given different weights if the results are to be representative of the U.S. population. Charles Prysby and Carmine Scavo developed such a data set for *SETUPS: Voting Behavior: The 2008 Election*.[3] The percentages in the tables for this section were calculated directly from that data set, although as described in Footnote 4, slight adjustments had to be made in the numerical frequencies.

---

[1] Charles Prysby and Carmine Scavo, *SETUPS: Voting Behavior: The 2008 Election* (Ann Arbor, MI: Inter-University Consortium for Political and Social Research and the American Political Science Association, 2009). Availble at www.icpsr.umich.edu/SETUPS2008. The frequency counts in this chapter are computed from the 2008 and, in a few cases, 2004 NES data sets. These studies were conducted by the Survey Research Center at the University of Michigan and are distributed by the International Consortium for Political and Social Research.

[2] The first major work to come out of this was Angus Campbell, Philip E. Converse, Warren E. Miller and Donald E. Stokes, *The American Voter* (New York: John Wiley, 1960). For an update see Warren E. Miller and J. Merrill Shanks, *The New American Voter* (Cambridge: Harvard University Press, 1996).

[3] Prysby and Scavo, *op. cit.*

2.1.1 Describing a Frequency Distribution

For public opinion and many other types of data used in political science, most of the time, an item has a limited number of categories and a substantial number of cases within each category. The best way to summarize such a **categoric variable** is to count the number or frequency of cases in each category. For example, the 2,102 respondents in the 2008 NES can be divided into a limited number of categories in terms of their action in the presidential election:

(1) those who voted for Barack Obama;
(2) those who voted for John McCain;
(3) those who voted for other candidates; and
(4) those who did not vote or did not say how they voted.

Technically, the **distribution** of a variable refers to the range and concentration of its values. The range represents all the possible values that it may take; and the concentration refers to how many or what proportion of the cases have a particular value. A **frequency distribution**, therefore, is a concise presentation of how many or, more commonly, what proportion of the cases are in the specific categories of an item. For example, a frequency distribution can tell us what percentage of the public voted for Barack Obama or John McCain or takes a pro-choice or pro-life position on abortion.

To create a frequency distribution, an individual or a computer must count the number of responses out of 2,102 that fall into each category. A single researcher, for example, could put each of the surveys into a different pile depending upon the answer to the question on presidential vote and then count the number of surveys in each pile. This obviously would be an extremely cumbersome and time-consuming process. Thus, normally the responses are entered into a computer data base; and a software package is then used to do the frequency count. Once the number of cases or respondents in each category is tallied by whatever measure, a table presenting this frequency count can then be printed out. It usually includes several columns of absolute numbers and percentages. While most of these are easy to understand, they will be introduced one at a time to underline the meaning of each type of data.

Table 2.1: Presidential vote in 2008 NES survey.

	Number	Percent	Valid percent
Barack Obama	842	40.1	53.8
John McCain	691	32.9	44.2
Other Candidate	31	1.5	2.0
TOTAL VOTING	(1,564)		100.0
Did not Vote/Did not Say	538	25.6	
TOTAL	2,102	100.1	

A central component of such a table is the number of cases, in this case survey respondents, who are in each category as in the frequency distribution for 2008 presidential vote in the first column of Table 2.1. This tells us what the four categories are and how many respondents fell into each one.[4] The resulting frequency count shows that Barack Obama had a significant lead of 842 to 691 over John McCain, that none of the other candidates received very much support (31 in total), and that there was a considerable number of nonvoters (538). This seems in line with what actually occurred.

Still, these raw numbers are not the easiest data to work with. It would be fairly difficult, for example, to compare category differences between two tables with different sample sizes. Rather, the percentage of respondents in a category, which is reported in the second column of the table, would make interpreting the table much easier because percentages provide a standardized measure that varies between 0 and 100 to assess and compare the size of each category. Thus, most frequency counts contain the percentage as well as the absolute number of cases in each category. The percentage is simply the category frequency divided by the total number of cases multiplied by 100. For example, the 842 Obama voters constitute:

$$100 \times (842/2{,}102) = 40.1\%$$

of the total sample.

---

[4]In the actual, unweighted sample, 1,564 people indicated for whom they voted, while 538 did not. In the weighted analysis, though, the weighting produced 1,591 voters. To make the total number of cases equal the actual number of respondents (2,102), the percentage for each category of voters (Obama, McCain, and others) was multiplied by 1,564 to estimate the number of cases for that category.

These percentages show that Obama led McCain by a margin of 40.1% to 32.9% among the NES respondents, with all other candidates getting only 1.5% of the vote combined. The last figure in the table on nonvoters shows that the NES sample differed from the American population in one important respect. The actual electorate had a turnout rate of approximately 62%, while 74.5% of the NES sample reported voting, which is far beyond the expected range of **sampling error** as will be shown in Chapter 8. To some extent, this may reflect misreporting whether they voted. However, simply participating in the NES survey may well have made some people much more interested in politics and political issues.

The data in Table 2.1 also look a little strange because these percentages are clearly lower than the ones that came flashing across American television screens on election eve in 2008, which ended with Obama having a 53% to 46% lead in the total popular vote. It is very easy to understand why this is so. By definition, nonvoters are not included in the actual share of the vote garnered by the political gladiators. Thus, in analyzing the presidential vote, it makes eminent sense to regard the nonvoters as **missing data** and calculate a candidate's percentage based on only those in the sample who claimed to be voters. For example, Barack Obama's percentage is computed by dividing the 842 respondents who voted for him by the 1,564 participants in the survey who reported their vote:

$$100 \times (842/1{,}564) = 53.8\%.$$

This produces what are sometimes called **valid percentages** as illustrated by the third column in the table which shows Obama winning over McCain by a margin of 53.8% to 44.2%, with other candidates gaining the support of 2.0% of the respondents. This is quite close to the final election returns and well within normal sampling error range (see Chapter 8).

2.1.2 Are Americans Conservative or Liberal?

A seemingly simple and straightforward way of assessing whether Americans are conservative or liberal is to ask the U.S. citizens how they place themselves in terms of partisanship, ideology, and issue positions. Given the very close recent elections, we might well expect that Americans would be fairly evenly divided between conservatives and liberals. However, even a brief review of public opinion data indicates that the situation is far more complex. This subsection reviews data on four areas of public opinion: (1) partisanship and ideology, (2) economic issues, (3) security issues, and (4) cultural issues. In each area, as we will see, the answer to the questions of whether Americans are liberal or conservative turns out to be not so simple after all.

The flip-flopping of slight advantages for Democrats and Republicans over the last several decades suggests that Americans should be fairly evenly divided in their party loyalties and ideological orientations. This expectation does not turn out to be the case, however, although the political implications of partisanship and ideology in the contemporary United States appear to be surprisingly different. Table 2.2 indicates the distribution of party identification at the time of the 2008 election. Part A at the top of the table presents a seven-point scale with three categories each of Democrats and Republicans (strong, weak, and leaning) and Independents in the middle. Part B presents the same data with just three categories: Democrats, Independents, and Republicans. Because the survey participants were prompted to express even mild

Table 2.2: Party identification, 2008.

A. Seven Categories	
Strong Democrat	20.2%
Weak Democrat	16.5%
Leans Democrat	15.6%
Independent	8.3%
Leans Republican	11.2%
Weak Republican	14.2%
Strong Republican	14.0%
TOTAL	100.0%
B. Three Categories	
Democrat	52%
Independent	8%
Republican	40%
TOTAL	100%

partisan preferences in the follow-up questions, there are only a few Independents (8.3% of the sample).

Both Part A and Part B of Table 2.2 have countervailing advantages and disadvantages. Part A allows us to gauge how enthusiastic the followers of the two parties are. For example, 20% of the population considered themselves strong Democrats, while a markedly larger portion (32%) were only weak or leaning Democrats. In contrast, the larger table makes it at least a little difficult to compare the number of Republicans and Democrats because three categories of each must be added together. It is fairly easy to see that the Democrats had an advantage, but figuring out exactly how big it is takes more effort than many readers are willing to invest. Thus, Part B, despite the fact that it contains less information, is often a better presentation because it directly shows a comfortable Democratic advantage of 52% to 40% in 2008. This one snapshot of partisan affiliation does mask some significant changes over the first decade of the 21st century. During the first half (2000–2005), the two parties were extremely close; and the Democrats then jumped to about a 10 percentage-point lead for 2006–2008. However, the Republicans soon started a comeback. For example, the Democrats' lead was cut to 47% to 42% in the fourth quarter of 2009.[5] Overall, therefore, there does seem to be a fairly even partisan balance.

One might expect the numbers of conservatives and liberals to parallel those for Republicans and Democrats since each ideology is widely associated with one of the parties. However, this turns out to be far from true, as demonstrated by the data in Table 2.3. The table shows that Americans lean toward the conservative end of the political

Table 2.3: Ideology, 2008.

Conservative	44%
Moderate	28%
Liberal	28%
TOTAL	100%

---

[5] Jeffrey M. Jones, "Democrat Support Dips Below Majority Level in 2009", *Gallup Reports*. Available at www.gallup.com.

spectrum fairly strongly as 44% of Americans identified themselves as conservatives in 2008, compared to 28% as liberals and another 28% as moderates. More broadly, conservatives have enjoyed a decisive advantage ideologically since the 1970s.[6]

This self-identification of the American public as primarily conservative is certainly inconsistent with its balanced or slightly pro-Democratic party loyalties. This suggests, in turn, that there may be other dimensions of ideology that affect voting and partisanship. Thus, it is desirable to look at how the citizenry stands on specific issues to see if more detailed results might give us a better insight into the dynamics of political competition in the U.S. in the early 21st century.

One central issue dimension revolves around whether or not the U.S. should have a large government that pursues redistributive policies. Part A in the top half of Table 2.4, for example, presents the percentage of Americans who wanted government spending cut, kept the same, or increased for four different government services that are generally supported by liberals: education, social security, child care, and the poor. American attitudes about these issues in 2008 were fairly liberal as slight majorities of 50% to 53% wanted to increase governmental spending in all these areas, while only 14% to 17% of the citizenry wanted to cut expenditures.

On a technical note, Table 2.4 represents a somewhat different type of frequency presentation than the preceding tables. Tables 2.1 to 2.3 are **simple full frequency counts** because they contain all the categories for just one item (i.e., presidential vote, party affiliation, or ideological identification) in a presentation. Part A in the top half of Table 2.4, in contrast, is a **complex full frequency table** because it contains the proportion of cases in all the categories for four variables — in this case, whether spending should be increased, cut, or kept the same for a particular government service. This has both an advantage and a disadvantage. On the one hand, it allows several or more than several items to be directly compared in the same table, making it easy to see that Americans were fairly liberal on all these issues. On the other hand,

---

[6]Robert S. Erikson and Kent L. Tedin, *American Public Opinion*, 6th Edn. (New York: Longman, 2001), p. 101.

Table 2.4: American attitudes toward government spending by area.

	Cut (%)	Keep same (%)	Increase (%)
A. Complex Full Table, 2008			
Public Schools	14	33	53
Social Security	15	33	52
Child Care	17	31	52
Poor People	14	36	50
B. Complex Partial Table	Increase (%)		
Public Schools	53		
Social Security	52		
Child Care	52		
Poor People	50		

it results in the table having a large number of entries which can become confusing or intimidating.

A simplified and perhaps more comprehensible presentation can be made with a **complex partial frequency table**, such as the one in Part B in the bottom half of Table 2.4. It is "complex" because it includes data on the four different items; and it is "partial" because it only reports the percentage of respondents in one category for each variable — those who wanted increased spending. The format of a complex partial frequency table has both advantages and disadvantages. On the one hand, it facilitates comparison by presenting just one figure or data point for each variable. On the other hand, by limiting the data array to just one category, it "throws away" information and may provide slightly misleading results. For example, the first column for 2008 in Part B shows that just over half the electorate wanted more spending in all of these areas. However, we cannot tell whether the people who did not want spending increases were satisfied with the *status quo* or actually wanted budget cuts. Consequently, it is impossible to determine from just these data whether liberals really had a small lead or a big lead over conservatives.

Yet, we certainly should not jump to the conclusion that all Americans are liberal on all economic issues. The major conservative initiative concerning budget politics in the early 21st century, of course, is to cut taxes. Table 2.5 shows that in 2004 Americans were enthusiastic

Table 2.5: Bush tax cuts, 2004.

Oppose Strongly	29%
Oppose	12%
Favor	18%
Favor Strongly	41%

conservatives on this issue (because tax cuts were not a central issue in 2008, they were not included in this data set). A large plurality (41%) strongly approved President Bush's tax cuts; and, overall, citizens favored the tax cuts by the substantial margin of 59% to 41%. Clearly, George Bush picked a popular issue by making tax cuts a centerpiece of his presidency. More broadly, this indicates that the public's attitude toward the role of government might be described as the desire for a "tax-cut and spend" policy, which explans why balancing the budget is so hard![7]

These data, hence, provide an explanation for why the federal budget often runs red ink. Conservatives blame Democratic social programs; liberals blame Republican tax cuts; and both of these interpretations probably have considerable validity. Yet, if we think about it, the public demands many liberal programs, as well as a conservative tax policy. Democracy tends to reward politicians who give citizens what they want — in this case, maxing out Uncle Sam's credit cards! It also means that Americans appear massively split or ideologically schizophrenic on economic issues. On the one hand, they tilt in the liberal direction on the role of government and want many of the programs that liberals advocate. On the other hand, they are staunchly conservative in their refusal to pay the taxes necessary to finance these programs.

The tragedy of September 11th greatly increased the importance of security issues in American politics. Part A in Table 2.6 indicates very strong public support for the conservative advocacy of greater governmental activism in providing domestic security. For example, 53% wanted to increase spending to fight crime versus only 14% who

---

[7] George Hager and Eric Pianin, *Balancing Act: Washington's Troubled Path to a Balanced Budget* (New York: Vintage Books, 1998).

Table 2.6: Attitudes about security issues, 2008.

A. DOMESTIC SECURITY ISSUES		
Increase Crime Spending		53%
Favor Death Penalty		70%
B. DEFENSE SPENDING		
Cut		28%
Keep Same		29%
Increase		43%
C. SUPPORT FOR WARS	Approve	Disapprove
War on Terror	60%	25%
Iraq War	25%	63%
Afghanistan War	23%	58%

wanted cuts in this area; and an overwhelming majority of 70% supported the death penalty. In some ways, Americans are just as conservative concerning international security issues, but at least one important caveat must be made about this pattern. In terms of resource priorities, there was significantly more support for increasing defense spending than cutting it (43% to 28%), as can be seen in Part B of the table. Still, not all of America's security initiatives won popular acclaim in 2008. In particular, while a strong majority of 60% approved the war on terror, approximately equal majorities disapproved the wars in Iraq and Afghanistan (see Part C). Clearly, Americans have not issued a blank check to their leaders in the security realm.

Cultural issues pit the conservative defenders of traditional values against the liberal advocates of personal freedom and growth. By implication at least, conservatives believe that society has the right and responsibility to protect itself and its institutions, such as the family and religion, from the effects of "slouching towards Gomorrah",[8] while liberals believe that it is immoral for society to stifle the individual. By the end of the 20th century, these "culture wars" had become quite

---

[8] Robert H. Bork, *Slouching Towards Gomorrah: Modern Liberalism and American Decline* (New York: ReganBooks, 1996).

Table 2.7: Views on abortion, 2008.

Pro-Life (Never; only for rape and incest)	42%
Intermediate (Only if clear need)	18%
Pro-Choice (Always)	40%

Table 2.8: Views on other "culture wars" issues, 2008.

	Support (%)	Oppose (%)
Gay Marriage*	39	35
Protect Gays from Job Discrimination	75	25
Gays in Military	79	21
Make Buying Guns Harder	48	52
Increase/Decrease Immigration	14	45

*26% said that they supported civil unions but not gay marriage.

strident.[9] Metaphorically in terms of popular culture, we might view this as an argument over whether *Mayberry RFD* or *Sex and the City* represents the "real" America.

Table 2.7 shows that Americans were fairly evenly split on abortion, one of the most passionate and polarizing cultural issues in contemporary American politics, in 2008. The pro-life position that abortions should never be performed or strictly limited to cases of rape and incest was supported by 42% of the NES sample, while 40% took the pro-choice position that it should always be allowed. This suggests, incidentally, why many politicians hate the abortion issue — no matter what position they take, they are sure to alienate many voters. On other cultural issues, U.S. citizens are all over the map ideologically. Table 2.8 shows, for example, that they were conservative concerning gay marriage which was approved by just over a third of the population, but quite liberal concerning protecting gays against job discrimination and having them serve in the military which were supported by three-quarters of Americans. Thus, public opinion diverges radically, even in what seems to be the same issue area. In addition, the public appeared

---

[9] James Davison Hunter, *Culture Wars: The Struggle to Define America* (New York: Basic Books, 1991).

to be decidedly conservative on immigration and fairly evenly split but slightly conservative on gun control.

2.1.3 The Overall Nature of U.S. Public Opinion

We started this chapter by posing a very reasonable question that, in theory at least, should be easy to answer: Are Americans conservative or liberal in their political beliefs? After examining a large amount of public opinion data, the answer to this easy question does not appear so easy after all. In part, this results from the fact that Americans' political beliefs are far from consistent. Thus, making an overall assessment can appear to be a daunting endeavor. The tables in this chapter should certainly have indicated that Americans have rather inconsistent attitudes about a wide variety of issues that can be ranked on a conservative-to-liberal dimension.

Overall, as summarized in Table 2.9, these attitudes in combination might form one of five different types of overall ideological positions. The first two are easy to understand. If most Americans are conservative on most issues, then there is a **conservative public**. Conversely, if most Americans are liberal on most issues, then there is a **liberal public**. Third, there would be a **polarized public** if a fairly even balance exists between strong conservatives and strong liberals on most issues. A fourth possibility is that the general citizenry is not happy with either extreme and, rather, takes a position in the middle of the ideological spectrum on most issues. In this case, we would probably say that the nature of public opinion indicates a **moderate public**. The final

Table 2.9: Possible structures of public opinion.

Type	Defining characteristic
Conservative	Most people are conservative on most issues.
Liberal	Most people are liberal on most issues.
Polarized	A fairly even balance exists between strong conservatives and strong liberals on many issues.
Moderate	Most people are in the middle of the ideological spectrum on most issues.
Split	A substantial number of conservative positions are supported by a strong majority, but so are a substantial number of liberal ones.

possibility is that the public is conservative on a considerable number of issue areas, but also liberal on many others. Here, we would have a **split public** or, to use more colorful language, one that is ideologically, but not necessarily psychologically, schizophrenic.

The evidence about the ideological hue of Americans is certainly complex. In terms of general orientations, they are fairly even in terms of party identification, but lean well to the conservative side in self-proclaimed ideology. However, this does not mean that all or even most of their political positions are conservative. The public is ideologically split on economic issues, being strongly liberal on some but just as strongly conservative on others; and the same is true for cultural issues. Finally, on security issues, Americans are generally conservative, but even here they do not necessarily agree with every conservative position. Overall, therefore, describing Americans as ideologically split or schizophrenic does not appear to be very far off the mark which provides a good explanation for why there has been no critical realignment over the last 40 years.

2.2 DATA ARRAYS AND GRAPHS: HOW DOES THE U.S. COMPARE TO OTHER DEVELOPED NATIONS?

In this section, we will compare the United States with 20 other advanced industrial democracies to see whether America is doing well or poorly relative to countries which have similar socioeconomic environments. The data used in these analyses are fundamentally different from the public opinion figures discussed in Chapter 2. There, the principal focus was on the individuals who participated in the 2008 NES survey. The data were then reported as the percentage of respondents who had a specific characteristic, attitude, or behavior, such as their presidential vote or attitudes about social security.

Here, we will be dealing with **aggregate data** which measure the characteristics of a set of social aggregates of individuals who compose particular industrialized nations. The data are presented as the value of a particular nation on the indicator in question, such as the U.S.'s economic growth rate or index of income inequality. Because of this difference in the nature of the data, different modes of presentation are more appropriate than the frequency counts or distributions used in the previous section. The first part discusses data arrays; and the second shows how graphs can be used to present these data in more visually attractive formats.

What should we expect about and conclude from these comparisons? John Kingdon reported that his students have had two general perspectives about America compared to other nations: (1) the United States is better than other countries and (2) conditions in other societies are fairly similar to the U.S.[10] As an aside, we might note a slight logical inconsistency. If social, economic, and political conditions really are fairly similar throughout the developed world, it might be hard to argue that any nation is better or worse than the others. Here, in fact, we are making these comparisons with the expectation that even advanced industrial societies have significant differences in their governments, economies, and societies. Citizens of the United States obviously have a vested interest in hoping that Professor Kingdon's students are correct in their first expectation. If they are, the U.S. really is doing quite well. Even if their second expectation that America's economic performance and social outcomes mirror those in the rest of the developed world turns out to be true, Americans can probably take more than a modicum of comfort that their country is in pretty good shape. Only if both expectations are incorrect and the U.S. turns out to have fallen behind most of the rest of the advanced industrial nations, then, there should be worry that doom and gloom may be at hand.

2.2.1 Data Arrays

For many of the economic, political, and social indicators examined here, almost every case (nation) has a different value. Thus, when the number of cases is fairly small, it makes sense simply to present a list of each case along with its value for the item in question, creating a **data array**. This is done in Table 2.10 for the gross domestic product (GDP) per capita[11] of the advanced industrial nations. Here, GDP is measured

---

[10] John W. Kingdon, *America the Unusual* (New York: St. Martin's Press, 1998), p. 1.
[11] National wealth is usually measured in terms of GDP or Gross National Product (GNP) per capita. For the purposes of this book, the fairly minor differences between GNP and GDP can be ignored. In essence, GNP measures all the goods and services

Table 2.10: Comparative wealth of industrialized nations, 2007.

Nations	GDP per capita*
Norway	US$53,477
United States	US$45,489
Ireland	US$45,027
Switzerland	US$41,101
Netherlands	US$39,225
Canada	US$38,500
Australia	US$37,565
Austria	US$37,119
Sweden	US$36,603
Denmark	US$35,961
United Kingdom	US$35,699
Belgium	US$35,358
Finland	US$34,718
Germany	US$34,391
Japan	US$33,626
France	US$32,686
Spain	US$31,586
Italy	US$30,381
Greece	US$28,423
New Zealand	US$27,431
Portugal	US$22,815

*Measured in Parity Purchasing Power (PPP).

in "purchasing power parity" (PPP). As anyone who has visited Tokyo knows, for example, the Japanese have high incomes, but they also pay very high prices, at least when Japanese yen are converted into U.S. dollars. The conversion to PPP takes care of misaligned exchange rates and different costs of living, thereby providing a good measure of the relative affluence of various nations.[12]

---

produced by the corporations and citizens of a specific nation (e.g., the United States) whether at home or abroad, while GDP measures the production within a given nation, whether by its own or by foreign corporations and citizens. Why one or the other is used here depends simply on how the data were reported in the various sources from which the data set was compiled.

[12] Of the variables used in this book to compare nations, GDP per capita in 2007 and tax burden and infant mortality in 2008 were taken from OECD, *OECD Fact Book, 2008* (Paris, OECD, 2010). Available at www.oecd.org. GDP per capita, the ratio of

At least in terms of relative affluence, the United States is doing quite well. It was the second richest nation in the world in 2007 with a GDP per capita of US$45,489, behind Norway at US$53,477, who was a major beneficiary of the surging oil prices at that time. Ireland was third and Switzerland fourth with GDP's per capita over US$40,000. Most of the rest of the developed nations (14) were in two packs with levels of wealth of US$35,000 to US$40,000 and US$30,000 to US$35,000. Finally, Greece, New Zealand, and especially Portugal were noticeably poorer than the rest of the developed world with GDP per capitas of under US$30,000.

Similarly, the data arrays in Tables 2.11 to 2.13 show very significant variations within the developed world in terms of the size of government, economic performance, and social outcomes. Table 2.11 presents data on the size of government as measured by the tax burden, that is, the proportion of a country's economy or GDP in 2006 that was devoted to the taxes of all levels of government. The Scandinavian welfare states of Sweden and Denmark have the largest governments as their tax burdens equaled nearly half (49%) of GDP. Conversely, Japan, the United States, and Switzerland had the smallest governments with tax burdens in the 28% to 29% range.[13] For the average annual economic growth from 1980 through 2004 reported in Table 2.12, the Irish had by far the most dynamic growth rate of 5.1%, far higher

---

government spending to GDP, the ratio of savings to GDP, life expectancy, and infant mortality in 2003, as well as the poverty rate in 2000 and economic growth over 1980–2004 were taken from OECD, *OECD Statistics* (Paris: OECD, 2005). Available at www.oecd.org. Economic growth for 1980–1999 and the Gini index of income inequality were taken from World Bank, *World Development Report, 2001* (New York: Oxford University Press, 2001); the infant mortality rate and the ratio of government spending to GDP before 2000 came from OECD, *OECD Health Data 2000* (Paris: OECD, 2000); and the rankings on the Human Development Index and India's infant mortality rate came from United Nations, *Human Development Report, 2002* (New York: Oxford University Press, 2002).

[13] This confirms the argument of Kingdon, *op. cit.* For comprehensive and sophisticated treatments of the differences among the role of government and public policies in developed nations, see Arend Lijphart, *Patterns of Democracy: Government Forms and Performance in Thirty-Six Countries* (New Haven: Yale University Press, 1999); Harold L. Wilensky, *Rich Democracies: Political Economy, Public Policy, and Performance* (Berkeley: University of California Press, 2002).

Table 2.11: Taxes' percentage of GDP, 2006.

Nations	Taxes % GDP
Sweden	49.5
Denmark	49.1
Belgium	44.5
France	44.2
Norway	43.9
Finland	43.5
Italy	42.1
Austria	41.7
Netherlands	39.3
United Kingdom	37.1
New Zealand	36.7
Spain	36.6
Portugal	35.7
Germany	35.6
Canada	33.3
Ireland	31.9
Greece	31.3
Australia	30.6
Switzerland	29.2
United States	28.0
Japan	27.9

than second place Australia with 3.6%. In comparative terms, the U.S. economy was quite good, ranking fourth with an average growth rate of 3.2% over this quarter of a century. In contrast, the United States had the highest rate of infant mortality in the developed world in 2006 of 6.9 per 1,000 live births (see Table 2.13). This was appreciably higher than the 5.4 of the next-to-last Canada and two-and-half-times higher than the world leaders (Japan, Sweden, and Finland) at 2.6 to 2.8.

Two important advantages of a data array are that all the data for a variable can be presented in a table and that the ranking of cases, which is often of primary interest, can be ascertained with a single glance. In addition, the relative values of the countries or cases can be highlighted, as is done in Tables 2.10 to 2.13, by adding blank lines to the data arrays to indicate significant breaks between how highly the individual nations scored on the item in question. Yet, a perusal of these

Table 2.12: Average annual economic growth rate, 1980–2004.

Nations	Economic growth rate (%)
Ireland	5.1
Australia	3.6
Norway	3.3
United States	3.2
Finland	3.2
New Zealand	2.8
Spain	2.7
United Kingdom	2.5
Japan	2.4
Canada	2.3
Denmark	2.3
Greece	2.3
Portugal	2.2
Netherlands	2.0
France	1.9
Austria	1.9
Sweden	1.8
Belgium	1.8
Italy	1.7
Germany	1.6
Switzerland	1.3

tables would also suggest to anyone who does not have a photographic mind that it does not take too many cases for much of the data to get lost in the shuffle.

If we ask what these results imply about the perceptions of Professor Kingdon's students, the answer is certainly far from clear. America is not the same as most other nations, but whether the nation looks good or bad is ambiguous. For example, it has a comparatively small government. Conservatives would generally applaud this state of affairs, but liberals would decry it. Furthermore, it seems well above average on economic performance but below average on social outcomes, although there is some possibility that other indicators might produce different results. Just as the public opinion data showed that the answer to the question of whether the United States is conservative or liberal is quite complex, it is hard to definitively say how well it is doing.

Table 2.13: Infant mortality rate, 2006.

Nations	Infant mortality (Per 1,000 live births)
Japan	2.6
Sweden	2.8
Finland	2.8
Norway	3.2
Portugal	3.3
Austria	3.6
Belgium	3.7
Ireland	3.7
Greece	3.7
Denmark	3.8
France	3.8
Spain	3.8
Germany	3.8
Italy	3.9
Netherlands	4.4
Switzerland	4.4
Australia	4.7
United Kingdom	5.0
New Zealand	5.2
Canada	5.4
United States	6.9

2.2.2 Graphs

Graphical presentations are normally more effective than data arrays for general audiences or even for specialists who do not like to squint at blurry rows of little numbers. The comparisons and relationships are easier to see; and the presentation is often more dramatic. Yet, graphs are not an unmitigated blessing for several reasons. They almost always contain less material than a data array, so the information that they provide is almost inevitably quite simplistic. This section, hence, describes several types of graphs and illustrates them with the data on the developed democracies.

Perhaps the most common type of graph is the **bar graph** which is used to compare quantities of something for a few cases. Bar graphs, thus, are very well suited for comparing the values that a few nations have on some indicator. For our illustration, we will compare the United States and Sweden, representing respectively a small government committed to *laissez-faire* capitalism and a highly developed welfare state. Thus, this would seemingly form a good comparison to test competing images or models of how *laissez-faire* democracies should differ from welfare states. In particular, conservatives argue that government intervention and interference in the economy lead to waste and inefficiency and, thus, predict that the U.S. should outcompete nations with larger and more redistributive governments, such as Sweden. In contrast, liberals argue that a welfare state is necessary to take the edges off raw capitalism and, consequently, predict that welfare states would have considerably better social outcomes than the winner-take-all United States.

The bar graphs in Figures 2.1 and 2.2 confirm both the conservative and liberal theories about the effects of big government. On the one hand, Figure 2.1 shows that economic growth was much higher in America than in Sweden during 1980–2004. On the other hand, as can be seen in Figure 2.2, infant mortality in the United States is well over double the rate in Sweden.

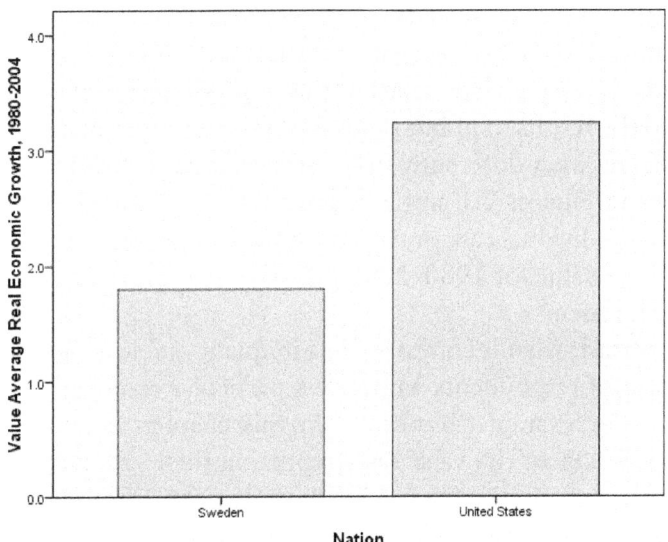

Figure 2.1: Comparing the economic growth rate for 1980–2004 in the U.S. and Sweden.

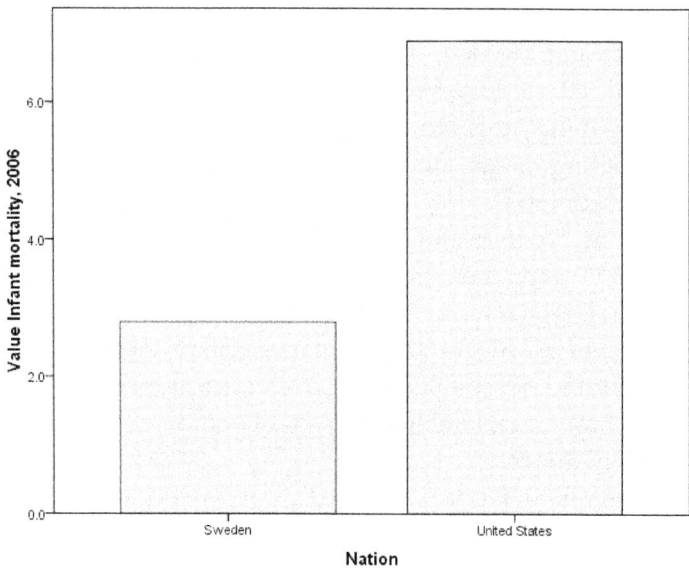

Figure 2.2: Comparing the infant mortality rate for 2006 in the U.S. and Sweden.

Graphs are a very popular form for presenting data because they are so attractive and easy to understand and interpret. They can provide, for example, a valuable alternate for presenting the information that is contained in frequency tables in the previous section. Applying bar graphs to the results of public opinion surveys requires conceptualizing the data somewhat differently than what we did for the socioeconomic indicators in Figures 2.1 and 2.2. For them, the basic datum was the value of an individual case or nation for the variable under analysis. For example, the value for 1980–2004 growth rate is 3.2% for America and 1.8% for Sweden.

In contrast, what is compared in a frequency table is the number or proportion of respondents who give a particular response to a survey question. For example, Table 2.1 in this chapter showed that 842 people or 53.8% of the valid cases reporting their presidential vote in 2008 supported Barack Obama, while 691 or 44.2% of the valid cases cast their votes for John McCain. The bar graph will look the same, incidentally, whether actual numbers of cases or valid percentages are used because, in either case, the proportionate height of the bars will

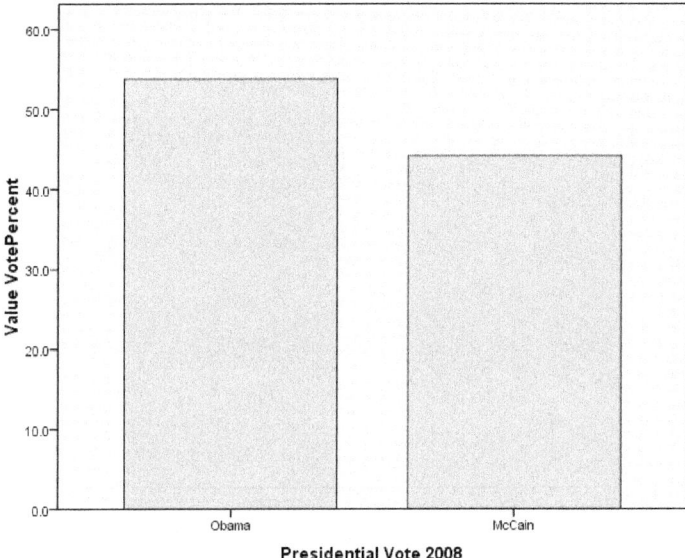

Figure 2.3: Support for Barack Obama and John McCain, 2008.

be exactly the same. Figure 2.3 presents the bar graph for presidential vote using percentages since it is easier to understand this standardized scale.

While bar graphs can be used in many different situations, two other types of graphs are applied to special types of data. Line graphs depict trends in a variable over time; and pie charts summarize the shares of something that add up to 100%, such as a budget. Even though bar graphs can be used in these situations, these two other types of graphs give a more attractive format visually; and, thus, they are often used.

In 2006, America clearly was a laggard in the developed world in terms of its comparatively high rate of infant mortality. Another way of assessing infant mortality in America is to examine change over time. Here, the answer to "How is the country doing?" is far different. Between 1960 and 2003, for example, the infant mortality rate fell by 73% from 26.0 to 7.0 per 1,000 live births.[14] Certainly, very substantial progress is being made. Figure 2.4 charts this rapid fall in

---

[14] Incidentally, this gives the opposite impression from the data on the current infant mortality rate in Table 2.13.

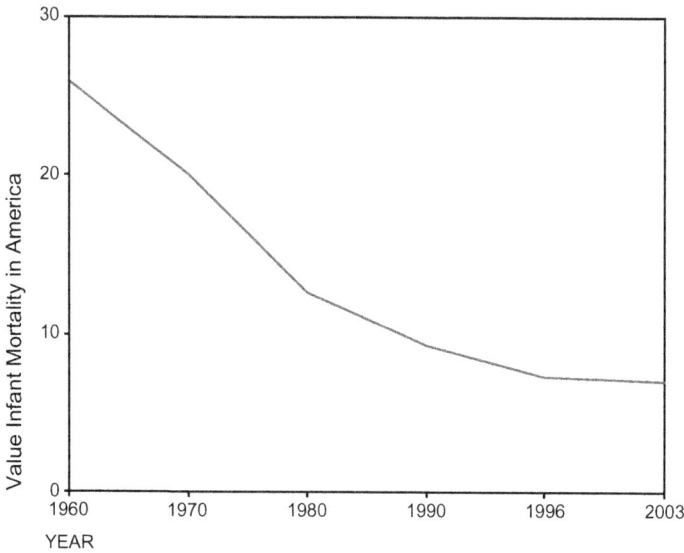

Figure 2.4: Line graph of the infant mortality rate in the United States, 1960–2003.

infant mortality with a line graph in which the line connects the data points for each year. It highlights the rapidly improving U.S. infant mortality rate and shows that the drop was sharper between 1960 and 1980 than between 1980 and 2003.

A second special situation in data analysis arises when the variable in question contains categories whose values sum to 100%, as national or state budgets do. In such cases, a pie chart may provide the best graphical technique for reporting the data. For example, Table 2.14 contains the percentage of the budget for the basic categories in the 2008 federal budget.[15] The pie chart in Figure 2.5 provides an attractive visual image of how much of the budget is consumed by different programs and areas. Social security and medicare constitute a third of the budget, which explains why reforming these programs is a leading objective of conservatives who want to reduce the budget deficit without raising taxes. The other two major items are human resources

---

[15]These data are taken from Office of Management and Budget, "Historical Tables" (Washington, D.C.: Office of Management and Budget, 2010). Available at www.omb.gov.

Table 2.14: U.S. Federal budget, 2008.

Medicare & Social Security	32.8%
Other Human Resources	29.0%
National Defense	20.1%
Physical Resources	5.3%
Other Functions	4.6%
Interest	8.2%
TOTAL	100.0%

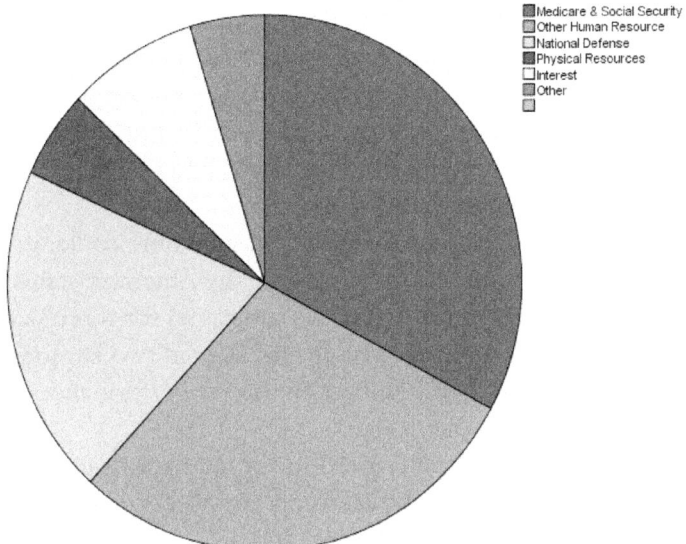

Figure 2.5: Pie graph of the U.S. Federal budget, 2008 (% of total budget).

at 29% and national defense at 20%, while nothing else except interest payments take up much over 5% of the budget.

EXERCISES

1. Go to the Gallup Poll web site (www.gallup.com) and access stories about two specific political issues (e.g., healthcare, economy, or immigration). Create frequency tables to report these data. Discuss the findings in terms of how conservative or liberal Americans are

and whether public opinion on each issue should be more helpful to Democrats or Republicans.

2. Table 2.4 showed that at the time of the 2008 elections Americans were liberal in terms of wanting an expansion of a variety of government services. Yet, within a year public opinion seemed to be demanding smaller, not larger, government. Why do you think this is so? Discuss what this means for the future direction of American politics and public policy.

3. Alan Wolfe concluded in his book *One Nation After All* that in the late 1990s the general American middle class citizenry, unlike the political elites, was not really polarized on cultural issues but, rather, displayed a fairly moderate consensus on most of these issues. Do you think that this is still true? Why or why not? Briefly describe how you could design a research project to find out whether Wolfe's findings are still true a decade later.

4. The StateMaster website (www.statemaster.com) contains a fairly large number of statistical indicators for the American states. Go to the website and get the data on two indicators for three states that you would like to compare. Present the data in two bar graphs and discuss which states have the best and worst performances on each indicator.

5. Time series data on the advanced industrial nations going back to approximately 1960 are available on the website of the Organization for Economic Cooperation and Development (OECD) at www.oecd.org. They can be found in the *OECD Factbook* under STATISTICS. Select one socioeconomic indicator and record the entire time series in a data array for a country in which you are interested. Then, present the data in a line graph. Discuss what the graph shows in terms of the change that occurs and whether or not this represents progress for the nation.

6. Conduct an anonymous survey of your class on about 10 political issues. Each student should report the results for two issues in frequency tables and bar graphs. Discuss the data in terms of how conservative or liberal the class is on each issue.

Part I
Designing Research Projects

Chapter 3

The Logic of Inquiry and Research Design

The discussion in Chapter 2 concerned the attributes of just one variable or, in statistics-speak, a single distribution. Frequency counts, for example, can tell us whether Americans are conservative or liberal in terms of their ideological self-identification, attitudes about abortion, or contentiousness about smut on TV. Data arrays and graphs, for their part, can tell us what the economic growth rate, life expectancy, or GDP per capita are in individual countries. Such information, in turn, indicates whether a specific nation (e.g., America) is performing well or poorly in the area in question. This certainly is important information; and many articles and books are written based on such results.

Still, analyzing or discussing only one item at a time is quite limiting because it cannot say anything concrete or definitive about the often vital question of why the distribution has the particular shape that it does. Indeed, political science devotes considerable effort to developing explanations for why specific variables or distributions have the values that they do. In essence, this involves asking and then answering the question of why. Why are some Americans Democrats while others are Republicans? Why do some nations have higher economic growth rates than others? Such questions turn our attention from the nature of a single variable to the **relationship** between two or more items. These efforts proceed at two interlinked levels. Theoretically, political scientists need to devise explanations for differences among individual citizens or developed nations. For example, it is generally assumed that wealthy Americans are more likely to identify themselves as Republicans than those who are less well endowed. Methodologically, they then have to devise and apply statistical techniques appropriate for testing whether or not these explanations actually hold.

This chapter provides an overview of how political scientists go about the first task. Sections 3.1 and 3.2 discuss political science concepts and their empirical indicators which form the basic building blocks for our theories. Section 3.3 considers the primary characteristics of empirical theory which involves establishing relationships among several variables in an analysis of politics. Finally, Section 3.4 describes the general process for constructing political science theories; and Section 3.5 develops the two specific theories around which most of the examples illustrating the statistical techniques described in this text will be organized.

3.1 CONCEPTS AND INDICATORS IN QUANTITATIVE RESEARCH

The discussion of American public opinion and of the differences among developed democracies in Chapter 2 revolved around several general concepts in the political science literature, such as whether an individual's ideology is liberal or conservative and whether or not a country has a welfare state. This calls attention to a two-step process in developing a quantitative study. First, the key concepts or topics of interest must be selected; and, second, strategies for measuring them must be devised that will produce quantitative indicators for each concept in the theoretical model. This section, hence, discusses the critical nature of the relationship between concepts and indicators in empirical research. The first subsection describes what concepts are; and the second discusses indicators and two somewhat different strategies for linking them to more abstract concepts in political science research.

3.1.1 Concepts

The building blocks of political science theory and analysis are called concepts.[1] **Concepts define what are considered to be basic or essential political phenomena and provide the rules or criteria for grouping cases into different categories.** For example, democracy has long been a central concept in political science; and countries have been classified as democratic or nondemocratic depending upon whether the citizens can choose and hold accountable their governments and political leaders and upon whether basic political and civil rights are protected. Democracies, in turn, are often conceptualized as to whether their form of government is presidential or parliamentary or as to the number and ideological orientations of major political parties competing for power in them.[2]

A more complex example is provided by the concept of ideology which can be defined as a basic set of political beliefs. Both political parties (another concept) and individuals are often classified as conservative or liberal based on these beliefs. Defining ideology as the division between conservatives and liberals, however, is far from unproblematic. Let us define conservatives, as was done in Chapter 1, as supporters of a strong national defense, a business-friendly environment, and traditional political values and as opponents of big government and redistributive services helping the poor. Most of us would think that this definition is fairly mundane, yet it implies several severe definitional conflicts. The first three conservative goals, for example, might well require a large and activist government to provide military protection, business subsidies, and prohibitions against immoral activities, all of which would draw strident liberal protests. This underlines the complexity and potential ambiguity of even well understood concepts in political science.

---

[1] Abraham Kaplan, *The Conduct of Inquiry: Methodology for Behavioral Science* (San Francisco: Chandler Publishing Company, 1964) Part II provides a much more detailed discussion of concepts in the social sciences.
[2] Giovanni Sartori, *Parties and Party Systems: A Framework for Analysis* (Cambridge: Cambridge University Press, 1976).

3.1.2 Linking Indicators to Concepts

In addition to their potential complexity, most concepts used in political science theory are fairly abstract which raises the question of how they can be applied to actual politics and government in the United States and elsewhere. In general, this involves finding logical connections between the abstract concept and measurable **indicators** that can be found in the real world. As a simple example, let us look at how we might measure the conservatism of a politician or voter. As indicated in Table 3.1, there are a number of attitudes and positions that are clearly conservative: self-identification as a conservative, support for small government, support for tax cuts, opposition to government intervention in the economy, opposition to welfare policies, support for a strong national defense, a pro-life position on abortion, and support for censoring pornography. Any one or some combination of these attitudes, hence, could be used to provide measurable indicators of the more abstract concept of conservatism.

More formally, the selection of the actual indicators of a theoretical concept is a key step in the research process that is termed the **operationalization** of the concept. That is, the researcher must move from an abstract definition of a concept of interest to a precise statement of how it will be measured in his or her quantitative study:

> *Conceptualization* is the refinement and specification of abstract concepts, and *operationalization* is the development of specific

Table 3.1: Example of concept and indicators.

Concept
Ideological Conservatism of an Individual

Indicators
Self-identification as Conservative
Supports Small Government
Supports Tax Cuts
Opposes Government Intervention in the Economy
Opposes Welfare Spending
Pro-Military
Pro-Life on Abortion
Supports Censorship of Pornography

research procedures (operations) that will result in empirical observations representing those concepts in the real world.[3]

For example, the abstract definition of a conservative as someone who opposes the development of a large welfare state can be operationalized by being defined or measured as support for cutting child care spending or reducing the general level of government services by respondents to the 2008 National Election Study (NES).

There are two very different approaches to operationalizing abstract concepts by specific measurable indicators in political science research that possess countervailing advantages and disadvantages.[4] The first is to use **a single operational definition** of the concept. For example, a person could be defined as a conservative if she or he placed themselves on the conservative end of the spectrum on general ideology or if they took a pro-life position on abortion. Conversely, the **multiple indicator** approach assumes that many concepts in political science are so complex that they cannot be adequately measured by a single indicator. Thus, the researcher should develop multiple indicators of a complex concept, such as conservatism, and use the much more voluminous data that they produce in defining and analyzing the concept.

The first approach has the advantage that each concept has a single, unambiguous operationalization, so that measuring and relating it to other variables is straightforward. The drawback, of course, is that it may be impossible to find a single operational definition that is really adequate. For example, the tremendous variation in the level of support for attitudes universally considered to be conservative in Chapter 2 certainly cautions against using any one of them by itself to measure conservatism. Conversely, the multiple indicator approach provides much richer information about a concept, but also raises the problem of how to combine it to provide quantitative results, although some very advanced techniques, such as structural equations

---

[3] Earl Babbie, *The Practice of Social Research*, 7th Edn. (Belmont, CA: Wadsworth, 1995), p. 132.
[4] For a much more detailed discussion of the operationalization of indicators, see *ibid.*, Chapter 6.

modeling, have been developed that can model and measure "latent variables" based on the relationships among multiple indicators.[5] There is, unfortunately, no universal principle for choosing between these two competing approaches. Rather, the contrasting advantages of each need to be weighed in the context of a specific research project. Moreover, the questions of reliability and validity discussed in the next section raise additional problems for linking abstract concepts to measurable indicators.

3.2 RELIABILITY AND VALIDITY

Linking a concept defined in abstract theoretical terms to the indicators that are actually used to measure it can raise problems beyond the initial choice of whether to use a simple operational definition or to apply multiple indicators. For example, an abstract concept to which we have already referred to repeatedly is a person's political ideology as denoted by a liberal-to-conservative scale. Certainly, a large number of indicators exist for whether a person is conservative or liberal: their own self-identification; their positions on tax cuts, abortion, social security spending, and numerous other issues; whether they were favorably or unfavorably disposed toward traditional values; and so forth (see Table 3.1).

The connection between overall or abstract conservatism and a person's responses to these questions might appear at first glance to be simple and even unquestionable. Yet, the linkage between concepts used in social science theory, such as a person's ideology, and the measures that are taken with regard to them is often a little and sometimes more than a little ambiguous or problematic. In Chapter 2, when we tried to measure how conservative Americans are, we got very different answers depending upon what indicator was used. This almost certainly reflected reality in that many people do have both conservative and liberal opinions on different subjects. In many instances, however, the fact that several indicators of a concept produce very different measurements of it can create major problems for the analyst.

---

[5] Rex Kline, *Principles and Practices of Structural Equation Modeling* (New York: Guilford Press, 1998).

A field study that was conducted several decades ago gives a good illustration of the fundamental problems that can arise when we try to reach conclusions about the nature of political or social reality based on indicators of an abstract concept. This research focused on alcohol consumption in a "dry" region, that is, an area where the sale of alcoholic beverages is illegal. The researchers used two different measures: (1) questions in an interview and (2) a surreptitious examination of the respondents' trash cans. Not surprisingly, the two indicators produced rather different results, with the second method showing much more drinking than the first.[6] The problem for the analyst, then, is to decide which measure of alcohol consumption better depicts life in the community being studied. In this case, it is fairly obvious that the second indicator is the more accurate. However, the choice is often not so clear cut. Moreover, the underlying assumption here should not be particularly welcomed by political scientists who routinely base their analyses and arguments upon public opinion data. After all, if people lie about their liquor consumption, why should they not lie about which politicians, parties, or policies they love and hate?

3.2.1 Reliability

In technical terms, the two major issues concerning how well an indicator measures a concept are the **reliability** and **validity** of the indicator in question.[7] **Reliability** is the simpler issue and **is defined as how constant the results produced by repeated measures of the indicator are**. In the physical sciences, where the nature of what is being studied is well understood, thinking in terms of the reliability of measuring instruments makes sense. For example, if a scale varies in the weight of a given mass of some element that it records in repeated

---

[6]Eugene J. Webb, Donald T. Campbell, Richard D. Schwartz and Lee Sechrest, *Unobtrusive Measures: Nonreactive Research in the Social Sciences* (Chicago: Rand McNally, 1966), Chapter 5.

[7]For a much more detailed discussion of reliability and validity, see Edward G. Carmines and Richard A. Zeller, *Reliability and Validity Assessment* (Beverly Hills, CA: Sage, 1979).

weighings, it is assumed that the scale is not reliable rather than that the actual weight changes.

In political science, though, reliability becomes somewhat more problematic. If we get different results at different times, does that mean that the measure is unreliable? Or has the concept in which we are interested changed? For example, the 2008 NES survey was conducted in two parts in which the respondents were interviewed both before and after the election. Suppose someone said that they were going to vote for John McCain in the pre-election interview, but then reported voting for Barack Obama in the post-election one. Does that mean that the NES question on presidential vote was not reliable or that the person changed his or her mind during the course of the campaign? Most political scientists and certainly the people who are associated with the NES project would argue for "real change", while a skeptic might be happy to conclude that this shows that polls are unreliable. In short, reliability can be easily estimated by comparing the results of several measurements taken at different points in time. However, if what is being measured can conceivably change over time, any conclusion about reliability is not very reliable — to make a pun.

3.2.2 Validity

Validity is the degree to which an indicator actually measures the concept in question. Establishing the validity of their measures should certainly be a high priority for political scientists. Yet, a quick review of the methods that are used for validating indicators strongly suggests that none are foolproof!

Probably, the most commonly used basis rests on what is called **face validity** in the sense that the linkage between the concept and the indicator is so obvious that it can be accepted at "face value". Much of the time this is reasonable. It certainly seems obvious that someone who calls themself a conservative, or who wants to downsize the federal government, or who is pro-life on abortion has at least some conservative political values. However, it is also easy to find cases where "face validity" falls on its face. Over half of Americans, for example, are liberal on such issues as social security, education, and environmentalism even though conservatives have a large lead over liberals in terms of ideological self-identification.

This brings us to three more sophisticated approaches for establishing the validity of the relationship between a concept and its measurable indicators. In **convergent validity**, several indicators of a concept are used. If all produce the same result, much more confidence can be given to their measurement of the concept. A more powerful technique is **criterion validity**, in which an indicator is compared to another one whose validity has already been established. Finally, the most powerful approach is probably **construct validity**. Here, the concept in question is part of a well-established theory; so that a single indicator can be compared to the results provided by a wide array of indicators of several other concepts. All these approaches make the very reasonable assumption that the greater the number of consistent results, the more confidence we can place in them. Yet, one can still wonder if validities can be established beyond a shadow of a doubt. Criterion and construct validities require that some concept-indicator linkages have been validated in the past — which could only have been done by face or convergent validity!

This leaves us with the not unreasonable reliance upon convergent validity. However, multiple indicators can and sometimes do produce multiple results as can be seen in Tables 3.2 and 3.3. Table 3.2, for example, reports public opinion in 1992 on three items that all have strong face validity as indicators of a person's support for the military. Yet, the results in the table are monumentally inconsistent. The first item suggests that Americans strongly support the military since 77% viewed it positively, in contrast to only 9% who expressed negative feelings. Moreover, almost four-fifths of Americans (78%) felt that maintaining a strong military was either very important or extremely important, while a mere 2% said that it was not an important national objective. In very sharp contrast, however, the citizenry in 1992 wanted to cut defense spending rather than increase it by the two-to-one margin of 44% to 22%. Clearly, there is a substantial validity problem here! Presumably, the first two indicators tapped general and positive feelings toward the military. The question on defense spending, in contrast, evidently elicited beliefs about spending priorities. Here, the

Table 3.2: Support for military, 1992.

Feelings towards Military	
Negative	9%
Neutral	14%
Positive	77%
TOTAL	100%
Importance of Maintaining a Strong Military	
Not Important	2%
Somewhat Important	21%
Very Important	42%
Extremely Important	36%
TOTAL	101%
Defense Spending	
Cut	44%
Keep Same	34%
Increase	22%
TOTAL	100%

Table 3.3: Decidedly contrasting results about Americans' views about gun laws.

1996	
Oppose Gun Control	53%
Favor Gun Control	47%
TOTAL	100%
2000	
Relax Gun Laws	4%
Keep Them the Same	37%
Make Gun Laws Stricter	59%
TOTAL	100%

combination of the end of the Cold War and the 1991–1992 recession presumably led many Americans to give higher priority to domestic than to defense outlays.

Table 3.3 compares Americans' views on gun laws in 1996 and 2000. Here, two somewhat different questions were used; and the results differ dramatically. In 1996, when people were simply asked whether they supported or opposed gun control, the public appeared slightly conservative as the nays held a slim majority of 53% to 47%. In contrast, the question was changed in 2000 to whether existing gun laws should be relaxed or made stricter. Given this option, Americans appeared to be quite liberal as they preferred tightening to loosening gun laws by an overwhelming margin of 59% to 4%. In the abstract, both questions would have face validity as measures of a person's attitude toward gun laws. Yet, the extremely contradictory results show that seemingly similar indicators do not necessarily produce similar results. The fact that the two questions were asked four years apart certainly raises the possibility of reliability problems or real attitudinal changes. Still, the difference is so great that it is almost impossible not to believe that they elicited different views or attitudes, even if the reasons for this remain murky.

These contradictory results should not be taken to mean that all public opinion or other social science research is meaningless. Rather, we need to weigh evidence carefully and try to make the best judgments or interpretations we can based on what can be found. For example, the validity problems that were illustrated by the data in Tables 3.2 and 3.3 strongly suggest the value of looking at several indicators or measures of a concept whenever it is possible.

3.3 CHARACTERISTICS OF EMPIRICAL THEORY

Empirical theory seeks to determine why things occur. To do this, it searches for cause-and-effect relationships among variables relevant to the study of politics.[8] Empirical theory has five principal elements or characteristics. These are that it involves explanation, specifying the expected relationships between two or more variables, simplification, abstraction, and testing the theory against reality.[9] The first subsection briefly summarizes these characteristics; and the second discusses the difference between deductive and inductive means of constructing theories.

---

[8] See the first section of Chapter 4 for a much more detailed discussion of empirical theory.
[9] Kaplan, *op. cit.*, Parts VIII and IX discusses this with much greater sophistication.

3.3.1 The Five Elements of an Empirical Theory

The first characteristic of empirical theory is that it involves **explanation** or asking and answering the question "why". Very simple examples of explanation are the expectations that wealthier people will be more conservative than poorer ones and that infant mortality rates will be lower in developed nations which have large welfare states than in those that do not. Both these are explanatory statements in the sense that variations in one variable — how conservative an individual American is or what the infant mortality rate in a specific industrialized nation is — are explained by the values of another variable — how high the family income of the citizen is or how high a priority a nation gives to its welfare state functions. Explanation, then, is based on an assumption of **determinism** or, more simply, that things happen for a reason. People do not just pick their political beliefs randomly out of thin air but adopt them based on their conditions in life. Someone who is poor will be likely to want government assistance and, thus, favor big government. Someone who is rich, in contrast, may see little direct benefits for themselves in government programs and resent high tax rates, thereby favoring small government.

Second, explanation *must* involve the **relationship between two (or more) variables**, rather than the description of just one factor or item. For example, the data in Chapter 2 showing that Americans are conservative on ideological self-identification and taxes while being liberal on education spending and split on abortion, do not and cannot offer any explanation for these attitudes in themselves. Rather, to explain why someone is conservative or liberal on any of these items, we must posit some characteristic, such as wealth or belief in traditional values, that should affect a person's political attitudes.

Similarly, just listing a country's infant mortality rate does not provide an explanation *per se*. However, there is a fundamental difference in the nature of the data sets on Americans' political attitudes and on national rates of infant mortality that results in the latter being at least suggestive of the explanations involved in empirical theory. The NES poll surveyed 2,102 "nameless and faceless" Americans, so there is little that might be said about how a particular John or Jane Doe responded. The national data set, in contrast, includes slightly over 20 nations. Thus, looking at their individual values might well suggest some explanations for variations in infant mortality rates. For example, the lower infant mortality in Sweden and the Netherlands compared to the U.S. implies that large welfare states might bring down infant mortality. It should be noted, though, that these simple two-or-three-nation comparisons can only suggest but not support or prove an explanation. This can only be done by including all the relevant countries in the analysis.

A third characteristic of empirical theory is **simplification** which means that the theory focuses upon a few important causes rather than everything that might have a tangential influence. For example, a theory of why some Americans identify themselves as Democrats and others as Republicans would probably include their degree of affluence and belief in traditional values, but not whether they had ever lived next door to Barack Obama or Mitt Romney or whether they invested in Microsoft right after Bill Gates left his garage or in Enron right before the bottom fell out. The key for a successful empirical theory, then, is to "cut to the chase". That is, to simplify the chaos of the political world by picking out what is most important, while simultaneously avoiding the error of oversimplification, such as leaving out vital explanatory factors.

While simplification may appeal to students because having only a few central causes to remember is much better than having to keep several dozen things in mind, the fourth characteristic of **abstraction** can be less attractive to those primarily interested in practical politics. This is because abstraction, or making generalizations about a large number of cases, moves away from the interesting dirt and details of politics to the more rarified air of empirical theory. A good example comes from theories about presidential elections. Historical treatments of why John Kennedy narrowly edged Richard Nixon in 1960 focus on such tantalizing tidbits as Nixon's "five o'clock shadow" and sweaty brow during the first televised debate, along with a recent rumor that Bobby Kennedy turned up the thermostat, or as the Democrats' alleged stealing of the elections in Illinois and Texas. When political scientists theorize about presidential elections, though, they take out the personalities and the sleaze and do things like divide candidates into incumbents and nonincumbents and hypothesize that incumbents win in good times and lose in bad times (see Table 1.2 in Chapter 1), which is admittedly less tantalizing than political gossip.

Finally, the fifth characteristic of empirical theory is that it **must** be subject to **testing against reality**. That is, you must be able to see whether or not the predictions of the theory hold true in the real world. This involves a three-stage process. First, the theory must be formulated in terms that can be measured in the real world of politics; second, data have to be gathered on the variables that are included in the theory; and, third, the data must be analyzed to see how well they conform to the theory. For example, a commonly applied theory about political attitudes in the United States is that people with high socioeconomic status (SES) will be more conservative than others. The first step in testing this theory would be to design several measures of each concept: income, education, and race could be used to measure SES, while Chapter 2 included numerous indicators of conservatism. The second stage would be to get data, either by accessing an existing data set like the 2008 NES or by conducting your own survey. Then, at the third stage, statistical analysis would be applied to see whether wealthier and more educated people actually are more conservative than other Americans.

3.3.2 From Whence Do Theories Come?

A fundamental question, of course, is how theories are constructed. In essence, the two approaches are **induction** or making generalizations from sets of descriptive facts and **deduction** or drawing implications from an existing theory to a new situation or context. A good example of this fundamental difference is provided by the two alternatives for developing the proposition or theory that affluence affects a person's view of the government in the United States with the wealthy opposing big government. One could conduct a survey that included questions on a person's income and whether he or she supported or opposed big government. If most of the wealthy opposed and most of the poor supported a large and activist government, the theory would have been arrived at inductively. If both the wealthy and the poor took the same position, either for or against big government, incidentally, there would be no association or relationship. Conversely, one can focus on the benefits and burdens of big government. Since government services are widely seen as primarily benefitting the poor[10] and government revenues as involving taxes on the rich, it would be easy to deduce from this that the less affluent would like big government and the more affluent would resent it.

Some who focus on the science in political science believe that deduction is more advanced and important than induction. Yet, deduction involves applying, extending, and perhaps modifying existing theory, which raises the question of where that theory came from originally. Ultimately, somebody had to look at a large and seemingly chaotic number of facts and impart order and comprehensibility to them by inductive theorizing. Thus, both approaches play vital roles in the development of political science theory.

3.4 CONSTRUCTING EXPLANATORY THEORIES

Once the concepts of interest and the actual indicators of them have been specified, we are ready for the next stage of the analysis which is to use **empirical theory** to derive hypotheses about the expected **relationships** among these variables. A **hypothesis**, in turn, is the cause-and-effect or causal linkage that is presumed to exist between two variables. For example, when we say that we expect wealthier people to be more conservative than poorer ones, we are really indicating: (1) that there are two variables, affluence and ideology, and (2) that most of the time the wealthy will have more conservative attitudes than the poor. Theories, at least in political science, usually encompass a considerable number of relationships, but here we shall start (and end) at the fairly simple end of theoretical complexity with only a small number of relationships included in the theory.

---

[10]The review of the federal budget in Chapter 2 (see Table 2.14) would suggest otherwise because middle class entitlements, like Social Security and Medicare, encompass a third of the budget, while defense, interest, and physical resources constitute another third.

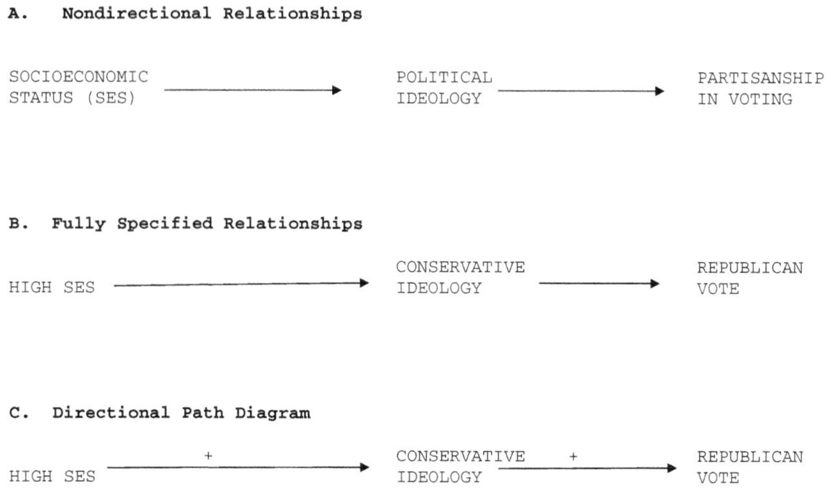

A. Nondirectional Relationships

SOCIOECONOMIC STATUS (SES) ⟶ POLITICAL IDEOLOGY ⟶ PARTISANSHIP IN VOTING

B. Fully Specified Relationships

HIGH SES ⟶ CONSERVATIVE IDEOLOGY ⟶ REPUBLICAN VOTE

C. Directional Path Diagram

HIGH SES —+⟶ CONSERVATIVE IDEOLOGY —+⟶ REPUBLICAN VOTE

Figure 3.1: The socioeconomic model of American voting.

3.4.1 Sketching a Theoretical Model

Figure 3.1 outlines what might be called the socioeconomic model of American voting. This is a two-step theory or model. The first step or hypothesis is that people with higher SES tend to be conservatives; the second is that conservatives tend to vote Republican. In the figure, arrows are used to show the direction of the expected cause-and-effect relationships. For example, the fact that the arrow goes from SES to political ideology in Model A at the top of Figure 3.1 denotes the assumption that a person's SES affects or causes his or her ideology and not the other way around.

Figure 3.1 contains three models which give alternate specifications of the same theory. Model A indicates that SES affects personal ideology which, in turn, influences partisanship in voting. This certainly is a simple theory which most political scientists would regard as valid without a second thought. What a second thought would indicate, however, is that while this model is not necessarily wrong, it is incomplete because it does not hypothesize or predict the exact nature of these two relationships. That is, it does not tell us, for example, how people with a specific ideology should be expected to vote. For example, would a conservative be expected to vote for Democratic, or Republican, or third party candidates? Model B, therefore, is necessary to state the **fully specified relationship**. This theory states that the normal expectation is that people with higher SES should be conservative ideologically which, in turn, should predispose them to vote for Republican candidates.

Model C at the bottom of the figure contains the same three variables in the same order as Model B, but it also adds the sign of the expected direction of the relationship (either positive or negative). The plus (+) sign for the arrow going from conservative ideology to Republican vote, for example, shows that people who have the first characteristic (conservatism) would be expected to be more likely than other Americans to have the other one (voting Republican). Specifying the expected direction of a relationship is especially important in the analysis of public opinion data because they contain many variables for which the direction of the scale is arbitrary. For example, ideology can be defined and measured *either* as conservatism or, standing the scale on its head, as liberalism. Figure 3.2, for example, shows the different directions of relationships that might be postulated between SES and ideology. The indicators of SES, such as income and education, should be positively related to conservative ideology but negatively related to liberal ideology.

Theoretical models, like Figure 3.1, are called **arrow diagrams** or **path models**. The reason for the term arrow diagram should be obvious since arrows are used to designate causal relationships with an arrow going from each cause to each effect in the model. These diagrams also show the path of influence or causality predicted by the theory. For example, according to Figure 3.1, SES influences a person's

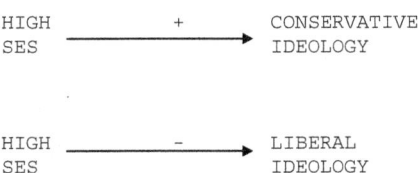

Figure 3.2: Possible specific hypothesized relationships in the socioeconomic model of American voting.

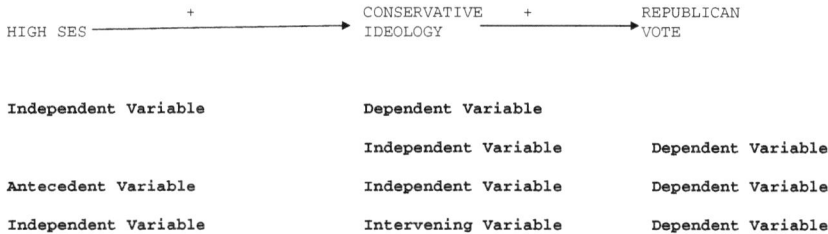

Figure 3.3: Terminology for cause-and-effect relationships in the hypotheses modeled by arrow diagrams.

ideology directly. In addition, because ideology has a direct impact on partisanship, SES has an indirect effect on whether she or he supports Democrats or Republicans that is exercised through ideology.

Political scientists have several terms for the variables that are involved in these relationships, as illustrated in Figure 3.3. The effect in a hypothesis is called the **dependent variable** because its value is considered to be dependent upon or explained by the cause. In contrast, the cause is the **independent variable** because, at least for the purpose of the specific hypothesis, its value is unexplained. When a model contains more than one hypothesis, the same variable may be an independent variable in some hypotheses and a dependent variable in others. For example, in the socioeconomic model of voting presented in Figure 3.3, conservative ideology is a dependent variable explained by SES but is also, in turn, an independent variable that explains Republican voting.

When considering a combination of three variables, furthermore, two other terms also come into play. If the primary hypothesis under consideration is the one linking the middle one (conservative ideology) as the independent variable to the last one (Republican vote) as the dependent variable, then the initial variable in the model (high SES) is called the **antecedent variable** because it is assumed to help structure the relationship between the independent and dependent variables. Conversely, if the principal hypothesis uses the initial item (high SES) to explain the final one (Republican vote), the middle one (conservative ideology) becomes an **intervening variable** because it mediates the effect that the independent variable exercises upon the dependent one.

3.4.2 Hypotheses

Hypotheses form the central feature of empirical theory and the arrow diagrams that summarize it. Thus, some attention needs to be paid to how to state and evaluate hypotheses. Robert Bernstein and James Dyer, for instance, have developed a concise overview of what constitutes a good hypothesis that is summarized in Table 3.4.[11]

Table 3.4: Bernstein–Dyer requisites for good hypotheses.

A. Hypotheses Must Contain

1. Two variables
2. A cause-and-effect statement linking them
3. The theoretical population to which the hypothesis applies
4. Generalizability
5. Absence of value judgments

Example: "The higher a person's SES in the United States, the more likely she or he is to hold conservative political views."

B. Common Errors in Hypotheses

1. Hypothesis only refers to one variable

   "Americans are conservative".
   "European countries have welfare states".

2. In the hypothesis, the relationship between the independent and dependent variables is not clear

   "SES is related to ideology".
   "National affluence influences infant mortality".

3. Hypothesis makes a value judgment

   "Conservatives have sold out to the rich".
   "Liberals are destroying America values".

4. Hypothesis lacks generality

   "Sarah Palin is more conservative than Nancy Pelosi".
   "The U.S. will have a higher economic growth rate than Sweden".

Source: Robert A. Bernstein and James A. Dyer, *An Introduction to Political Science Methods*, 3rd Edn. (Englewood Cliffs, NJ: Prentice Hall, 1992), pp. 6–8 and 11–12 — examples not in original text.

---

[11] Robert A. Bernstein and James A. Dyer, *An Introduction to Political Science Methods*, 3rd Edn. (Englewood Cliffs, NJ: Prentice Hall, 1992), Chapter 1.

Consider the hypothesis:

> The higher a person's SES in the United States, the more likely she or he is to hold conservative political views.

This straightforward statement neatly illustrates each of the five components that, according to Bernstein and Dyer, a good hypothesis must have, as summarized in Part A at the top of the table. The two variables are SES and conservative ideology; the causal linkage between them is that people with high SES tend to be conservatives; American citizens form the theoretical population; the generalization in the hypothesis applies to over 100 million voters; and there is no value judgment about whether conservatives (or liberals) are good or bad or ugly.

This might make theory building and hypothesis construction appear very easy, but it is also very easy to make critical mistakes that invalidate the hypothesis, as listed in Part B in the bottom half of Table 3.4. First, such statements as "Americans are conservatives" or "European countries have welfare states" may or may not be true, but they are not actual hypotheses because they only refer to one variable — the ideology of individual Americans or the institutions created by European governments. Second, the exact nature of the expected relationship may not be specified. To say that "SES is related to ideology" or that "national affluence influences infant mortality" does not indicate the exact nature of the relationship. Rather, a good hypothesis would be: "Wealthier people are more conservative"; or "Wealthier nations have lower infant mortality rates". Third, while denouncing one's political enemies is certainly popular both on the campaign trail and in friendly and not-so-friendly bull sessions, arguments such as "Conservatives have sold out to the rich" or "Liberals are destroying American values" are simply value statements, not theoretical hypotheses.

Finally, a hypothesis that just names two individual cases is not appropriate because there is no generalization to a broader population, although such a generalization may be implicit. For example, to say that Sarah Palin is more conservative than Nancy Pelosi might be taken to imply that Republican politicians are more conservative than Democrats and that people from smaller communities are more conservative than political leaders from large metropolitan centers. Similarly, one might expect that the U.S. would have a higher economic growth rate than Sweden because its *laissez-faire* policies provide a much better climate for business than the larger welfare state in Sweden. The specific variables and theoretical population should be explicitly stated in the hypothesis, though.

3.4.3 What Disproves a Hypothesis?

The next question concerns how we go about showing that hypotheses are true or false. In philosophical logic and many hard sciences, hypotheses are considered to represent **universal statements**. That is, they are assumed to be always true; and, if we can find evidence of even one instance when they are not, the hypothesis and the theory on which it is based are **falsified**. For example, in a chemistry lab, if the same chemicals are mixed in the same proportions under the same conditions, the results will always be the same. This is not so, however, for most social science theories. Consider what might be taken as the almost self-evident hypotheses that wealthy Americans are more conservative than poorer ones. If we look at George H. Bush or George H.W. Bush, we find wealthy individuals who are conservatives, as the hypothesis predicts. However, what about Ted Kennedy who was just as wealthy if not more so and quite liberal?

We could very quickly find an exception, I dare say, to every hypothesis in empirical political theory. Still, if most rich people identify themselves as conservatives while most poor people call themselves liberal, it would seem that a valid relationship does indeed exist. Consequently, political science and the social sciences, in general, view their hypotheses as containing **statistical statements** which are defined as statements that are **true more often than would be expected by random chance**, as will be discussed in more detail in the later chapters on specific statistical techniques.

The idea of statistical statements also raises a technical point about how to establish them. So far, we have discussed hypotheses in this section in positive terms. That is, the hypotheses are stated as relationships that are expected to be found — for example, wealthier Americans will be more conservative than those who are less affluent.

Technically, in contrast, relationships are measured in terms of the probability that the **null hypothesis** of no difference is true (i.e., that the rich and the poor are similar ideologically). When this probability, as measured by standard statistical theory, is low, **the null hypothesis is rejected**, indicating that there is indeed a significant linkage between the variables in the hypothesis.

Finally, the concept of statistical statements also implies that empirical theory rests upon **contingent conclusions**. This means that even if the evidence is in line with their theories, political scientists believe that new evidence may show that the theory is incomplete or incorrect. Examples of contingent conclusions being radically revised are easy to find, even in the supposedly hard sciences. For example, Einstein's theory of relativity went far beyond Newton's theory of gravity. Even more dramatically, 200 years ago, the generally accepted theory in medicine was that the sick should be bled either by being cut or having leeches suck them. Luckily, this theory has long been discarded — which probably contributes to the major increases in life expectancy over the last century or so! Returning to the more humble relationships considered in this text, Japan went from having an exemplary political economy during the 1970s and 1980s to recording one of the worst economic records in the developed world over the last 20 years. Consequently, scholars have switched their focus from what Japan did right[12] to what it did wrong.[13]

3.5 DERIVING TWO SIMPLE THEORIES

The five chapters in Parts III and IV of this book describe techniques for testing hypotheses by measuring how strong the relationships are between specific variables. The discussion of these techniques will be organized around evaluating two simple theoretical models. The first seeks to explain the ideology and partisanship of American citizens; and the second examines the support for competing conservative and liberal

---

[12] For example, Ezra F. Vogel, *Japan as Number One: Lessons for America* (Cambridge: Harvard University Press, 1979).

[13] For example, Richard Katz, *Japan, the System that Soured: The Rise and Fall of the Japanese Economic Miracle* (Armonk, NY: M.E. Sharpe, 1998).

perspectives upon the consequences of big government. Focusing our analytic attention upon a limited number of questions should make the statistical results more meaningful and comprehensible.

As indicated both in the discussion of economic issues in Chapter 2 and in the illustration of the difference between induction and deduction earlier in this chapter, it is very widely, if not universally, assumed in the study of American politics that the wealthy tend to be conservatives and the poor tend to be liberals because of their clashing economic interests or the "politics of rich and poor".[14] This constitutes what might be called the two-stage socioeconomic model of voting sketched in Figure 3.1. At stage one, people with higher SES are viewed as being more likely to be conservative; and at stage two, high SES and conservatism are predicted to lead to supporting Republicans at the polls.

The discussion in Chapter 2 of the growing importance of cultural issues for the U.S. politics also suggests that people with traditional values should be more conservative than other Americans as well. This creates a third stage to our explanatory model that is diagramed in Figure 3.4. For the first stage of the model, let us hypothesize that people with high SES will be more likely than others hold traditional values, reflecting their "establishment" concern with the social, economic, and political *status quo*. In the second stage, people with high SES and

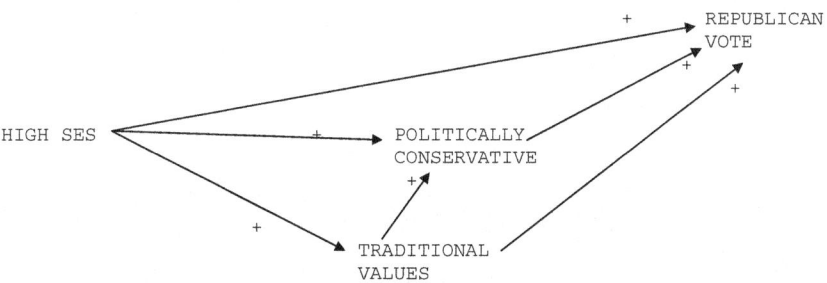

Figure 3.4: Model of relationships among high SES, traditional values, political conservatism, and republican voting.

---

[14] Kevin Phillips, *The Politics of Rich and Poor: Wealth and the American Electorate in The Reagan Aftermath* (New York: Random House, 1990).

traditional values are both predicted to hold conservative political views. Finally, people with high SES, traditional values, and conservative views all should be more likely than citizens with other characteristics and attitudes to support Republican candidates at the polls.

The comparison between the United States and Sweden in Chapter 2 suggested two hypotheses reflecting contradictory ideological hues. First the very good economic performance of the *laissez-faire* U.S., especially compared to the low growth recorded by Sweden with its large welfare state, supports the conservative theory that big government undercuts or is negatively related to economic performance. In contrast, the leading position of Sweden in terms of social outcomes, as well as America's mediocre record in this area, suggests that big government leads to or is positively related to better social outcomes. The one-stage model in the top half of Figure 3.5 depicts these two relationships.

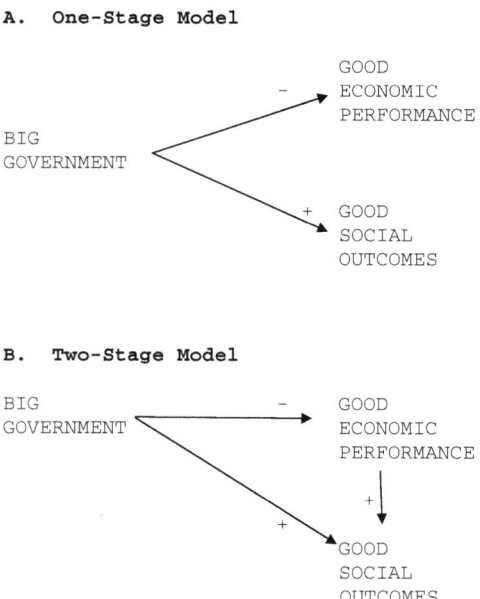

Figure 3.5: Model of relationships among big government, good economic performance, and good social outcomes.

These two hypotheses are contradictory in the sense that one posits that big government produces good effects (the liberal view), while the other predicts that it will have negative consequences (the conservative position). Yet, they are not *logically contradictory* in that both may be true, at least in the short term. Perhaps, we should hope that this does not turn out to be the case because of the policy dilemma that it would create: increasing or decreasing the size of government to produce better outcomes in one area would, simultaneously, lead to worse outcomes in the other. If both hypotheses are supported, therefore, complex issues of policy trade-offs arise which would probably be far more welcomed by scholars who love to debate than by political officials whose careers get destroyed when bad things happen.

Finally, there is also the possibility of a two-stage relationship. In particular, better economic performance should ultimately enhance social outcomes because economic growth creates more resources for the entire society. The bottom half of Figure 3.5 diagrams this relationship. Here, the policy inconsistency or trade-off is most manifest. The direct impact of larger government on good social outcomes is positive. However, the indirect influence is negative since larger government leads to worse economic performance which would be expected ultimately to undercut social outcomes. Thus, in contrast to the consistent theoretical model of American voters in Figure 3.4, the model of national performance in Figure 3.5 is clearly somewhat inconsistent in the relationships that it derives.

EXERCISES

1. Discuss how you would apply the concept of "activist government" in an analysis of the advanced industrial democracies. Specify three possible indicators of activist government that could be directly measured. What would each of them tell you about how activist a government is?
2. Select three indicators of the ideological conservatism of Americans. How would you try to establish the validity of each indicator?
3. Find an article that includes statistical analysis in one of the following journals: *American Journal of Political Science, American Political*

Science Review, or the *Journal of Politics*. What is one hypothesis that is tested in the article? What concepts and indicators of them are included in the hypothesis? How is the validity of the indicator or indicators established?

4. International Relations (IR) focuses on the relations among nations. Specify three concepts that you think should be important in this field. Then give hypotheses about the relationships that would be expected to hold among them.

5. Suppose you are trying to test the hypothesis that men will be more likely than women to say that they are more in agreement with Sarah Palin than Nancy Pelosi with data from a survey of the students in your research methods class. Which of the five characteristics that a hypothesis must contain are not included in the proposed study? Which of the four errors in hypothesis writing are present? How would you correct these problems?

6. Specify a theory that would link the following four variables from a data set for the developed democracies: (1) poverty rate, (2) total government spending as a percentage of GDP, (3) average school years that the population has completed, and (4) GDP per capita. Give a specific hypothesis for each relationship in your theoretical model. Then, illustrate this theory with an arrow diagram.

Chapter 4

Approaches to the Study of Politics

It should not take much exposure to the subject to realize that political scientists differ considerably in their perspectives. Most noticeably, some are conservatives; and a much larger number are liberals. Some emphasize quantitative research, while others disdain it. More subtly perhaps, some approaches to political science focus on description or "just the facts", while others give pride of place to interpretation and explanation and still others are primarily concerned with ethical questions. More broadly, this suggests that there are competing approaches (or to give them a more impressive-sounding name) paradigms in political science. Such a conclusion might be somewhat surprising or confusing to students, but it reflects a situation that exists in other disciplines, even the hard sciences.

This chapter gives an overview of the nature of political science in order to put the type of quantitative analysis described in this book into perspective by showing how it relates to the wide variety of efforts involved in the study of politics. In particular, it examines three general subjects. Section 4.1 describes the three basic types of analysis that are involved in research about politics. Section 4.2 takes a much broader focus and charts how the primary emphasis or paradigm in political studies has changed dramatically over time. Finally, Section 4.3 outlines three alternative strategies for establishing a relationship between two variables, such as whether or not wealthier American people are more likely to take politically conservative positions than other Americans.

4.1 TYPES OF POLITICAL ANALYSIS

Political scientists engage in a wide variety of activities in their scholarship. In essence, the work of political scientists can be classified into three intellectual tasks: (1) description, (2) normative or ethical theory, and (3) empirical or explanatory theory. **Description** deals with the question, "What is it like?" **Normative theory** applies moral or ethical precepts to answer the question, "Is it good or bad?" Finally, **empirical theory** seeks to explain political phenomena and events by seeking out "Why did it happen?" Many articles and books, of course, contain a combination of these different types of analysis; and a good case could probably be made that the insights, which can be gained from one type, would probably be distinctly limited without an appreciation of the other modes of analysis.

4.1.1 Description

The basic activity in political science, as in most fields of study, is **description** in the sense that most political science research primarily involves description. This should not be very surprising. After all, until you know what something is through descriptive research, it is impossible (at least logically) to try to determine whether it is good or bad (normative theory) or to link its nature to some explanatory factor (empirical theory). Anyone who has read a basic textbook about American government, for example, has encountered a description that encompasses 300–400 pages of innumerable facts about what the government is like. The central point here is that until we find out what the institutional characteristics of the government are and how they are used, abused, or ignored in practice through painstaking descriptive research, we will not be able to say very much about American politics.

Moving on to a more concrete example, Chapter 2 included a substantial amount of descriptive materials about the nature of Americans' political attitudes. The discussion in that chapter was organized around the simple descriptive question, "Are Americans conservatives or liberals?" The answer to this question, though, turned out to be anything but simple. In terms of ideological self-identification, Americans are clearly conservative. Yet, in terms of their stances on individual issues, they are conservative on many (as would be expected from their self-identification), liberal on many more, moderate on some, and polarized between strong conservatives and strong liberals on at least a few. Thus, public opinion in the United States can only be described as ideologically split.

This example also suggests that even a straightforward and unbiased description of what Sgt. Friday of *Dragnet* would term "just the facts" does not always or inevitably produce results about which everyone can agree. Regarding the data on Americans' ideologies, conservatives could credibly claim that, especially in view of citizens' ideological self-images, they are Number One, while liberals could puncture their balloon by pointing to the many important issues on which Americans continue to want an activist government. From a more analytic and less partisan perspective, some analysts could decry the lack of political information in the American public that results in such ideological incoherence, while others could castigate the political elites and parties for continuing to purvey their outdated ideologies when Americans quite evidently are demanding a new public philosophy.

4.1.2 Normative

The study of politics certainly involves important ethical issues, giving rise to a long-standing tradition of **normative theory**. Some issues raise important moral concerns. Perhaps the best example is abortion, which involves a horrible and unresolvable conflict between the most fundamental rights of women, championed by pro-choice groups, and of the unborn, championed by pro-life groups. Politics itself can be viewed normatively. For example, important strands of classical political theory view democracy and citizen participation in politics as critical for the moral development of individuals.[1]

At one level, obviously, statistics really have nothing to contribute to normative theory. Whether Americans are overwhelmingly pro-choice or overwhelmingly pro-life or, as they actually are, almost evenly split

---

[1] For example, Michael J. Sandel applies such an approach to American political history quite insightfully in *Democracy's Discontent: America in Search of a Public Philosophy* (Cambridge: Harvard University Press, 1996).

between the two positions has nothing to do with the momentous ethical issues involved in the abortion debate. Yet, description and data can indicate whether or not a normative position is realistic. For example, beginning with the early public opinion and voting studies in the 1940s and 1950s,[2] the view that American democracy rests upon an informed and activist citizenry was shown to be quite unrealistic and, therefore, is now considered clearly untenable.

4.1.3 Empirical Theory

For many political scientists, the most important activity in our discipline is **empirical theory**. As described in more detail in Chapter 3, empirical theory seeks to explain political phenomena, such as why some citizens are more conservative than others, why particular types of candidates triumph on the hustings while others are forced to contain their tears on election eve, why some nations have better economic or social performances than others, and so forth. For example, comparing the United States to Sweden in Chapter 2 suggests that welfare states will have better social outcomes but worse economic performance than nations committed to *laissez-faire* policies. Specifically, government policy is used to explain variations among developed nations in the economic and social realms.

4.2 CHANGING FASHIONS OR PARADIGMS IN POLITICAL STUDIES

The previous section showed that the study of politics involves three very distinct types of research activities. Given this variety of scholarly concerns, it should not be very surprising that the study of politics has passed through eras when its emphasis changed considerably from one paradigm or way of doing analysis to another. This section, hence, provides an overview of these changing paradigms or fashions that have dominated political studies at one time or another. It begins by outlining Thomas Kuhn's argument that the key factor in the history of

---

[2] Angus Campbell, Philip E. Converse, Warren E. Miller and Donald E. Stokes, *The American Voter* (New York: John Wiley, 1960).

science has been the successive development of broad paradigms that define the principal problems for and methods of scientific inquiry; and the historical evolution of paradigms in political science is then presented.

4.2.1 Scientific Paradigms

To the uninitiated, science is an impressive, if not imposing, endeavor conducted by physicists, mathematicians, biologists, and others of their ilk. Universal laws applicable to all phenomena can be stated in precise (if generally incomprehensible) mathematical formulations and verified or disconfirmed by replicable experiments whose results can be easily evaluated by the initiates of the discipline in question. This certainly contrasts with the social sciences, in which fundamental disagreement about theoretical frameworks, or even basic facts, is ongoing and seemingly not amenable to rational resolution. There is also the view that science is essentially a cumulative process. That is, the facts and experimental results are added to each other over time in a building-block approach as knowledge expands in a linear manner.

However, Thomas Kuhn presents a much different picture of the history of science in *The Structure of Scientific Revolutions*.[3] He contends that science has advanced through a series of revolutions in which one way of viewing the world, which he calls a **paradigm**, is replaced by an alternative formulation. A paradigm, according to Kuhn, is an accepted model of scientific practice that dominates a particular field of inquiry. It provides the general theoretical framework within which research and discussion are carried out, sets the research agenda by posing questions that are considered worthy of analysis, and delineates the methodology considered appropriate for scientific inquiry. In contrast to the construction of paradigms, most research constitutes **normal science**, which accepts the basic assumptions of the overarching paradigm and seeks to find new facts or to supply more detailed proofs within its framework.

---

[3]Thomas S. Kuhn, *The Structure of Scientific Revolutions*, 2nd Edn. (Chicago: University of Chicago Press, 1970).

A good example of two radically contrasting paradigms comes from the field of astronomy. The traditional, or Ptolemaic, astronomy assumed that the earth was at the center of the universe with the moon, planets, and stars revolving around it. Geometrical and mathematical systems were then derived to fit astronomic observations within this paradigm. The Copernican revolution in astronomy assumed that the earth and planets rotated on their axes and revolved around the sun. Surprisingly, its ability to supplant the Ptolemaic paradigm did not come from any great superiority in its predictions. Rather, it was a growing crisis of confidence in the traditional system that led to the acceptance of a successor paradigm with a radically different view of the universe:

> With respect both to planetary position and to precession of the equinoxes, predictions made with Ptolemy's system never quite conformed with the best available observations. Further reduction of these minor discrepancies constituted many of the principal problems of normal astronomical research for many of Ptolemy's successors.... For some time, astronomers had every reason to suppose that these attempts would be as successful as the ones that had led to Ptolemy's system. Given a particular discrepancy, astronomers were invariably able to eliminate it by making some particular adjustment in Ptolemy's system of compounded circles. But as time went on, a man looking at the net result of the normal research effort of many astronomers could observe that astronomy's complexity was increasing far more rapidly than its accuracy and that a discrepancy corrected in one place was likely to show up in another.... In the 16th century, Copernicus' co-worker, Domenico da Novara, held that no system so cumbersome and inaccurate as the Ptolemaic had become could possibly be true of nature.[4]

In sum, Kuhn concluded that paradigms are not really subject to scientific evaluation and comparison, but are accepted and rejected because of their ability to solve acute problems of interest to a specific scholarly community. Paradigms fall into question when anomalies within them are perceived serious enough to constitute an acute crisis. A new paradigm can do one of several things. It can incorporate important new phenomena into the subject matter of a discipline, such as

---

[4] *Ibid.*, pp. 68–69.

new classification schemes in botany or geology; it can correct false assumptions, such as the Copernican revolution; or it can subsume existing scientific theory into a more encompassing framework, such as Einstein's theory of relativity did to Newtonian physics.

In the social sciences, paradigm construction and change are much more common than in the physical sciences. Because universal laws applicable to all phenomena or relationships akin to $E = MC^2$ evidently cannot be developed, it is always easy to find instances or cases that do not fit a particular theoretical framework. The challenge for theory in political science, therefore, is to winnow inconsequential deviant cases from fundamental anomalies that create an acute crisis for a paradigm — a process that, as you might imagine, is far from being noncontroversial. Moreover, the nature of the critical questions that interest scholars are probably more subject to rapid change in the social sciences, as we shall see in the next subsection.

4.2.2 The Evolving Nature of Paradigms in Political Studies

If contemporary political scientists cannot reach consensus on a single paradigm for their field, it would certainly be expected that the leading paradigms in the study of politics would have changed considerably over time. Harry Eckstein, for example, developed an interesting model of succeeding paradigms in the study of politics that, with some adaptions and deletions, is summarized in Table 4.1.[5] In this model, over the last several centuries, the study of politics has evolved through six radically different stages or paradigms: (1) Machiavelli's practical advice on strategies and policies for gaining and maintaining power; (2) Montesquieu's attempt to find general patterns in political regimes; (3) the grand theories explaining the evolution of human history by Hegel and Marx; (4) a focus on the formal institutions of government that went through several stages — the philosophical or normative basis of government, concern with constitution-building, and formal-legal

---

[5] Harry Eckstein, "A Perspective on Comparative Politics, Past and Present". In *Comparative Politics*, Harry Eckstein and David Apter, Eds. (New York: Free Press, 1963), pp. 3–32.

Table 4.1: Changing paradigms in political studies.

Paradigm	Analytic focus	Methodology
Policy Prescription Machiavelli	Policy advice to a Prince	Crude induction or anecdotes

General Patterns
  of Government
  Montesquieu
	Types of government and their relationship to economic and social environment	Logical deduction and observation of political settings

Historicism Hegel and Marx	Grand theories explaining historical development of politics and economics	Abstract theory illustrated by detailed historical examples

Formal Institutions
  I. Normative basis
  II. Democratization
  III. Traditional Political Science
	I. Social contract theory
	II. Constitution-building
	III. Formal-legal studies
		I. Philosophical studies
		II. Propose constitution
		III. Describe legal forms

Behavioralism
  I. Informal politics
  II. Scientific approach
	I. Parties and interest groups
	II. Public opinion and aggregate data on governments
		I. Case studies
		II. Statistical analysis

Return to Theory
  I. Economic
  II. New institutionalism
  III. Post-modernism
	I. Apply economic logic to politics
	II. Effects of institutions
	III. How context shapes power relations
		I. Rational actor theory
		II. Complex case studies
		III. Deconstructing conventional assumptions

Source: Harry Eckstein, "A Perspective on Comparative Politics, Past and Present". In *Comparative Politics*, Harry Eckstein and David Apter, Eds. (New York: Free Press, 1963), pp. 3–32 except for the categories of "Return to Theory" and "Normative Bases" of "Formal Institutions".

studies; (5) political behavioralism which had two very different stages, focusing first on informal politics and then on quantitative data and the scientific method; and, most recently, (6) a "return to theory" that is yet far from establishing a consensus about what theory should be.

Machiavelli's *The Prince* represents a primer on how to get and maintain power that was penned by the author with the Machiavellian design — which failed! — of gaining political employment. Machiavelli justified the various strategies and policies that he proposed by what Eckstein rather dismissively calls the crude induction of offering a few anecdotes that were consistent with his conclusions.[6] Today, such policy and campaign advice is certainly prominent and, if the screaming heads on *Crossfire* are any evidence, still rather crude. For example, George W. Bush's advisor and campaign manager Karl Rove had a strongly Machiavellian reputation that was lauded by conservatives and Republicans and decried by liberals and Democrats.[7]

Montesquieu in his *The Spirit of the Laws* took a much more sophisticated approach. This work, according to Eckstein, sought to distinguish among different types of governments and relate their characteristics and policies to the nature of their societies and other aspects of the context in which they operated. Eckstein was struck by how modern this appears in its sophisticated view of the relationships among society, government, and policy and by what a break it constituted from Machiavelli's much more simplistic view of politics.[8]

The third stage in Eckstein's model of the development of political science moved to much grander theorizing in the form of what has been termed historicism. These were theories, like those of Hegel and Marx, which conceptualized history as a series of stages through which humankind ascended from more primitive to more advanced social, economic, and political relations. They combined an abstract principle concerning the driving force behind these progressive transformations — for example, changing relationships concerning the control of the means of production in Marxist theory — with massive historical descriptions that ostensibly validated the theories. A major crisis in political theory occurred when most of the profession reached the conclusion that these brilliant theories were flawed and unpersuasive. If the best and the brightest of political thinkers, like Hegel and Marx,

---

[6] Ibid, pp. 6–7.
[7] James Moore and Slater Wayne, *Bush's Brain: How Karl Rove Made George W. Bush President* (Hoboken, NJ: John Wiley, 2003).
[8] Eckstein, *op. cit.*, pp. 7–8.

could be grossly wrong, the very enterprise of political theory came into question.

This created a revolution in the study of politics aimed at reducing, if not eliminating, interpretive error. Political thought, for example, became a separate field that focused upon what past political thinkers had written, not how their thought could be applied to the contemporary political world. The study of actual politics, in turn, came to emphasize formal-legal studies in large part, according to Eckstein, because nobody could argue about its subject matter:

> The emphasis in the study of politics upon formal-legal arrangements is thus a natural outgrowth of the positivistic reaction to historicism, simply because primitive positivism, in attempting to restrict the role of thought, naturally leads the analyst to steer clear of the more inchoate data. Primitive, unadulterated positivism insists upon *hard* facts, indubitable and incontrovertible facts, as well as facts that speak for themselves — and what facts of politics are harder, as well as more self-explanatory, than the facts found in formal-legal-codes?[9]

As indicated in the fourth part of Table 4.1, however, the genesis of formal-legal studies includes two previous and more intellectually compelling stages of which one has been acknowledged by Eckstein. As Eckstein notes, the 19th century was the great age of constitution-making. Thus, the immediate cause of the formal-legal approach was not necessarily a search for hard facts but the much more exciting and intellectually stimulating reason that this was where the action was in political studies in the late 19th century, when historicism crashed. Somewhat more distantly perhaps, the concern with constitution-making itself can be seen as the descendant of the attempts to define the basic social contract underlying government of such diverse theorists as Hobbes, Locke, Burke, and Rousseau.[10] In any event, though, formal-legal studies dominated the study of politics from the late 19th century through the 1950s, coming to be called traditional political science.

---

[9] Ibid, p. 10.
[10] George H. Sabine, *A History of Political Theory*, 3rd Edn. (New York: Holt, Rinehart, and Winston, 1961), Chapters 23, 26, 28 and 29.

While it lost its status as the dominant paradigm in political science during the 1960s, formal-legal studies, like political thought in the late 19th century, turned into an autonomous subfield as constitutional law became increasingly important for legal education.

Over time, traditional political science came under increasing challenge for missing what was most important about politics. This led to the behavioral revolution that focused on what actually happened in the political world, as opposed to what was written down in constitutions and legal statutes. As summarized in the fifth line of Table 4.1, two very different stages can be distinguished in the behavioral approach to studying politics. The first, which began to emerge as a distinct subfield a little before World War II, focused on the informal politics of political parties, interest groups, and elites, based on the almost self-evident argument that this was where "the action was" that determined what government really did. By the early 1960s, though, this strand of political studies was being pushed aside by the transformation of political behavioralism to a scientific revolution emphasizing quantitative data analysis and the development of testable laws explaining political activities.

This second type of behavioralism held sway in the discipline from sometime in the 1960s to the late 1980s or early 1990s and, in fact, took credit (or blame) for the science in political science. Its emergence represented a confluence of two separate trends, one theoretical and one concerning data availability. At the theoretical or philosophical level, science and positivism became increasingly prestigious; such that most of the social sciences, including political science, tried to emulate the scientific method. Probably more importantly, though, the development of public opinion surveys and the growing collection of aggregate data on governmental units created huge amounts of quantified data that simply had not been available before.

An observer with a sense of irony could note a strong parallel between political behaviorism and the formal-legal studies of traditional political science that it supplanted as the dominant paradigm in the discipline. Both started by finding something new and exciting — constitution-making for formal-legal studies and first informal politics and then new types of political data for behaviorism. Over time, however, the excitement of the paradigm shift faded; and what Kuhn called the normal science of dealing with the available data took over. However, the data sources specified by the paradigm increasingly became seen as limiting research by excluding important areas of concern to the scholarly community. Thus, by the 1980s and 1990s, political scientists were beginning to turn their studies to subjects that went beyond what could be subjected to quantitative analysis.

Perhaps the key element in this emerging new stage of the study of politics is a renewed interest in broader theory. However, as the bottom row of Table 4.1 indicates, there is certainly no consensus on what the fundamental theoretical orientation should be, as three rather divergent approaches are easy to identify. The first might be called economic theory since it applies economic logic to model and predict the decisions of individuals and governments,[11] leading to what is called the rational actor theory whose advocates now hold a leading position in political science. A second, much different theoretical approach has been called the new institutionalism. It defines institutions more broadly and informally than the formal-legal approach and argues that such institutions have important consequences for governmental practices, political policies, and social and economic outcomes.[12] Finally, post-modern theory has issued a sharp challenge to conventional political theorizing and especially to positivist assumptions and quantitative data analysis. The post-modernists argue that the ostensibly scientific distinction between values and facts is untenable, that the context of political and social action is all important for understanding its meaning, and, therefore, that theorists should emphasize the critical "deconstructing" of conventional interpretations and research methodologies in the social sciences.[13]

---

[11] The classic work in this field is Anthony Downs, *An Economic Theory of Democracy* (New York: Harper & Row, 1957). For an excellent study applying this approach to government policy see Ronald Rogowski, *Commerce and Coalitions: How Trade Affects Domestic Political Alignments* (Princeton: Princeton University Press, 1989).

[12] James G. March and Johan P. Olsen, *Rediscovering Institutions: The Organizational Basis of Politics* (New York: Free Press, 1989).

[13] Joe Doherty, Elspeth Graham and Mo Malek, Eds., *Post-Modernism and the Social Sciences* (New York: St. Martin's Press, 1992).

4.3 ALTERNATIVE STRATEGIES FOR SHOWING A RELATIONSHIP

Even within the field of quantitative behavioral studies, there are three major approaches for assessing whether or not an explanatory relationship exists. The first is the **experimental approach** in which rigorous control of the environment allows all but the central factors in the experiment to be randomized and, thus, eliminated as possible alternative explanations. Second, statistical analysis explicitly controls for the effects of other variables in what is termed **quasi-experimental designs**. Finally, **case studies** use detailed analysis, both quantitative and qualitative, of a small number of cases to justify conclusions. This section discusses the advantages and disadvantages of each approach to suggest some of the strengths and limitations of the statistical approach used in this book. The first subsection lays out the logic of experimental design in some detail. The second and third discuss **quasi-experimental designs**. Finally, the last one gives an overview of quantitative case studies.

4.3.1 The Logic of Experimental Design

Perhaps because of its wide-spread utilization in the hard sciences, the experimental approach is often considered the gold standard for social science research. In the physical world, elements and materials will always be the same. For example, heating one unit of hydrogen or carbon dioxide will always produce the same effect if environmental conditions, such as pressure, are held constant no matter what particular atoms and molecules are involved in the experiment. Thus, in the physics and chemistry experiments that are inflicted upon many political science students by university requirements, the student is issued some materials and a set of instructions about what to do with them. Students who make the experiment come out correctly get A's, while others suffer the consequences.

This process is diagramed in Part A of Figure 4.1. For example, several chemicals are mixed together and heated to set off a chemical reaction producing a new chemical compound. Part B of Figure 4.1 then transforms this logic to the social science setting, adding the

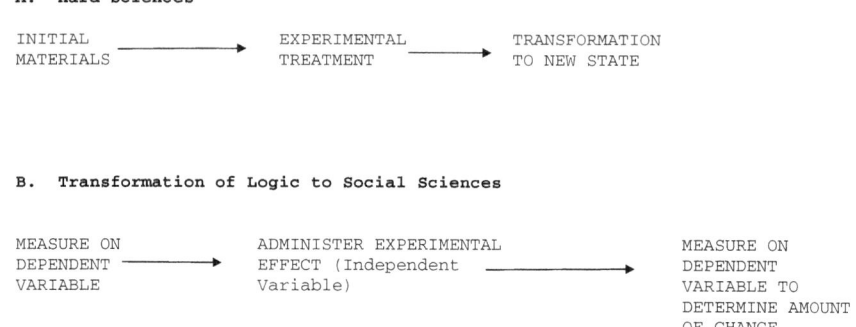

Figure 4.1: Overview of experimental method.

terminology of cause-and-effect in social science theory: **independent variable** is used to denote the cause, while **dependent variable** is used to refer to the effect.[14] The **logic of experimental design** is that the variable which is assumed to be the effect or dependent variable should first be measured for some group of subjects at what might be called "time 1". Then, at "time 2" an experimental effect is administered, which becomes the "independent variable". Somewhat later at "time 3", the dependent variable is measured again. If the independent variable exerted a causal impact, the value of the dependent variable would have changed. In contrast, if it does not change, then there is clearly no association between the independent and dependent variables.

For example, suppose the dependent variable is how conservative a person considers himself or herself. In the United States, as we have seen, two fairly distinct strands of conservatism focus upon economic and cultural issues respectively. We might hypothesize, then, that a film sympathetic to the working poor might make people more liberal, while one that is an expose of the sex industry would push its viewers in a conservative direction. To test these hypotheses, subjects could be shown these films; and their before and after levels of conservatism could then be compared.

---

[14]This terminology is discussed in much more detail in Chapter 3.

Fortunately or unfortunately, depending upon your perspective, dealing with human subjects in experiments is a much more complex (though perhaps less risky) process than handling hydrochloric acid for two important reasons. First, unlike working with physical matter, it is not tenable to assume that we are replicants of each other. Second, humans may be affected by numerous outside events besides what happens in the experiment. Thus, if the stock market crashes, or war breaks out, or a prominent politician is caught in a financial or sexual scandal between the pre-test and post-test in the experiment, these events might affect the subjects' ideological orientations, in addition to any influence exerted by the experimental effect itself.

Consequently, experimental designs in the social sciences tend to be more complex and sophisticated, as sketched in Figure 4.2. Most fundamentally, two different groups of subjects are required. One is the **experimental group** to which the **experimental treatment** is administered; and the other is the **control group** which does not receive the experimental effect. For the experiment to show that the treatment affects the dependent variable, therefore, both of two conditions must hold. First, a significant change must occur in the experimental group after the treatment is received. Second and, in addition, this effect cannot also occur in the control group because

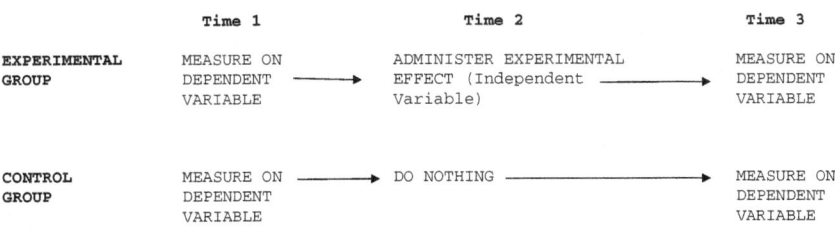

Figure 4.2: Modification of experimental method for dealing with human subjects.
Source: Adapted from Earl Babbie, *The Practice of Social Research*, 7th Edn. (New York: Wadsworth, 1995), p. 235.

Table 4.2: Possible outcomes for experiment testing whether viewing video on working poor makes people more liberal.

Results in experimental group	Results in control group	Implications for hypothesis
Subjects do not become more liberal	Results immaterial	Hypothesis disconfirmed
Subjects become more liberal	Subjects become more liberal	Hypothesis disconfirmed
Subjects become more liberal	Subjects do not become more liberal	Hypothesis supported
Subjects become more liberal	Subjects become more liberal but to a significantly lesser extent than experimental group	Hypothesis is supported

this would suggest that some factor external to the experiment has affected both groups similarly.[15]

Table 4.2 summarizes this logic for the hypothesis that watching a video about the problems facing the working poor in the United States would make Americans more liberal. For the hypothesis to be supported, obviously the experimental group must become more liberal after watching the video. If its attitudes do not change or if it actually becomes more conservative (row #1 in the table), the hypothesis is clearly disconfirmed; and the results for the control group are meaningless or immaterial for the analysis. As indicated in rows #2 and #3, the finding that the experimental group has become more liberal does not necessarily validate the hypothesis. If the control group which did not see the video also becomes more liberal (row #2), the supposition would be that both groups were affected by some external events. Only if the experimental group becomes more liberal while the control group does not (row #3) would the hypothesis be supported. Finally, both the video and some external event might be working

---

[15] Donald Campbell and Julian Stanley, *Experimental and Quasi-Experimental Designs for Research* (Chicago: Rand McNally, 1963) provide the classic treatment of experimental design for the social sciences and discuss more sophisticated designs than the one presented here.

separately to change the subjects' attitudes in a liberal direction. In this case (row #4), both groups would become more liberal, but the change would be significantly greater in the experimental group, thereby supporting the original hypothesis.

This type of research design obviously puts a critical premium upon the selection of the experimental and control groups always on one and sometimes on a second key criterion. First, the experimental and control groups must always be composed of essentially the same type of people. In the hypothetical experiment in Table 4.2, for example, if the experimental group had members who were more susceptible to liberal messages than the control group because of their income, race, or gender, even results consistent with the hypothesis might well reflect the difference between the two groups rather than the impact of the video. Comparability is usually assumed to be assured by the random assignment of participants to the control and experimental groups. However, unless the number of participants is fairly large, such an assumption is probably somewhat problematic. Second, questions can also arise about the population to which the results of an experiment can be generalized. Of necessity, experiments involve fairly small groups who may not be representative of the full population. For example, college students, who often comprise the subjects for psychological and political science experiments, almost certainly differ from other Americans in many important attitudes and behaviors.

Experiments face the problems of establishing validity (see Chapter 3). Theorists usually distinguish between problems of **internal validity** that concerns the manner in which the experiment itself is conducted and of **external validity** that concerns whether or not the results of an experiment can be generalized to a broader population. A carefully done two-group experiment in which subjects are randomly assigned to the experimental and control groups (see Figure 4.2) is generally sufficient to establish internal validity. However, the problems of external validity can raise more complex design questions. For example, care must be taken to ensure that the participants in the experiment are representative of the groups about which inferences are being made. In addition, more elaborate procedures, such as an experiment utilizing four groups (two experimental and two control), are often needed to overcome the problems associated with possible **interactions** between the experimental test and the broader environment.[16]

As an illustration of this important technique, experimental designs following the logic of Figure 4.2 are often used in medical research when one group of patients receives a treatment and another one a placebo to see whether the treatment produces beneficial results. A recent example of this concerns several studies of hormone replacement therapy (HRT) for post-menopausal women. HRT clearly reduced some of the direct symptoms of menopause and was thought to help strengthen bones and prevent heart disease and Alzheimer's. Conversely, there were fears that HRT contributed to breast cancer. In July 2002, a huge study of over 16,000 women was halted when it became apparent that HRT produced elevated levels of both breast cancer and heart disease; and, in the summer of 2003, a study of over 4,000 women was reported in which the Alzheimer's rate was double for women over 65 who received HRT as opposed to a placebo.[17] These findings have countervailing implications about the research project. On the one hand, it represents high quality research based on huge national samples whose results are clearly beyond question. On the other, it certainly raises the question of how the medical establishment could have been so wrong about HRT for so long!

4.3.2 Quasi-Experimental Designs and the Statistical Approach

Experimental designs are fairly limited in political science research, even in quantitative studies, for two complementary reasons. First, it is hard to do experiments on many research questions. Certainly, even putting the daunting ethical questions aside, it would be hard to conceive how to set up experiments about, for example, governmental policy responses to economic crises, the need for medical care in a

---

[16] Earl R. Babbie, *The Practice of Social Research*, 7th Edn. (Belmont, CA: Wadsworth, 1995), pp. 242–246.

[17] Breastcancer.org, "June 2003 Updates on HRT Harms" and "Hormone Replacement Theory May Double the Risk of Alzheimer's Disease". Available at www.breastcancer.org.

society, or national security issues. Second, there are already huge amounts of valuable and interesting nonexperimental data on citizens, governments, and other entities relevant for political analysis. The two data sets used in this book demonstrate that numerous questions can be posed and explored about the ideological views of Americans and the public policies of advanced industrial nations. Putting these two factors together, therefore, explains why experimental research remains fairly limited in political science.

When the requisites for an experimental design can only be approximated by alternative techniques, the resulting studies are said to be based on **quasi-experimental designs**. In experiments, the random assignment of subjects into experimental and control groups is assumed to ensure that the two groups are similar except for exposure to the treatment involved in the experiment. Consequently, many experiments really involve only two factors or variables. The first is the experimental treatment itself which is the cause in the relationship under consideration; and the second is the effect which is measured before and after the experimental treatment is administered (see Figure 4.2). By far, the most common type of quasi-experimental design in political science is to collect data on a fairly large number of variables for a single group, such as the respondents to the 2008 National Election Study (NES) survey. Explicit **statistical controls** can then be used to determine whether other factors are influencing or contaminating the specific cause-and-effect relationship of interest to a researcher.[18]

The two sets of analyses of American public opinion and the attributes of developed democracies, for example, represent the statistical approach to ensuring that relevant factors are controlled when the relationship between two variables is measured. Both these data sets, but especially the one on citizen attitudes in the United States, contain a far larger number of variables than would be possible to assemble in an experimental research situation. Thus, it is possible to introduce variables that might affect the relationship in a hypothesis directly into the analysis, rather than simply assuming that the randomization of

---

[18]Thomas D. Cook and Donald T. Campbell, *Quasi-Experimentation: Design and Analysis Issues for Field Settings* (Chicago: Rand McNally, 1979).

subjects has eliminated all the confounding effects. For example, one might suspect that the hypothesis that people with higher incomes should have more conservative attitudes would be affected by the race or gender of the respondent. In an experimental situation, the assumption would be made that the experimental and control groups were essentially the same in their make-ups by race and gender. For the alternative approach of using statistical controls, separate analyses could be computed for African-Americans and whites and for men and women.

The statistical approach, therefore, certainly has several analytic advantages. It permits examining many relationships at the same time and explicitly tests what effect, if any, particular control variables have upon the relationship under consideration. In short, it can provide substantially more statistical information than can be generated by experimental designs. The choice between experimental and statistical research designs, hence, should be made according to the objectives of a particular study. As indicated above, for example, many important topics in political research simply are not amenable to the experimental approach; and existing quasi-experimental data sets contain lodes of valuable information. More theoretically, the experimental design is more appropriate for treating one key relationship, while the statistical approach is better for modeling the relationships among a broader set of factors.

4.3.3 Types of Quasi-Experimental Designs

There is an important difference concerning the time frame between the logic of experimental designs and the quasi-experimental design used in analyzing the 2008 NES survey. The classical experimental design sketched in Figure 4.2 explicitly uses time to measure change and establish cause-and-effect relationships. That is, the effect of the experimental treatment is estimated in terms of the change between the pre-test and the post-test of the experimental group relative to the control group on the item in question. The attitudes and characteristics of the NES respondents, in contrast, were all measured at the same time. To test the hypothesis that wealthier people should be more conservative than less affluent ones on economic issues, the attitudes of the rich and poor at one point in time (November 2008) are compared. In the abstract, there is no reason to prefer one type of explanatory logic to the other. Making this distinction, though, does highlight the facts that there are several distinct types of quasi-experimental designs and that they require somewhat different types of statistical analysis.

The NES and developed nations' data sets represent **cross-sectional** analysis. Here, the values of the cases are compared at a particular moment in time. For example, Table 4.3 presents the values of the infant mortality rate and the ratio of all government spending to GDP for the 21 advanced industrial countries in 2003. A quick eye-balling of these data suggests support for the liberal hypothesis that

Table 4.3: A cross-sectional analysis: Infant mortality and government size in the developed world, 2003.

Nations	Infant mortality	Government spending % GDP
Australia	4.8	36.0
Austria	4.5	51.2
Belgium	4.3	52.0
Canada	5.4	41.6
Denmark	4.4	56.0
Finland	3.1	51.1
France	3.9	54.6
Germany	4.2	48.9
Greece	4.8	47.2
Ireland	5.1	33.3
Italy	4.3	49.0
Japan	3.0	38.2
Netherlands	4.8	47.9
New Zealand	5.6	—
Norway	3.4	48.7
Portugal	4.1	46.0
Spain	4.1	39.5
Sweden	3.1	58.3
Switzerland	4.3	35.7
United Kingdom	5.3	43.6
United States	7.0	37.1

countries with bigger governments will have better social outcomes. For example, the United States with its comparatively small government has the highest infant mortality in the developed world; and many of the European countries with large states have low levels of infant mortality. Still, this relationship between government size and infant mortality is obviously not perfect since Japan's small state has not prevented it from having the lowest rate of infant mortality in the world. Hence, to fully assess this relationship, we shall have to wait until we have covered the appropriate advanced statistical technique. This is regression analysis, which is described in Chapter 11.

In contrast to cross-sectional studies, **time series designs** explicitly measure the relationships between how variables change (or do not change) over time, analogously to the logic of a classical experimental design. Table 4.4 presents the data on the infant mortality rates and government size in America for every year from 1960 through 1996. Here, the relationship is less clear at a superficial glance. The infant mortality rate dropped fairly steadily over these four decades, but the size of government grew more sporadically and has been, surprisingly perhaps, fairly constant since the mid-1970s. Normal regression analysis can be applied to this data set which would use the size of government in a given year to explain the infant mortality rate. However, since the key factor is really the rate of change between years, more advanced econometric techniques (which are well beyond the scope of this text) are the most relevant for modeling this relationship.

Finally, a **pooled** analysis combines the cross-sectional and time series designs by providing time series of the same variables for several cases. For example, the time series on infant mortality and government size in the United States can be expanded by adding similar data for the other 20 developed nations. Again, this can be analyzed by either normal regression or by more advanced econometric techniques. If ordinary regression is applied, each combination of year and unit constitutes an individual case to create a "pooled cross-sectional analysis". For example, if Sweden were added to the United States in the data set presented above, there would still be only two columns of data with the years for Sweden being coded after or below those for the U.S. Given that quantitative analysis of the developed nations

Table 4.4: Time series analysis: Infant mortality and government size in the United States.

Year	Infant mortality	Government spending % GDP
1960	26.0	27.2
1961	25.3	28.6
1962	25.3	28.6
1963	25.2	28.6
1964	24.8	27.9
1965	24.7	27.4
1966	23.7	27.2
1967	22.4	30.5
1968	21.8	30.8
1969	20.9	30.6
1970	20.0	31.8
1971	19.1	31.8
1972	18.5	31.5
1973	17.7	30.6
1974	16.7	32.2
1975	16.1	34.7
1976	15.2	33.4
1977	14.1	32.4
1978	13.8	31.5
1979	13.1	31.5
1980	12.6	33.5
1981	11.9	34.0
1982	11.5	36.3
1983	11.2	36.6
1984	10.8	35.3
1985	10.6	36.2
1986	10.4	36.7
1987	10.1	36.5
1988	10.0	35.6
1989	9.8	35.4
1990	9.2	36.5
1991	8.9	37.9
1992	8.5	37.8
1993	8.4	37.1
1994	8.0	36.0
1995	8.0	35.9
1996	7.8	35.5

often suffers from the small number of cases (countries), this technique is particularly popular in that field.[19]

4.3.4 Quantitative Case Studies

Both experimental designs and statistical research work from what might be called "closed data sets". Data are gathered on a set of cases — subjects in an experiment, respondents to the 2008 NES survey, or the 21 developed democracies. Various types of data analyses are then performed upon the cases. Significant relationships are established by showing that one variable is related to another among the cases in the data set. In quantitative case studies, a somewhat different technique is applied. First, different types of data are gathered for only one or a very small number of cases; and the quantitative data are often supplemented by qualitative descriptions and interpretations as well. The basic mode of analysis, then, is to reach conclusions about political relationships, not using statistical results over a substantial number of cases, but trying to generalize from what was observed in only one or a few cases.

An excellent example of this approach is provided by Harold Wilensky's chapter on "The American Welfare Mess in Comparative Perspective" in *Rich Democracies*.[20] Wilensky evaluates and challenges the conservative critique of welfare policy in the United States which argues that welfare programs give incentives for unwed mothers to live in social dependency, thereby creating a self-perpetuating cycle of poverty and dependency that moves on from one generation to another. He presents a wide variety of data from the U.S. on the level of welfare payments among states, fertility rates of welfare and non-welfare women, the typical length of participation in welfare programs, the racial composition of welfare recipients, and welfare as a percentage of national and state budgets which are inconsistent with the conservative theory. We should note, though, that this does not necessarily validate liberal arguments about what welfare policies would work better.

---

[19] For example, see Harold L. Wilensky, *Rich Democracies: Political Economy, Public Policy, and Performance* (Berkeley: University of California Press, 2002).
[20] *Ibid.*, Chapter 8.

This analysis, thus, represents a statistical case study in the sense that a number of statistical results from one case are combined to test a hypothesis about public policy. Wilensky then goes on to supplement this case study by a statistical study comparable to the ones discussed in the previous subsection. If the conservatives are correct that the provision of welfare sets off the pathologies of social dependency, these effects should be greater in larger welfare states that provide more generous programs. This hypothesis does not turn out to have much support since the United States is marked by such social outcomes as a very high teenage pregnancy rate, despite its comparatively limited welfare supports. This also shows the advantage of testing theories with different types of analyses since convergent findings increase our confidence in their validity.

Compared to the experimental and statistical research designs, this approach has a distinctive advantage and disadvantage. On the one hand, we cannot be as confident of the results as in the other two approaches. For the "closed" data sets in experimental and quasi-experimental analyses, the statistical results themselves indicate how strong the relationships under consideration are with very considerable precision. For the statistical case approach, in contrast, the melding of different results, especially when they are qualitative in nature, inevitably must rely upon the judgment and interpretation of the researcher, rather than just what the data themselves show.

This disadvantage of more contestable findings is offset, however, by the limitations of a single data set which may not contain all the information relevant to the analytic question at hand. Considering and integrating several streams of evidence, therefore, could in many instances produce more sophisticated and meaningful conclusions. For example, let us take the conservative hypothesis that big government hurts economic performance. During the 1980s, there was considerable statistical evidence for this proposition if government size was correlated with real economic growth rate. In this statistical comparison, both the United States and Japan had small governments and high growth compared to other advanced industrial nations. Yet, those who engaged in case studies of Japan found that it had a highly interventionist government. Indeed, the Japanese experience was generally used, not to validate the conservatives' *laissez-faire* logic, but to serve as the foundation for the theory that strong development states play a leading role in promoting industrial transformation.[21] While we can leave conservatives and liberals to fight over what the classification of Japan's political economy means for their theories, this example certainly should underline the point that we sometimes need multiple streams of evidence to avoid overly simplistic conclusions.

EXERCISES

1. Find an article about current American politics on the website of Real Clear Politics (www.realclearpolitics.com). Summarize the major points in the essay. What are the descriptive, normative, and/or explanatory parts of the article?
2. Give one major argument for and one against the government's redistributive policies to help the poorer members of society. Indicate how each one could use descriptive, normative, and explanatory analysis to support its contentions.
3. Briefly describe a reading that you have done for one of your political science courses. What paradigm in political studies does it best represent. Why does it fit into this paradigm?
4. The analysis of public opinion in the first half of Chapter 2 represents the Behavioralism II paradigm. Discuss how it shows both the strengths and weaknesses of this approach.
5. Describe how you would construct an experimental design to evaluate whether listening to speeches by Newt Gingrich makes people more likely to support Republican candidates.
6. Describe how you would construct a quasi-experimental design to explain which type of people like and dislike President Obama.

---

[21] Jeffrey A. Hart, *Rival Capitalists: International Competitiveness in the United States, Japan, and Western Europe* (Ithaca: Cornell University Press, 1992); Chalmers A. Johnson, *MITI and the Japanese Miracle: The Growth of Industrial Policy, 1925–1975* (Stanford: Stanford University Press, 1982).

Chapter 5

The Relationship of Qualitative Approaches to Quantitative Analysis

Anyone who has read much, or even a little, of the books and articles in contemporary political science should be quite aware that much of the literature in this field does *not* involve quantitative results. Thus, **qualitative analysis** probably remains the dominant method for conveying information and findings in political science. Still, even if actual numbers are not involved in many studies and research reports, what they do is often surprisingly similar to the quantitative data presented in this text. Indeed, many researchers talk in terms of qualitative data which are "observations not easily reduced to numbers".[1] Researchers, thus, try to reach conclusions or, more colorfully put, solve jigsaw puzzles based on data and information that, at the conceptual level, differ from those used here only in being less easy to quantify than the answers to a survey, such as the 2008 National Electron Study (NES) poll, or the social and economic measures that nations have long compiled.

This chapter presents overviews of the leading types of qualitative analyses in political science today. Section 5.1 contains brief summaries of three approaches: (1) elite interviews, (2) conceptualizations of

---

[1] Earl Babbie, *The Practice of Social Research*, 7th Edn. (Belmont, CA: Wadsworth, 1995), p. 280.

political institutions and systems, and (3) field studies or political anthropology. Each of these summaries begins with a description of the approach, gives an example or two of studies that apply it, and indicates how it might be related to some form of quantitative analysis. Section 5.2 then describes a fourth type of analysis, content analysis, in somewhat more detail.

5.1 QUALITATIVE APPROACHES TO POLITICAL STUDIES

This section summarizes three important types of qualitative analysis that are often used in political science: elite interviews, conceptualizations of political institutions and systems, and field studies or political anthropology. As will be seen, there is a significant amount of overlap among the applications of these approaches in the sense that they are used for similar purposes. More surprisingly, perhaps, it is also easy to discern several important similarities between them and the quantitative analyses that are described in this text.

5.1.1 Elite Interviews

Many studies focus on political elites, either government officials or those who have strong informal influence over political outcomes and policies. One obvious approach for gathering materials about political leaders is to conduct elite interviews with them. There are two broad reasons that such research may be valuable. First, elites have specialized and often rare knowledge about how governments work and policies are made. Consequently, anyone wishing to understand many important political events and phenomena must somehow gain access to this specialized knowledge. Second, the characteristics and attitudes of the elites themselves are a potentially important factor for determining what governments do and how policies are constructed.

There are several very important differences between elite interviews and broad or mass public opinion surveys, such as the NES studies. In mass surveys, the central objective is to measure attitudes in the general public. Thus, polls need to select fairly large samples that are representative of a society or population. In addition, most of the questions in such a survey tend to be structured or close-ended — that is, the respondents are given a set of potential answers from which one or more are selected. This is done to facilitate the interview process, both because many respondents may not be able to articulate options and because it allows shorter interviews, thereby minimizing respondent fatigue and impatience. The situation is dramatically different for most elite interviews. Participants in the study are selected exactly because they are assumed to possess specialized knowledge — that is, they are unrepresentative of the general public by design and even necessity. Moreover, most questions in many elite interviews are open-ended without a menu of options because the elites are assumed to have very detailed and nuanced knowledge and opinions which would be oversimplified or distorted by the structured interview schedules used in mass surveys.[2]

For example, Bob Woodward's *Plan of Attack* that was based on a large number of interviews with top officials in the Bush administration provides a far more detailed and insightful analysis of American policy toward the war with Iraq than could a study of "open" sources, either quantitative or qualitative.[3] Woodward's Introduction provides an excellent summary of both the strengths and weaknesses of research-based elite interviews:

> The aim of this book is to provide the first detailed, behind-the scenes account of how and why President George W. Bush, his war council and allies decided to launch a pre-emptive war in Iraq to topple Saddam Hussein.... The decision making leading to the Iraq War — concentrated in 16 months from November 2001 to March 2003 — is probably the best window into understanding who George Bush is, how he operates and what he cares about. I have attempted, as best I can, to find out what really happened and to provide some interpretations and occasional analysis.... The most elusive parts of any history are often the critical moments in the debates and the key turning or decision points that remain secret for years.... This history presents many of these moments, but I am aware that I have not found all of them.[4]

---

[2] Herbert J. Rubin and Irene S. Rubin, *Qualitative Interviewing: The Art of Hearing Data* (Thousand Oaks, CA: Sage, 1995).
[3] Bob Woodward, *Plan of Attack* (New York: Simon & Schuster, 2004).
[4] *Ibid*, pp. x–xi.

The first two sentences in the quotation indicate that the book is directed at both analytic aims of elite interviewing: understanding an important political dynamic (the decision-making that led to the war in Iraq) and gaining insight into a political leader (President George W. Bush). Woodward's candid interviews with and extensive quotations of President Bush and many leading members of his administration, as well as more anonymous participants in these momentous decisions, gives his book far more analytic insight and value than any other conceivable approach could have. Detailed quotations and attributions of attitudes and positions certainly show the importance of open-ended interviews that can gather far more sophisticated information than the structured surveys necessary to produce quantitative data.

Yet, these very advantages come with several drawbacks as well. As Woodward himself indicates, even his extensive study inevitably missed some key events and decisions. Moreover, one can certainly question the total honesty of his respondents, many of whom had an eye on how they would be portrayed in history. One relevant finding or insight from *Plan of Attack* for our question of whether Americans are conservative or liberal is surely that strong policy and personal disagreements and rivalries existed even among members of President Bush's foreign-policy "team". Thus, a significant amount of information provided to Woodward was almost certainly shaped by internal political considerations. Last but by no means least, Woodward's own interpretations certainly affect the picture painted by the book, raising questions about the extent to which his conclusions are affected by his own political biases or analytic assumptions.

There are no tables or graphs (if one discounts a single map) in *Plan of Attack*; and the book's emphasis on who said or did what in particular situations would appear to be the antithesis of a quantitative methodology. Yet, a moment's thought suggests that there is some analogy between Woodward's qualitative analysis and the way in which numbers are used in this text. In particular, the section on Levels of Measurement in Chapter 6 discusses how nominal scales are used to designate different categories in a variable and that ordinal scales can be used to measure how strongly someone approves or disapproves of an item. Applying this logic to *Plan of Attack*, for example, we might construct a nominal classification of reasons for going to war in Iraq: (1) Iraq's presumed possession of weapons of mass destruction (WMD), (2) Saddam Hussein's links with al Qaeda, (3) Iraq's threat to Israel, (4) Iraq's threat to neighboring Arab countries, and (5) Saddam's vicious rule, to name a few. Individual administrative figures could then be ranked on how they rated each of these potential threats. Whether this would provide any more insight than the existing qualitative analysis is certainly arguable, but at least a quantitative logic can be discerned.

Bob Woodward, of course, is a journalist not a political scientist. Still, work based primarily on elite interviews or, in some instances, more indirect observation of political elites, is very important in academic political science as well. For example, probably the leading scholar on the U.S. Congress is Richard Fenno whose technique of "soaking and poking" has been the basis for nearly 20 books regarding Congress which revolutionized the study of that institution.[5] Similarly to *Plan of Attack* but on a far broader scale, Fenno's soaking and poking have greatly enriched our understanding of how Congress operates, the relationships that actually exist between legislators and their constituents, and what a wide variety of congressional leaders are actually like. Thus, both dimensions of elite studies are well represented in Fenno's work.

5.1.2 Conceptualizing Political Systems

The comparability to quantitative analysis becomes stronger when we move on to the second form of qualitative analysis of conceptualizing political institutions and systems. These analyses are often at least partially based on elite interviews, but also bring in additional materials to support conclusions about how the system really works. A good example comes from the longstanding and still unresolved debate over the nature of community power structures. On the one hand, scholars

---

[5] The phrase "soaking and poking" to describe Fenno's methodology comes from Richard F. Fenno, Jr., *Home Style: House Members in Their Districts* (Boston: Little, Brown & Co., 1978), p. 249. See also, Richard F. Fenno, *Watching Politicians: Essays on Participant Observation* (Berkeley: Institute of Government Studies, University of California, 1990).

dating back to Robert Dahl based on his detailed study of politics in New Haven, Connecticut[6] have argued that politics in many local communities is basically pluralistic with no really dominant groups or figures and with different people and groups participating in different types of decisions. In stark contrast, many other analysts report detailed case studies, such as Clarence Stone's book on *Governing Atlanta*,[7] that find city and local politics to be dominated by narrow, generally business-oriented elites.

The conceptualization of the American political system by Theodore Lowi in his path-breaking *The End of Liberalism* presents another good example of highly influential qualitative analysis which represents a creative synthesis of vast materials on the nature of politics in America. As many scholars do, Lowi argued that the New Deal of Franklin Roosevelt represented a fundamental break with the previous operations of national government in the United States — so fundamental in fact that, he argued, it constituted a "Second Republic". The tremendous increase in the powers and activities exercised by the national government during New Deal, according to Lowi, were accompanied by the Roosevelt administration's decision in allowing interest groups to participate in policy-making to an unprecedented extent, as a means of securing their acquiescence to the expansion of federal power. Over time, policy-making fragmented into "iron triangles" consisting of these interest groups, the federal agencies administering policy in a narrow area, and specialized congressional committees. The result by the late-1960s was a combination of the growing power of vested interests in narrow issue domains and gridlock when powerful interest groups clashed.[8]

This picture of American politics, incidentally, was reinforced two decades later by journalist Hedrick Smith, who was probably unaware of Lowi's analysis, in *The Power Game* which described the abstract

---

[6] Robert Dahl, *Who Governs? Democracy and Power in an American City* (New Haven: Yale University Press, 1961).

[7] Clarence N. Stone, *Regime Politics: Governing Atlanta, 1946–1988* (Lawrence: University of Kansas Press, 1989).

[8] Theodore J. Lowi, *The End of Liberalism: The Second Republic of the United States* (New York: W.W. Norton, 1979).

processes American politics proposed by Lowi with much more gripping anecdotes, again (like Woodward) showing the contribution that an insightful journalist can make to political science. Smith's analysis of *The Power Game*, though, is more like academic political science than *Plan of Attack* in the sense that it proposes conceptual categories for understanding how things work in Washington. For example, he discusses different types of power, including both "porcupine power" and "the soft side of power", distinguishes between "big games of power" that include nationally prominent issues and political leaders and the more subterranean politics of bureaucratic competition and interest group lobbying. Based on these descriptions, he then presents typologies of these different "power games".[9]

The conceptualization of the post-New Deal polity in America as representing **interest group liberalism** creates a category that can be used for further analysis, for example, explaining different political outcomes before and after the New Deal. In fact, a similar conceptualization of political systems in comparative politics — **corporatist decision-making** — can be applied to our quantitative comparisons of politics and policy outcomes in the developed democracies. This theory is that some governments have what is called corporatist styles in which the government negotiates major policies fairly formally with a limited set of representatives of major social forces, such as business, labor, and the church, as opposed to the more raucous battling among interest groups and governments that marks such nations as the United States.[10]

Harold Wilensky has developed a complex historical model of democratic corporatist nations based on how different social forces participate in the political regime. In particular, he discerns the four different forms of corporatism listed in Table 5.1 (leftist, Catholic, leftist-Catholic, and corporatist without labor), as well as a group of six nations, which turn out to be those with British heritage, that

---

[9] Hedrick Smith, *The Power Game: How Washington Works* (New York: Random House, 1988).
[10] Harold L. Wilensky, *Rich Democracies: Political Economy, Public Policy, and Performance* (Berkeley: University of California Press, 2002), Chapter 2.

Table 5.1: Wilensky's classification of political economies.

Left Corporatist
Denmark
Finland
Norway
Sweden

Catholic Corporatist
Germany
Italy

Left-Catholic Corporatist
Austria
Belgium
Netherlands

Corporatist Without Labor
France
Japan
Switzerland

Least Corporatist
Australia
Canada
Ireland
New Zealand
United Kingdom
United States

Not Classified
Greece
Portugal
Spain

Source: Harold L. Wilensky, *Rich Democracies: Political Economy, Public Policy, and Performance* (Berkeley: University of California Press, 2002), p. 118.

have not developed corporatist institutions. He argues that each form of corporatism has important implications for the types of political economy and social policy that have evolved in these developed nations. This suggests that the corporatist form of government could be used as an explanatory factor for why the advanced industrial societies differ in terms of government size and socioeconomic outcomes. Indeed, Wilensky's sophisticated statistical analyses do demonstrate that corporatism exercises a powerful impact upon public policies and socioeconomic outcomes in the developed world.[11]

5.1.3 Field Studies

Field studies, or what might be called political anthropology, also seek to define a specific political community, institution, or setting. The basic approach and assumptions are somewhat different than in the qualitative conceptualizations of governmental systems just described. Field studies assume that communities, including their political process, are very complex social structures, which probably contain unique features. Thus, they aim at detailed and nuanced descriptions of single communities rather than the formulation of a more abstract concept, such as interest group liberalism or corporatist decision-making that can be applied to different political or social systems. This is because most field studies assume that the social context exerts a decided impact upon what people do and, in particular, upon how they interpret their own and others' actions. Consequently, such studies usually require long and direct observation of a community or social setting; and, methodologically, they raise complex issues of how the researcher should relate to the people being studied.[12]

Field studies are much more prevalent in anthropology and sociology than in political science. A classic and extremely influential sociological field study was conducted by Robert and Helen Lynd in Muncie, Indiana in the mid-1920s. Their book, *Middletown, A Study in American Culture*,[13] was both highly influential at the time and

---

[11] *Ibid.*, Chapter 2.
[12] John Lofland, *Analyzing Social Settings* (Belmont, CA: Wadsworth, 1984); Maurice Punch, *The Politics and Ethics of Fieldwork* (Newbury Park, CA: Sage, 1986); William B. Shaffir and Robert A. Stebbins, Eds., *Experiencing Fieldwork: An Insider View of Qualitative Research* (Newbury Park, CA: Sage, 1991).
[13] Robert S. Lynd and Helen Merrell Lynd, *Middletown: A Study in American Culture* (NY: Harcourt, Brace & Company, 1929). Also see Robert S. Lynd and Helen Merrell Lynd, *Middletown in Transition: A Study in Cultural Conflicts* (NY: Harcourt, Brace & Company, 1937).

path breaking in the sense that it showed the value and insights that could only be attained by a field study. The Lynds' methodology did make more use of social science conceptualization and quantitative indicators than most field studies. Muncie, called Middletown in the book, was selected because the Lynds saw it as a typical or ordinary American community; and the Lynds gathered huge amounts of quantitative data on everything from the explosion in the number of appliances and conveniences in Muncie homes to measures of a growing division between the business/professional and working classes in the city to club memberships and Church attendance to the nature of disagreements between children and parents. Still, the qualitative nature of the study is clear in the Lynds' argument that few generalizations are possible about the community's complex social fabric:

> On the contrary, the attempt to reveal interrelations in the maze of interlocked, often contradictory institutional habits that constitute living in Middletown has led to few general conclusions save as to the inchoate condition of this small modern community and the extent and complexity of the task confronting social science.[14]

A recent example of a modified field study that is highly relevant to the themes under investigation in this book is Alan Wolfe's Middle Class Morality Project. Wolfe sought to study the social and political values of middle class Americans to test the theory that the United States is polarizing into separate nations in a culture war. He selected eight middle class suburbs or communities in different regions of the U.S. that also differed somewhat on demographic factors, such as religion and race. A researcher lived in each community for 3–6 months; and detailed interviews were conducted with 25 residents in each community.[15] This project, therefore, involved substantially less immersion in the communities than a normal field study, but Wolfe consciously sought to blend the advantages of qualitative field studies and quantitative

---

[14] Lynd and Lynd, *Middletown*, (1929) p. 496.
[15] Alan Wolfe, *One Nation, After All: What Middle-Class Americans Really Think About God, Country, Family, Racism, Welfare, Immigration, Homosexuality, Work, the Right, the Left, and Each Other* (New York: Penguin, 1998), Chapter 1.

sociology and certainly reflected the underlying philosophy of political anthropology in his rationale for the project:

> I believe that we need to listen to the voices of ordinary people speaking about matters so central to modern morality.[16]

Wolfe's conclusions are well reflected in his book's title: *One Nation, After All.* Wolfe's interviews indicated that, unlike conservative and liberal intellectuals who had instituted a full-scale culture war by the late-1990s, middle class Americans were much more moderate and similar in their views and took a combination of conservative and liberal positions. Wolfe's analysis also illustrates the value and contribution that qualitative analysis can add to the raw numbers of quantitative studies. For example, he found that the American middle class is highly ambiguous about family values. These findings are conveyed both in quantitative and in qualitative forms. Table 5.2 reproduces his quantitative assessment of how the 200 participants in the study felt about family values: a little less than a quarter were conservative, only 2% were liberal, almost half were ambiguous in that they expressed both conservative and liberal values; and almost another fifth felt that

Table 5.2: Middle class views about the family in Wolfe's "middle class morality project".

	Number	Percent
Traditional: Strong support for conventional nuclear family	43	22
Post-Modern: Strong support for new family forms	4	2
Ambiguous: Combination of Traditional and Post-Modern values	90	45
Realist: Pragmatic accommodation to social change (i.e., working women) necessary	37	19
Insufficient Information to classify	26	13
TOTAL	200	101

Source: Alan Wolfe, *One Nation, After All: What Middle-Class Americans Really Think About God, Country, Family, Racism, Welfare, Immigration, Homosexuality, Work, the Right, the Left, and Each Other* (New York: Penguin Books, 1998), p. 100.

---

[16] *Ibid.*, p. 37.

families needed to accommodate themselves to such social change as working women and easier divorce procedures.

Such numbers probably convey far less meaning and nuance than detailed quotations. The need to look beyond our stereotypes of conservatives and liberals is probably conveyed more convincingly than in the table for most readers by the following extended excerpt from and about Katherine Mullins (a pseudonym), a businesswoman who lives in the Tulsa suburb of Broken Arrow:

> Here is an American who believes that if government would just get out of the way, America would come to respect merit and individual initiative far more than it currently does. Katherine Mullins speaks in the language of classic American libertarianism.
>
> And how does a libertarian raise her children? Conservatives, who presumably like what Katherine Mullins has to say about the economy and personal responsibility, would not be pleased to hear what she has to say about family values or religion. For Mrs. Mullins, work comes first and the family after: "When there's a job to be done, you do not just quit at five because you think you have got to come home to help the kids or to bathe", she asserts with some finality. "The kids would have to understand that is what it is all about, and that working just a little harder gets you something just a little more".[17]

5.2 CONTENT ANALYSIS: ATTACHING NUMBERS TO QUALITATIVE MATERIALS

Content analysis was developed as a technique for analyzing the content of communications. It can and has been applied to written documents, live speeches, video and audio recordings, and internet postings. The primary objective is to describe systematically the themes expressed in these communications which can then be attributed to their authors or presenters. The basic analytic interest, in turn, often is with the characteristics of the content of the message itself and what it represents — for example, what issues are emphasized by a political candidate, what attributes of a product are emphasized in

---

[17] *Ibid.*, p. 90.

an advertising campaign, or what types of articles are emphasized by particular magazines or journals. Sometimes, in more sophisticated content analyses, the goal of the analysis is to draw more indirect inferences from the messages under examination — for example, the psychological disposition of the author of speeches or diaries.

Content analysis has many obvious applications in the study of political science. It is particularly well suited to describe the policy positions of nations, parties, or individual politicians. For example, the number and nature of official statements warning Saddam Hussein of American concerns about Iraq issued by the Bush administration during the September 2001 to March 2003 period would be an important indicator of the U.S. policy. The strong differences that existed among countries on Iraq, further, could be examined by comparing the positions taken by their Presidents and Prime Ministers in speeches and official statements. Likewise, the strategies of Barack Obama and John McCain during the 2008 presidential election could be studied by analyzing the content of their speeches in terms of the issues that they discussed and the positions that they took on these issues.

The classification of content analysis as a qualitative technique is admittedly at least a little ambiguous. The documents, videos, etc. that provide the initial materials or data are clearly qualitative in nature. However, much if not most of content analysis involves transforming these qualitative materials into one kind of quantitative indicator or another, such as the number of references to Iraq in the acceptance speeches of Bush and Kerry or whether a particular speech by Jacques Chirac (during his presidentship of France) or Tony Blair (during his prime ministership of Great Britain) supported or opposed military action in Iraq.

There are two responses to the questions about treating content analysis as a qualitative technique, though. First, qualitative content analyses are an important part of the field.[18] Second, as will be seen, all but the most simplistic content analyses involve decisions about how to treat or code materials that involve qualitative judgment. This again

---

[18] Richard L. Merritt, *Systematic Approaches to Comparative Politics* (Chicago: Rand McNally, 1970), pp. 83–85.

underlines the analogies that exist between quantitative and qualitative approaches, which suggest that they are just as much complementary as competing. Or, in terms of the metaphor used throughout this text, both are intrinsic to the process of putting together the jigsaw puzzles which political scientists regard as important and central to their discipline.

This section on content analysis has two major parts. The first part describes content analysis that is highly relevant to the themes discussed in this text — Howard Gold's study of the *Conservative Shift* in American politics between the 1960s and late 1980s.[19] The second then discusses the major elements in content analysis, using Gold's study as a central illustration of these techniques.

5.2.1 Gold's Application of Content Analysis

Howard Gold was primarily interested in tracing and explaining the widely perceived "conservative shift" in American politics from the liberalism of 1960s during the administrations of John Kennedy and Lyndon Johnson to the conservatism of the 1980s under the presidencies of Ronald Reagan and George H.W. Bush. He focused upon three primary subjects or areas: (1) the public policies of our national government, (2) the positions of our two major parties, and (3) general public opinion. The first he assessed by providing a brief summary of what the Carter and Reagan administrations did in the areas of taxes, budgets, social welfare, education, public employment and training, regulatory policy, civil rights, and social issues. Public opinion was analyzed by presenting trends in political attitudes, such as the ones analyzed in this book, between 1960 and 1988.

Gold applied content analysis as his central methodology for examining the second topic or question of whether the Republicans and Democrats had become more conservative over the period under analysis, particularly between the mid-1970s and the late-1980s. He subjected two sets of documents to content analysis. First, the platforms or statements of issue positions that each party adopts at its presidential

---

[19] Howard J. Gold, *Hollow Mandates: American Public Opinion and the Conservative Shift* (Boulder, CO: Westview, 1992).

nominating conventions every four years were used to indicate the general policy stances of Republicans and Democrats. Second, the acceptance speeches of party nominees at the conventions were used to measure the specific views of presumably the most important leader in each party.

Tables 5.3 and 5.4 report the results of Gold's content analyses of the Republican and Democratic party platforms respectively. Each

Table 5.3: New conservative planks in Republican platforms, 1976–1988.

Issue areas	New policies	Years
Economic Issues		
Government and Economy	Balanced Budget Amendment	1980, 1984, 1988
	Enterprise zones	1980, 1984, 1988
	Repeal rent control laws	1988
Health and Welfare	Remove ineligible from welfare	1976, 1980
	Tighten food stamp eligibility	1976, 1980
Education	Abolish Dept. of Education	1980
	Tuition tax credits	1976, 1980, 1984, 1988
	Public school vouchers	1988
Cultural Issues		
Education	Pledge of Allegiance in schools	1988
Women's Rights	Oppose Equal Rights Amendment	1980
Abortion	Amendment banning abortion	1976, 1980, 1984, 1988
	Oppose public funds for abortion	1980, 1984, 1988
	No public funds for organizations supporting abortion	1984, 1988
Prayer	Amendment for nonsectarian prayer	1976
	Voluntary school prayer	1980, 1984, 1988
	Prayer in child care facilities	1988
Law and Order	Support death penalty	1980, 1984, 1988
Courts	Support pro-Life judges	1980, 1984, 1988
	Restrict Fed court jurisdiction	1984
	Support judges' pro-family values and judicial restraint	1980, 1984, 1988
Race	Oppose racial quotas	1976, 1980, 1984, 1988

Source: Howard J. Gold, *Hollow Mandates: American Public Opinion and the Conservative Shift* (Boulder, CO: Westview Press, 1992), pp. 44–45.

Table 5.4: New conservative planks in Democratic platforms, 1976–1988.

Issue areas	New policies	Years
Economic Issues		
Government and Economy	Anti-recession grants to stimulate private sector	1976
	Industrial de-regulation	1980
	Emphasize private sector job creation	1980, 1984
Housing	Private capital for public housing	1984
	Employer-assisted housing	1988
Education	Private responsibility for strengthening higher education	1984
Health	Call for healthcare cost containment	1984
	National health insurance a *long-term* goal	1984
Welfare	Neo-conservative critique	1976, 1980
	Call for workfare	1976, 1980
Cultural Issues		
Law and Order	Fed support for victims' rights	1980, 1984, 1988
	Reject social causes of crime	1984

Source: Howard J. Gold, *Hollow Mandates: American Public Opinion and the Conservative Shift* (Boulder, CO: Westview Press, 1992), p. 36.

table lists the new conservative policy positions that were included in the party's platform beginning in 1976. That is, only issue positions that had not been part of the party's platform before 1976 qualified as a measure of a "conservative shift". These tables list the issues and the years between 1976 and 1988 that they appeared in the platform for each party.[20]

It is widely perceived that Ronald Reagan's nomination in 1980 represented a major conservative shift in the Republican Party which was transmitted into national policy with his decisive victories in the 1980 and 1984 elections. Moreover, his strong challenge to President Gerald Ford in 1976 pushed the Republican platform rightward in that year as well. The data in Table 5.3 provide strong empirical support for this image, as Gold found that more than 20 conservative planks were

---

[20] *Ibid.*, Chapter 3.

added to the Republican platforms between 1976 and 1988 with most first appearing in 1976 or 1980. Looking more closely at the specific issues also indicates that cultural issues were emerging as central for Republicans since almost two-thirds of the issues listed in the table were in this area.

Perhaps a little more surprisingly, Table 5.4 shows that the Democratic Party was moving in a markedly conservative direction as well. In fact, Gold was able to identify 12 conservative additions to Democratic platforms between 1976 and 1988. Still, a closer examination indicates a very significant difference between these conservative shifts in the Democratic and Republic Parties. The new conservative positions in the Democratic platforms in Table 5.4 almost exclusively concerned economic issues, with the only conservatism on cultural issues being expressed in the area of law and order. More dramatically, in materials included in Gold's text but not in his table, the Democrats actually added two important *liberal* planks to their platform on central cultural issues, expressing support for abortion rights in 1976 and gay rights in 1980.[21] Thus, the two parties appeared to have begun polarizing on culture-war issues in the early-1980s.

5.2.2 An Introductory Overview of Content Analysis

Content analysis, as the primary technique for systematically studying communications, originated in the field of journalism which was (and is) concerned with the nature and impact of the mass media and with questions about how it treated the political world, as well as with methodologies for analyzing these issues:

> In primitive form, it flourished during the 1930s. Students of journalism and others ascertained attention patterns, as indicated by column inches or occasionally by word counts, for wide varieties of newspapers and other publications; they compared patterns of attention to political events over time in the same publications; they contrasted political interest in large metropolitan dailies to that in small-town weeklies; they spent much time with questions of appropriate sampling and validation techniques.[22]

---

[21] *Ibid.*, p. 35.
[22] Merritt, *op. cit.*, p. 64.

Projects based on content analysis range from fairly simple designs that a single researcher can apply to extremely complex projects that involve large teams. Likewise, the actual analysis may be easy to execute by someone without advanced expertise or may involve complex statistical analysis or the application of sophisticated computer programs to even code the data or the utilization of expert judges. Finally, content analysis is similar to other qualitative approaches in that questions can be raised about whether the quantification of materials robs them of important nuance.

The primary objective of content analysis is to implement a "data-reduction process by which the many words of texts are classified into much fewer content categories".[23] This process, as outlined in Tables 5.5 and 5.6 below, can be thought of as involving two major stages or types of analytic decisions. First, of course, comes the selection of what to study both in terms of the substantive subject matter and in terms of the material that will be subjected to content analysis. Second, the question of "How will it be studied?" must be posed and answered. This involves both conceptualizing how the study will be conducted (Parts I to III in Table 5.6 below) and devising the concrete procedures for quantifying the data (Parts IV and V in Table 5.6) The initial choice of subject matter will be determined by a researcher's substantive interests in most cases. Once the topic is selected, though, the specific

Table 5.5: Major dimensions of what will be analyzed.

	Dimension or question	Application in study of *conservative shift*
I.	Substantive research question or problem	Whether a party adopted a new conservative position
II.	Materials containing information on this topic	1. Party platforms 2. Acceptance speeches of nominees
III.	Will all of materials or a sample of them be subjected to content analysis?	All platforms (1976–1988) and acceptance speeches (1960–1988) included in the study

---

[23] Robert Philip Weber, *Basic Content Analysis*, 2nd Edn. (Newbury Park, CA: Sage, 1990), p. 15.

Table 5.6: Major dimensions of how content analysis will be conducted.

Dimension or question	Application in study of *conservative shift*
I. Form of analysis	
1. Components in communication(s)	Both Platforms and Speeches
2. Document or communication as a whole	No
II. Focus of analysis	
1. Substantive meaning	Both Platforms and Speeches
2. Structural characteristics (e.g., length or prominence)	No
III. What is coded	
1. Manifest content (e.g., words)	Platforms
2. Latent content (e.g., themes)	Speeches
IV. Type of data	
1. Presence/absence	Both Platforms and Speeches
2. Combinations of themes	No
3. Scale (e.g., like–dislike)	No
V. Who does analysis	
1. Single researcher	Both Platforms and Speeches
2. Panel of judges	No
3. Computer program	No

form of content analysis that will be applied is highly dependent upon the resources available for the project.[24]

Table 5.5 outlines the three major decisions that must be made about the question of what will be analyzed. The left column in the table lists each of these three decisions or questions in the abstract; and the column on the right illustrates this by indicating what Howard Gold did in his study of the conservative shift in party positions in the United States. The first step is to select a research problem or question. Once the subject of the research is specified, the materials that will be content analyzed need to be selected. This, in turn, is a

---

[24] For good general overviews of content analysis, see Klaus Krippendorff, *Content Analysis: An Introduction to Its Methodology* (Beverly Hills, CA: Sage, 1980); Jarol B. Manheim, Richard C. Rich and Lars Willnat, *Empirical Political Analysis: Research Methods in Political Science*, 5th Edn. (New York: Longman, 2002), Chapter 9; Merritt, *Systematic Approaches*, Chapter 3; and Weber, *Basic Content Analysis*.

two-stage process. First, the researcher must find a communication or set of communications that contain materials relevant to the subject at hand. Second, a decision must be made about whether all the materials, or just a sample of them, will be used in the study. The key factors here, quite obviously, are how voluminous the materials are and how many resources are at the disposal of the researcher.

Gold's central research question was whether a conservative shift had occurred in the issue positions of one or both of America's two major political parties between the 1960s and the late-1980s. Since the national parties in the United States are fairly weak or even dormant except during presidential campaigns, he selected the campaign rhetoric associated with presidential elections to serve as the source of documents and materials on how Democrats and Republicans viewed the major issues of the day at any particular moment. Once having made this general strategic decision about what to study, he then had to select specific documents for his content analysis. He chose the party platform to represent the positions of the party as a whole and the nominee's acceptance speech to tap the views of the party's pre-eminent leader. Because these two sources constituted a fairly limited number of documents that could be analyzed by a single researcher, there was no need to employ sampling. These two sources were certainly not the only potential ones that could have been included in Gold's study. He might, for example, have included all the speeches of a candidate that were covered by the *New York Times*, which almost certainly would have been so large a number that sampling would have become necessary.

Once the general subject matter and materials have been selected, it is necessary to make a series of decisions about how the content analysis will be conducted. Table 5.6 summarizes five such components of any content analysis. First, a fundamental decision concerns whether the unit of analysis is the components (words or themes) within documents and recordings or whether the entire communication should be treated as a single item. Both of Gold's content analyses represent the first type of approach. New conservative issue positions (i.e., those that had not been adopted before 1976) were identified in the party platform; and each of these components was then reported in Tables 5.3 and 5.4. Similarly, the number of conservative and liberal themes in each

The Relationship of Qualitative Approaches to Quantitative Analysis 115

acceptance speech were also tallied for a separate analysis. Conversely, each acceptance speech or platform might be conceptualized as a single item or unit of analysis and measured in terms of whether or not they mentioned tax cuts or health care, for example.

The development of computerized data bases, in particular LEXIS/NEXIS, makes such item analysis quite easy, even for extremely large and complex sets of materials.[25] There is a danger, though, that applying such technology to many items without considering the context of some communications may produce misleading results. For example, in the 2004 presidential campaign, George Bush and John Kerry differed strongly on whether the war in Iraq was a vital component of the war on terrorism. Thus, one might hypothesize that the terms "Iraq" and "war on terror" would appear together in many more Bush speeches than Kerry speeches. However, just counting the number of speeches or items in which both appear might be misleading if Kerry mentioned both, not to support Bush's thesis that Iraq is an integral part of the war on terror, but to refute it directly.

A second important question concerns whether content analysis is substantive or structural in nature. Substantive content analyses focus on the meaning of documents and recordings, such as the number of liberal or conservative themes in acceptance speeches. In contrast, structural analysis is primarily concerned with the nature of a communication to indicate its importance. For example, news stories can be coded according to their length in column inches or whether they are accompanied by a large headline or photograph to indicate their relative prominence. In short, substantive content analysis measures *what* is said, while structural content analysis examines *how* it is said.[26] As Table 5.6 indicates, Gold focused on substantive, not structural, analysis.

The third major decision involved in content analysis is whether the study will search for manifest or latent themes. Manifest content analysis records actual words or phrases. For example, Gold's study of the Republican and Democratic platforms selected only issues that were

---

[25] Manheim, Rich and Willnat, *op. cit.*, p. 165.
[26] Manheim, Rich and Willnat, *op. cit.*

specifically named or included in these documents. In contrast, latent content analysis moves beyond specifically stated words or phrases to identify underlying themes in the document. For example, Gold used his own interpretation of what constituted a conservative or liberal theme, not a count of actual words, to determine how many themes representing each ideology were present in the presidential acceptance speeches. Very often, the choice between manifest and latent content analysis involves a painful trade-off. Manifest content analysis provides hard data whose nature is usually unquestionable. However, we often are interested in more complex ideas than can be measured by such an approach. Latent content analysis, in contrast, can often produce more interesting and theoretically relevant categories, but at the cost of introducing possible interpretive bias into the study.

The first three parts of Table 5.6 really concern the conceptual strategy for doing a content analysis. Parts IV and V, then, move to the level of how the numerical codings and analysis will actually be done. Part IV describes the form that the data will assume. Many studies just code the presence or absence of the words or latent themes in a document or recording, as was done in Gold's content analysis. This can take several forms: the count of the number of times this content appears in the communication, a rating of whether or not the item as a whole contained this word or theme, or the percentage of text devoted to a particular concept. Sometimes, such data analysis moves from the counting of single themes to a **contingency analysis** of when and/or how often two themes go together. Usually, dictionaries of the words and themes that will be included in the content analysis need to be prepared beforehand. It is also valuable to engage in a **pre-test**. That is, some documents not included in the final content analysis should be coded as a way of testing and fine-tuning the preliminary dictionary.

A different type of data is to code categories in terms of a scale. For example, how conservative or liberal is a speech or a politician's views on an issue like abortion? How strongly did a prime minister from another country support or oppose military action in Iraq? How much like or dislike toward a political figure, such as Nancy Pelosi or Sarah Palin, does a newspaper editorial or television commentary express? This type of scaling has both advantages and disadvantages. On the one hand, sharper distinctions can certainly be drawn; and more sophisticated statistical analysis is often possible. On the other hand, there is the trade-off that the foundation for such ratings is usually far less precise than for simpler coding schemes.

Finally, Part V lists the three major possibilities for who will do the content analysis: (1) a single researcher, (2) a panel of judges, or (3) a computer software package. Of course, large projects may involve all three for different segments of the research, but the type and identity of primary analysis does much to define the scope of the project. Given the limits of the time and capability of any individual, any study by a single student or scholar will almost inevitably face significant resource limits. For example, Howard Gold's selection of just two types of documents to analyze the conservative shift of the political parties in the United States almost certainly stemmed from the fact that he had to do the analysis itself. In addition, the limitations on what a single researcher can accomplish can be greatly expanded by computer analysis. However, this requires specialized expertise in the computer programs in question; and the preparation of data for computer analysis may well require the work of a fairly large team.

For projects with more resources, the utilization of panels of judges can have several important advantages. First, having several judges means that much more work can be done than by a sole coder. Second, the judges may possess specialized knowledge that is unavailable to a single researcher. For example, content analysis in comparative politics often requires experts about the different countries in the study.[27] Perhaps most importantly, having multiple judges provides a means for checking for the possibility of interpretive bias in latent content analysis when the coder has to apply personal judgments in coding underlying themes or in rating the content on a scale with several points instead of just noting its presence or absence. Simply put, substantial agreement among the judges, which is termed the degree of **intercoder reliability**, gives far more credence to the results than the interpretation of one scholar or student.

---

[27] Merritt, *op. cit.*, Chapter 3.

EXERCISES

1. Briefly describe how you would design a study based on elite interviews of the dramatic battle over healthcare legislation in 2009 and 2010. Who should be included in the interviews? What should be the major questions in the interviews? What conclusions do you think that you could reach based on such a research project?
2. Qualitative analysis can be used to conceptualize political systems. Briefly describe how the Tea Party Movement conceptualizes the federal government in the United States. How convincing do you think this perspective is? Why?
3. Describe how you would design a field study to examine how Americans feel about the role of government. What would you do to make the findings representative of our citizenry? What would be your general strategy for eliciting information? What specific topics would you include in the study?
4. Conduct a content analysis of the acceptance speeches of John McCain and Barack Obama in 2008. Make sure that your content analysis includes the major themes in each speech and the specific positions that the candidate took on the issues that they addressed. Briefly describe what you did in terms of the five dimensions included in Table 5.6.
5. Perform a content analysis on two articles which support and two which oppose the current presidential administration that are available on the web site of Real Clear Politics (www.realclearpolitics.com). Make sure that your content analysis includes the major themes in each article and the reasons that it supports or opposes the President. What does your analysis imply about the strengths and weaknesses of the administration?

Part II
The Foundations for Statistical Analysis

Chapter 6

Some More Complex Issues in Interpreting Data

Chapter 2 introduced political science data by showing how frequency tables and graphs can present them in simple and easy-to-understand formats. However, using these data can raise several more complex issues. This chapter, then, considers three methodological issues associated with the data in Chapter 2. Section 6.1 shows **how data presentations, especially graphs, can be distorted,** to give misleading impressions. Section 6.2 discusses some problems that can arise referring to several **different types of percentages**. Finally, in Section 6.3, we consider the **levels of measurement** that are appropriate for different types of data.

6.1 THE DANGERS OF DISTORTION

Because graphs are often read at a quick glance, their meaning may be distorted, either inadvertently or deliberately, by how they are presented. That is, while seeing is believing, seeing can also be deceiving! Such problems can easily arise in the interpretation of truncated bar graphs. The bottom or the start of these graphs are not zero, as they were in all the bar graphs in Chapter 2. Rather, they start at a level that allows all the different data points to be displayed. This can save considerable space in the graph and provide a greater visual emphasis of differences among the cases.

However, manipulating the scale of a graph can produce very different impressions, as can be easily seen in the two bar graphs in Figure 6.1 on life expectancy in the U.S., Sweden, and Japan. The first graph is a full one which compares the figures of 77.2 in the United States, 80.2 in Sweden, and 81.8 in Japan. While someone with either a sharp eye or good glasses should be able to see that Japan has the highest and America the lowest life expectancies among these three nations, the differences are infinitesimal. The second graph is a partial or truncated one, which begins at 76 instead of zero. This produces an exceedingly different impression. Here, the United States seems to have a very poor performance on this social indicator, while Japan has a considerable lead over Sweden. Incidentally, the second truncated graph is the one produced by default by a popular software graphing program. Thus, care certainly needs to be taken in presenting graphs. Otherwise, what you see may be largely determined either by what a computer mindlessly spews forth or by what someone else wants to show!

The danger that a quick look at a graph can give the wrong impression is often multiplied when **pictographs** are used. Instead of a simple bar whose height represents the value of an individual case for a variable, a pictograph uses a picture or symbol to give a more striking representation. Pictographs can be very attractive visually and, thus, are used fairly often in place of bar graphs. The problem with them, however, is that these pictographs are in two dimensions, so that it is very easy to distort size differences. A good example of this is used in a popular text called *How to Lie with Statistics* which compares the average wage rates in the United States and another hypothetical nation.[1]

In this example, wages in the U.S. are assumed to be twice as high; and this is represented in one graph by the American worker having two money bags, while his counterpart only has one. The problem of dimensionality comes out in the second graph which gives the two workers money bags of different sizes. Since the U.S. worker made

---

[1] Darrell Huff, *How to Lie with Statistics* (New York: W.W. Norton, 1954), pp. 66–70.

Some More Complex Issues in Interpreting Data 123

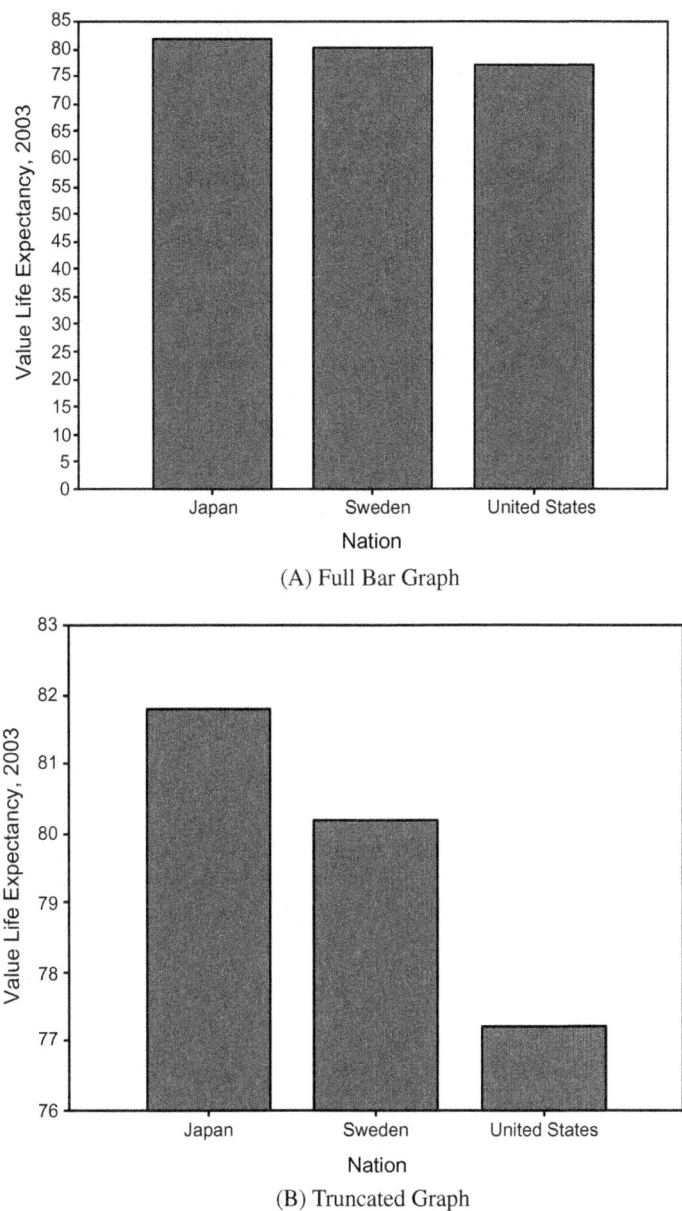

(A) Full Bar Graph

(B) Truncated Graph

Figure 6.1: Bar graphs for life expectancy, 2003.

twice as much, the person who constructed the graph gave him a money bag that was twice as wide and twice as high. Consequently, with two dimensions that are twice as big, the U.S. worker now gets a money bag that is *four times* as big as his counterpart from the other country. This is clearly a huge distortion. The only question about it would be whether it was deliberate or not. That is, did the compiler forget basic arithmetic and geometry? Or, did he or she intentionally mean to mislead the viewer, perhaps to make Americans happier with their incumbent administration?

Pictographs can be dangerous, consequently, if you do not pay close attention to the dimensions of the graph. Fortunately, while the second graph shows the gross distortions that a pictograph can display, the first indicates how to solve the problem of distorted dimensions quite easily. What you need to do is to make comparisons by changing the number of items depicted by the picture in the graph. For example, the number of bags of money that a worker has can be used to represent the amount of his or her salary. In contrast, if the size of a two-dimensional figure are manipulated for comparative purposes, grossly distorted dimensions will almost inevitably emerge.

These examples of misleading graphs involve visual impressions that depart from reality. Sometimes, though, serious questions can arise over exactly what reality is. A subtle and ambiguous example involves changing what is being compared as is done in Figure 6.2. Here, data on infant mortality are used to test the liberal argument that welfare states are able to provide better social outcomes for their citizens than a *laissez-faire* political economy, such as America. When infant mortality in the United States is compared to that in Sweden in the first bar graph, this argument receives strong support as the U.S. rate is twice as high as in the welfare state. However, if a developing nation like India is added to the comparison as is done in the bottom graph, the difference between the United States and Sweden looks trivial. Here, the question is not misleading the reader by distorting the graph but, rather, involves the theoretical question of what should be included in the analysis in the first place.

The distortions that can easily occur in graphs illustrate the broader point that Darrell Huff makes in *How to Lie with Statistics* that just

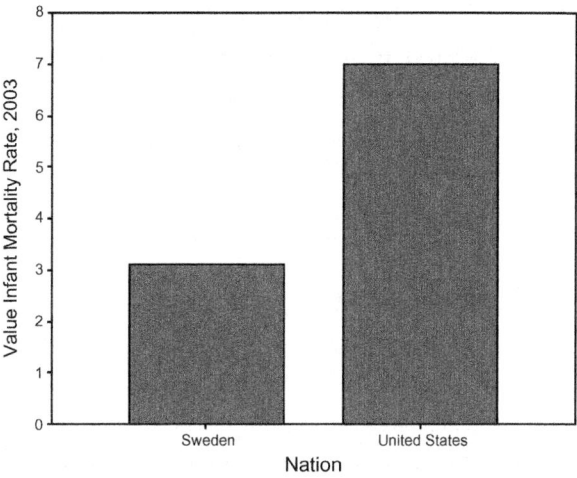
(A) Bar Graph for the United States and Sweden, 2003

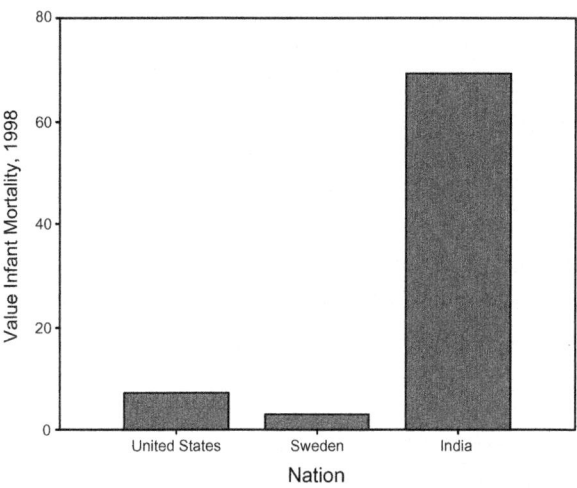
(B) Bar Graph for the United States, Sweden, and India

Figure 6.2: Bar graphs for infant mortality.

because there are "hard" numbers does not mean that these numbers tell the "whole truth and nothing but the truth".[2] The fact that Huff's text is still in print without any revisions almost 60 years after

---

[2] *Ibid.*

its initial publication in 1954 certainly implies that the problem of false impressions created by partial and misleading statistics has yet to be solved. No wonder, Mark Twain was quoted as saying that there are three kinds of lies: "lies, damn lies, and statistics!" In fact, Huff proposed the concept of **statisticulation** which he defines as "misinforming people by the use of statistical material".[3]

6.1.1 Types of Statisticulation

Several types of statisticulation can be distinguished. Unlike Mark Twain, this discussion does not consider statistics to form a separate class of lying. Rather, it takes the distinction between lies and damn lies as the basis for separating minor and major instances of the misuse of statistics. Thus, let us define lies as "slight, perhaps inadvertent, distortions" and damn lies as "flagrant attempts to mislead". This creates the three forms of statisticulation summarized in Figure 6.3. The first type refers to the degree of distortion in a presentation. Here, lies are separated from damn lies by the degree to which they misrepresent reality. For example, the truncated bar graph on economic growth rates in Part #A of Figure 6.4 is a fairly minor distortion which somewhat overstates America's better economic performance, while the one on life expectancy in Part #B would clearly make the list of gross distortions or damn lies because it makes Japan's and Sweden's trivial advantage over the U.S. on this social indicator look huge.

Such distorted graphs can easily be drawn inadvertently. However, sometimes the distortions are deliberately introduced by an analyst hoping to make his or her point seem stronger than it actually is. For example, a conservative would probably emphasize the better economic performance of the *laissez-faire* United States compared to Sweden with its large welfare state and, therefore, like the overstatement of this difference in Part #A of Figure 6.4. In contrast, a liberal who believes that America's *laissez-faire* political economy leads to poor or unfair social outcomes would be overjoyed at the huge distortion about how much higher life expectancy is in Sweden than in America in

---

[3] *Ibid.*, p. 100.

TYPES OF STATISTICULATION

TYPE OF STATISTICULATION	MINOR FORM (Lies)	GROSS FORM (Damn Lies)
DEGREE OF DISTORTION	Small Distortion that does not change meaning greatly	Huge Distortion that fundamentally changes conclusion drawn from graph or statistical table
REASON FOR MISLEADING INFORMATION	Misleading information inadvertent	Misleading information deliberately provided, usually for purposes of political manipulation
INCOMPLETE EVIDENCE	Partial results support wrong conclusions	False data (a damn lie by any definition)

Figure 6.3: Types of statisticulation.

Part #B of the figure. Consequently, we can make another distinction between lies and damn lies in statistical presentations. A lie is a simple mistake in setting up the scale of a graph or reporting another type of statistic without any thought of what its effects are, while a damn lie is explicitly distorting the graphical and statistical evidence to mislead the audience.

This brings us to a third dimension of misleading numbers. A number may be accurate and represent the "truth". Yet, what it shows may be far from the "whole truth". For example, as noted in the last paragraph, conservatives would generally prefer the government policies of the U.S. to Sweden, while liberals would generally prefer Sweden's welfare state. Conservatives could support their preference by citing America's much higher economic growth rate, while liberals could cite Sweden's lower infant mortality rate as evidence that their type of government works better. Both these statistics are accurate and factual by themselves. Yet, they certainly do not represent the whole truth because both ignore the fact that the U.S.'s higher economic growth is counterbalanced by Sweden's lower infant mortality. This suggests a third way of categorizing the lies and damn lies in statisticulation. A lie is presenting accurate but only partial information, while a

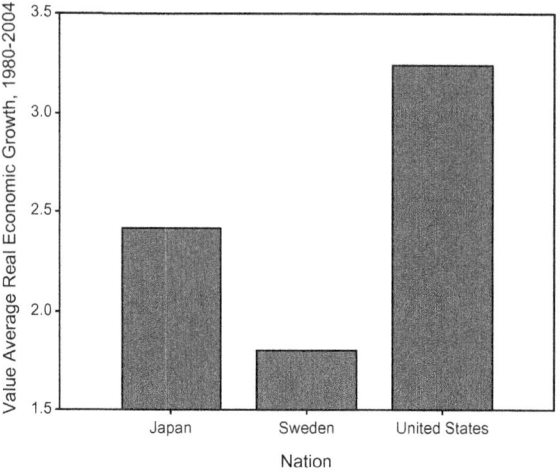

(A) Slight Distortion (lie): Economic Growth Rates

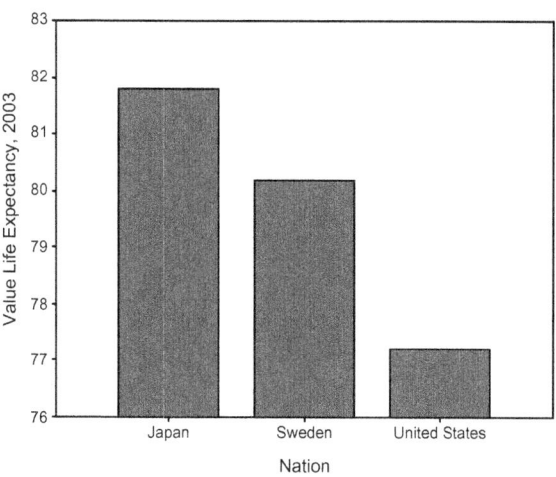

(B) Gross Distortion (damn lie): Life Expectancy

Figure 6.4: Distortions with truncated bar graphs.

damn lie is actually lying about the statistics themselves (e.g., claiming that Sweden has a higher growth rate than the U.S. or that America has a lower infant mortality rate than Sweden).

This is not to argue, however, that all statistics are misleading because some can and are abused as well as used — which might seem like be heresy indeed for a research methods book. Rather, the reader or consumer of statistics needs to think carefully about whether the statistical information is complete or whether what is not included might change the implications of the findings. Thus, common sense and skepticism are important for understanding statistical information.

6.1.2 Reagan and Income Inequality: Ignoring the Trend

Statisticulation can occur, not just in partisan propaganda pieces, but in mainstream and well respected analyses as well. A good example is *The Politics of Rich and Poor* by Kevin Phillips[4] which became a best seller in the early 1990s, as well as being used as a text in political science classes. Phillips' basic thesis was:

> The Republicans rode such a wave into office in 1969 as a middle-class, anti-elite correction, successfully squelching social permissiveness and disorder. But then, during the 1980s — and not for the first time in U.S. history — Reagan's GOP became a high-powered vehicle not only for capitalist revitalization, but also, as we have seen, for the accumulation of wealth by a relatively narrow elite. Twice before, the genius of the system has generated an electoral correction to such Republican excesses, raising the possibility of another in the 1990s.[5]

Phillips, in short, pictured Reagan as a reverse Robin Hood who stole from the poor and gave to the rich and predicted that these policies would lead to a popular backlash which might allow the Democrats to recapture the White House — which, incidentally, they did two years after *The Politics of Rich and Poor* rolled off the presses. One might expect that such an argument would come from a liberal Democrat. However, part of the power of Phillips' analysis came from his strong Republican credentials during the Nixon presidency, including his authorship of the book *The Emerging Republican Majority*, which predicted that Nixon's victory in 1968 heralded a change from Democratic

---

[4] Kevin Phillips, *The Politics of Rich and Poor: Wealth and the American Electorate in the Reagan Aftermath* (New York: HarperCollins, 1990).
[5] *Ibid.*, p. 33.

to Republican domination of U.S. politics.[6] Phillips, hence, appeared to be a Nixon Republican who feared that Reagan had undercut the political gains that Nixon had engineered for the Republican Party.

Phillips justified his argument with the data presented in the top half (Part #A) of Table 6.1 on individual income inequality in the United States as measured by the relative shares of total income going to the richest fifth and the poorest fifths of the population. Clearly, these data show that the rich got proportionately richer and the poor got proportionately poorer between 1969 and 1988. In 1969, the richest fifth of the population received 40.6% of all income and the poorest fifth got 5.6% with the ratio between them being 7.25:1. Two decades later, the top fifth's income share was 44.0% and the bottom fifth's was 4.6%, producing an inequality ratio of 9.57:1. At least according to economic historians, this represents a huge change. According to Phillips, this proved his point that Reagan was a reverse Robin Hood, although he did not use that term.

Given the large tax cut favoring the rich that Reagan sponsored in 1981, most readers found this a convincing argument. However, a slightly closer look at the table raises significant questions. Obviously, Reagan's policies could only affect income distribution during, but not before, he became President. Yet, income inequality increased only slightly less during the 1970s than during the Reagan administration in the 1980s. Moreover, although Phillips certainly could not be blamed for not presenting these data, the figures on the inequality in household incomes after Reagan left office in Part #B of Table 6.1 are completely incongruent with the image of Republican responsibility for greater inequality in late 20th century America. During the first Bush administration (1989–1992), there was no change at all in the degree of income inequality. In sharp contrast, under Democrat Bill Clinton, income inequality jumped between 1992 and 2000 to almost exactly the same extent that it had during the Reagan presidency. Clearly, America is experiencing a long-term trend of growing income inequality; and the Reagan years do not really stand out in terms of this

---

[6] Kevin P. Phillips, *The Emerging Republican Majority* (Garden City, NY: Anchor Books, 1970).

Table 6.1: Income inequality in the United States.

A. Individual Income Inequality

Year	Share of the poorest fifth	Share of the richest fifth	Ratio between income shares
1969	5.6%	40.6%	7.25
1980	5.1%	41.6%	8.16
1984	4.7%	42.9%	9.13
1988	4.6%	44.0%	9.57

Source: Kevin Phillips, *The Politics of Rich and Poor: Wealth and the American Electorate in the Reagan Aftermath* (New York: HarperCollins, 1990), p. 13.

B. Household Inequality

Year	Share of the poorest fifth	Share of the richest fifth	Ratio between income shares
1988	3.8%	46.3%	12.18
1992	3.8%	46.9%	12.34
2000	3.6%	49.8%	13.83

Source: "Historical Income Tables — Income Inequality" (Washington, D.C.: U.S. Census Bureau, 2003). Available at www.census.gov.

trend. Rather, rising inequality is due almost certainly to the transition from the Industrial Age to the Information Age sketched in Chapter 1 (see Figure 1.1) because of the loss of highly paid jobs for fairly unskilled workers in the manufacturing sector.[7]

This would appear to be a strong case of statistics being used in a misleading manner. When we look back to the three dimensions of statisticulation in Figure 6.4, a mixed picture emerges about how serious the statisticulation is. In terms of the third criterion of incomplete evidence, this would be a minor form in that accurate data are reported, but the full story or whole truth is not told. In terms of the degree of distortion, the depiction of the trend would probably qualify as a major or gross distortion. However, when looking at the reason

---

[7] Lester C. Thurow, *The Future of Capitalism: How Today's Economic Forces Shape Tomorrow's World* (New York: William Morrow, 1996), pp. 248–254.

for providing a misleading interpretation, it is clearly inadvertent, rather than deliberate and manipulative. If Phillips had wanted to mislead, he could have just given the data on the increase in inequality during the Reagan years. Instead, by including all the data that were reprinted in Part #A of Table 6.1, he actually provided the material to challenge his own thesis — which might suggest that he should have hired a more competent research assistant!

6.2 WHY SIMPLE PERCENTAGES ARE NOT ALWAYS SO SIMPLE

The nature of percentages is usually considered a simple topic, but it can sometimes become confusing when we try to make it too simple! Table 6.2 provides the data used to illustrate these points by comparing the percentage of conservatives, moderates, and liberals in 2000 with the distribution of ideological affiliation in the population in 1992. One major difference between the results for these two years is clearly an artifact of how the question was asked. In 2000, respondents were prodded strongly to pick either conservative or liberal, while they were not in 1992. Consequently, there were a lot more moderates in 1992 (31%) than in 2000 (7%).

None of the problems that can arise in interpreting percentages really result from anything that is hard to understand or even to compute. Rather, percentages can mean somewhat different things, thereby creating some confusion if one is not careful to examine how a specific percentage is being used. Table 6.3, hence, defines the four principal types of percentage measures and provides an example of how to calculate each from the data in Table 6.2.

Table 6.2: Americans' ideological position.

	2000		1992	
	Number	Percent	Number	Percent
Liberal	591	36	237	28
Moderate	109	7	332	31
Conservative	923	57	364	41
TOTAL	1,623	100	933	100

Table 6.3: The simple but potentially confusing world of percentages.

I. **Simple Percentages**
One number divided by another (times 100).
   A. **Proportion a category is of the whole**

   $$\text{Category Percent} = 100 \times (n_{\text{cat}}/N),$$

   where n_{cat} is the number of cases in a category, N is the total number of cases in the frequency table. Example for Conservatives in 2000 in Table 6.2:

   $$100 \times (923/1{,}623) = 57\%.$$

   B. **Relation between any two numbers**
   Example, the number of conservatives relative to liberals:

   $$2000\text{: } 100 \times (923/591) = 156\%,$$
   $$1992\text{: } 100 \times (364/237) = 154\%.$$

II. **Percentage-Point Difference**
The difference between two percentages.
Example for 2000:
Conservatives outnumber liberals by $57\% - 36\% = 21\%$ or percentage points — this is NOT the percentage difference between them.

III. **Percentage Difference**
The percentage-point difference between two figures measured as a percentage of either the lower or higher figure.
Example for difference between conservatives and liberals in 2000:

   There are $100 \times (21\%/36\%) = 58\%$ more conservatives than liberals.
   There are $100 \times (21\%/57\%) = 37\%$ less liberals than conservatives.

IV. **Percentage Change over Time**
The percentage increase or decrease from a base figure between an earlier and later point in time.
Examples:
Conservatives between 1992 and 2000:

   $$100 \times ((57\% - 41\%)/41\%) = 39\% \text{ increase.}$$

Liberals between 1992 and 2000:

   $$100 \times ((36\% - 28\%)/28\%) = 29\% \text{ increase.}$$

The most common use of a percentage is to measure what proportion of a whole is constituted or represented by a particular part of it. For example, almost every student can automatically calculate that answering 45 out of 50 questions results in a score of 90% and a well deserved A! That is, the correct part of the test (45 out of 50 questions) is equivalent to getting 90 out of a 100 questions correct. A **simple percentage**, then, is easily calculated by dividing the number of cases in a category by the total number of cases for the variable. This figure is then multiplied by 100 to convert it from a decimal to a whole number between zero and 100. Part A under "Simple Percentages" in Table 6.3 gives this calculation for conservatives in 2000. Of the 1,623 people in the sample who answered the question, 923 considered themselves conservatives — which works out to a goodly majority of 57%, compared to 36% liberals and 7% moderates. Looking at the percentages for 1992, conservatives also held a comfortable plurality of 41% to 28%, even though Bill Clinton won the election.

While simple percentages are often used, as in the preceding example, to measure how big a part is of the whole from which it is taken, they can be used to assess the relationship between any two numbers. For example, in 2000, there were 923 conservatives and 591 liberals in the NES sample. Thus, as indicated by Part B under "Simple Percentages" in Table 6.3, conservatives composed 156% more of the sample than liberals. Correspondingly, in 1992, there were 154% more conservatives in the sample than liberals, indicating that the ratio between adherents of these two ideologies stayed fairly stable during the 1990s. Methodologically, this example also shows that, in certain instances, it is possible to have simple percentages over 100%.

The second type of percentage is also very easy to understand. This is the difference between two percentages. For example, Table 6.2 shows that in 2000 conservatives had an advantage over liberals in Americans' self-identification of 57% to 36% or 21% (percentage points). What is slightly confusing here is that while the difference — $57\% - 36\% = 21\%$ — is written in terms of percentage signs, the result or difference between two percentages is actually expressed in terms of **percentage points**. For example, conservatives had a lead over liberals of 21 percentage points in 2000, compared to 13 percentage points ($41\% - 28\%$) in 1992.

At first glance, this distinction between percentages and percentage points might be considered worthy of attention only by someone who is cramming to play the statisticians' version of *Trivial Pursuit*.

However, this is an extremely important distinction because it is often confused with the **percentage difference** between two percentages, which can differ radically from the percentage-point difference. A simple percentage is calculated from the proportion between two things, often a part and the whole from which it is taken. The percentage difference, correspondingly, is the absolute difference between two items as a proportion of one of the two things being compared. For example, the percentage difference between conservatives and liberals in 2000 is calculated by dividing the percentage-point difference (21%) by either the percentage of conservatives (57%) or percentage of liberals (36%) in the sample and then multiplying by 100 to convert the resulting decimal to a whole number.

Certainly, this is potentially confusing because the percentage difference between two items may well differ substantially, depending upon which one is used as the base for the calculation. For example, the computations reported in Table 6.3 indicate that in 2000 there were 58% more conservatives than liberals when the 36% of liberals in the sample is used as the base, while there were 37% less liberals than conservatives when the 57% of conservatives in the sample is used as the base. Both these figures, moreover, are substantially greater than the 21 percentage-point lead that conservatives held over liberals. As Darrell Huff argues in *How to Lie with Statistics*,[8] such situations are not only confusing but create opportunities to present deliberately misleading results. For example, a conservative would probably stress that there are 58% more conservatives than liberals, while a liberal would probably say that the conservative advantage is only 21% and fail to make the distinction between percentage-point and percentage differences.

A special type of percentage difference is the **percentage change over time**, which represents the percentage by which some item increases or decreases between two points in time. Here, there is no question about which time should be used as the base since the change is always measured from the earlier time point. For example, the calculations in Table 6.3 show that the percentage of self-identified conservatives in the NES samples increased by 39% between 1992 and

---

[8] Huff, *Op cit.*

Table 6.4: Changes in the U.S. budget priorities.

	Federal budget, 1980	Federal budget, 1999	Percent change 1980–1999
Health and Medicare	9%	19%	111%
Social Security	20%	23%	15%
Other Human Resources	24%	20%	−17%
Defense	23%	16%	−30%
Physical Resources	11%	5%	−55%
Interest	9%	13%	44%
Other	4%	3%	−25%
TOTAL	100%	99%	

Calculating Percentage Change over time in Health Priority: Percentage Change = (19% − 9%)/ 9% = 111%

2000, while liberals had a 29% increase. As another statistical nit, note that the proportion of conservatives had to grow more than that of liberals in order to keep the ratio of conservatives to liberals the same as the number of conservatives stayed at just over 150% of that of liberals. Here again, each side can cite a figure that makes it look a little better — conservatives that their share of Americans' loyalties grew more than liberals'; and liberals that they kept the conservatives' relative advantage from expanding.

A more politically relevant example, perhaps, is provided by the data in Table 6.4 about changes in America's federal budget between 1980 and 1999. Playing with these figures certainly shows that it is easy to create confusion through "statisticulation". For example, consider the role of interest in the federal budget. Someone who wanted to emphasize the problems of budget deficits would say that it had skyrocketed by the percentage increase of 44%, while someone who wanted to de-emphasize it would claim that it had only inched upward by four percentage points.

Overall, it is very clear that the rapidly escalating health costs during the 1980s and 1990s had a major impact on the federal budget as health spending's share of the budget more than doubled from 9% to 19%. For state governments, incidentally, the impact was probably even greater. For example, the Medicaid program of health assistance for the poor, which the states share with the federal government, has been called the

Pacman of state budgets because it has grown so fast that it gobbled up all available state revenues. At the federal level, the squeeze of increased health expenditures on other areas or priorities created a strange set of political bedfellows whose share of the budget dropped: other human resources (i.e., social services), national defense, and physical resources, like infrastructure. On a methodological note, these data also show that negative percentage changes over time are probably almost as likely as positive ones, unlike most of the other percentage measures where negative figures are fairly rare.

A final potentially confusing characteristic of percentage changes over time raised by *How to Lie with Statistics* is that a percentage decrease followed by an equal percentage increase does not bring you back to where you started.[9] Thus, a decrease of 30% in the value of a stock portfolio followed by a 30% recovery still leaves the owner with a loss. For example, if you have an investment of $100 which loses 30% (or $30) of its value, the new value is $70. However, if it then gains 30%, this is only 30% of $70 or $21, giving a new value of $91 or $9 less than you started with. Correspondingly, if your investment first gained and then lost 30%, you would still only have $91. The 30% gain would get you up to $130, but a 30% loss from this would cost you $39, dropping the new net worth back to $91.

6.3 DIFFERENT SCALES OR LEVELS OF MEASUREMENT

The two data sets used in Chapter 2 are fundamentally different and, consequently, require different techniques for analysis. A data set can be thought of as a huge matrix or spreadsheet in which each column represents one item or variable and each row or line represents one case on which the variable is measured. For the data set on the characteristics of developed nations, each column contains the values for a specific variable for each of the 21 nations. For example, the average annual economic growth rates for 1980–2004 were 3.2 for the United States and 1.8 for Sweden (see Table 2.12 in Chapter 2).

---

[9] *Ibid.*, p. 111.

The version of the 2008 NES survey compiled by Charles Prysby and Carmine Scavo in *The 2008 Election*[10] contains 2,102 rows of data, one for each respondent, and 189 columns, one for each of the NES variables that they included in the data set. The nature of the data in this spreadsheet is fundamentally different as well. These public opinion data are **categoric variables**. That is, they have a fairly small number of categories, generally with a substantial number of cases in each category; and each category has a specific number (or **code**) that represents the different answers to the survey question. Unlike the values for infant mortality or GDP per capita which are important in themselves and were presented in the graphs and data arrays in Chapter 2, these codes are simple aids to help the computer manipulate the data and, thus, were not included in the frequency tables presented there.

Given the fundamentally different nature of these two types of data, they have to be treated in distinctly different ways. More formally, the data on the developed nations are termed **interval data** because the intervals between them represent real quantities. For example, the U.S.'s GDP per capita of $45,489 in 2007 is $12,803 more than the GDP per capita of $32,686 in France. One cannot make such a quantitative comparison between the category codings in the NES data set. Thus, they are considered to have a lower **level of measurement**. The level of measurement of these variables, in turn, can be divided into **nominal** and **ordinal**, depending upon whether or not the codings form a scale that goes from less to more of something.

6.3.1 The Nominal Level of Measurement

The simplest level of measurement is a **nominal scale** in which there is no order or relationship among the categories. While nominal variables are not that common in public opinion, several, such as religion and region, are quite important for many political analyses. For example, Americans are divided into many religions, such as Baptists, Catholics, Jews, Methodists, Muslims, and Presbyterians, to name just a few.

---

[10] Charles Prysby and Carmine Scavo, *SETUPS: Voting Behavior: The 2008 Election* (Ann Arbor, MI: Inter-University Consortium for Political and Social Research and the American Political Science Association, 2009). Available at www.icpsr.umich.edu/SETUPS2008.

Table 6.5: Codes for religious affiliation.

1	Mainline Protestant
2	Evangelical Protestant
3	Catholic
4	Other Christian
5	Jewish
6	Other
7	None
9	Not ascertained

These religions can be divided in a variety of ways, such as Christians and non-Christians or Catholics and Protestants. Yet, it is probably impossible to devise a scale on which all religions could be placed along a single dimension that goes from less to more of some quality. Thus, religion is usually treated as a nominal variable. Table 6.5, for example, reports the codings for the seven categories of religion (Mainline Protestant, Evangelical Protestant, Catholic, other Christian, Jewish, other, and none) used in *The 2008 Election* data set. Clearly, there is no single dimension that can capture the differences among these religious affiliations.

6.3.2 The Ordinal Level of Measurement

The second level of measurement that a categoric variable may have is **ordinal**. In ordinal variables, the categories can be ranked from less to more or lower to higher. However, the size of the distance between the categories cannot be measured or compared. Most public opinion data are at the ordinal level of measurement. For example, Table 6.6 presents a five-point scale of views about spending to aid the poor that goes from strong opposition to strong support. While such scales may appear to have equal divisions between their categories, this is not really the case. For the item on spending for the poor, respondents indicated how much and what kind of change they wanted in this area. Clearly, this is a scale of support for spending to help the poor. Yet, while the categories follow a logical progression, there is no guarantee that they really represent equal distances in attitudes about helping

Table 6.6: Ordinal scales for spending to help the poor.

1	Cut considerably
2	Cut a little
3	Keep same
4	Increase a little
5	Increase considerably

Table 6.7: Examples of ordinal codings.

Categories	Codes	Categories	Code #1	Code #2
Family Income		Ideology		
Under $15,000	1	Strong Liberal	1	−4
$15,000–$34,999	2	Liberal	2	0
$35,000–$49,999	3	Weak Liberal	3	6
$50,000–$79,999	4	Moderate	4	50
Over $80,000	5	Weak Conservative	5	100
		Conservative	6	213
		Strong Conservative	7	888

the poor. Moreover, each category undoubtedly contains people with substantially varying support or opposition to aiding the poor.

The logic of this coding should be easy to see in the two examples of ordinal variables presented in Table 6.7. The first variable in this table is family income which was changed from an interval to an ordinal variable by putting people into broad income categories (e.g., those with family incomes of $35,000 to $49,999) rather than recording their actual income. This was done in order to facilitate showing how family income is related to public opinion items through the technique of crosstabulation (see Chapter 9). For family income, each category represents a higher income than categories that have smaller numbers as their codes — a family with an income of $66,000 (coded 4) is obviously wealthier than one with an income of $20,000 (coded 2).

Ideology is the second variable included in Table 6.7. Although the scale of ideology from liberal to conservative does not involve such a neatly measurable commodity as money, it also fulfills the requisite for an ordinal scale since the higher a code a person receives, the more conservative she or he is — a weak conservative (coded 5 in the first coding scheme) is more conservative than a moderate (coded 4) and both are more conservative than a liberal (coded 2). Two coding schemes are presented for ideology. The first looks rational, going from one to seven. The second looks crazy, ranging from −4 for strong liberals to 888 for strong conservatives with no apparent pattern for the difference between one category and the next. Yet, both are entirely correct for an ordinal variable! The only limitation on the coding scheme is that higher numbers are used for higher ranking categories.

The two items included in Table 6.7 — family income and ideology — also illustrate a significant difference that exists between two types of ordinal variables. For income, the direction is **apparent** in that people in higher income categories have more money than those in lower ones. Ideology, in contrast, represents a case where the direction is **arbitrary**. In Table 6.7, ideology is measured on a scale of conservatism. That is, liberals receive low scores and conservatives receive high scores. Yet, it makes just as much sense to represent ideological self-identification by a liberalism scale in which the coding scheme is flip-flopped. Finally, these two frequency tables show the convention that an ordinal variable is placed in the table with the **lowest score in the first row** and the **highest score in the bottom row**, right above the TOTAL.

6.3.3 The Interval Level of Measurement

In contrast to the public opinion data which have a few discrete categories at the nominal or ordinal level of measurement, the data on the conditions that exist in the advanced industrial nations create **continuous variables** that are at the **interval level of measurement**. That is, the values of such variables as GDP per capita or the infant mortality rate can be measured so they have a multitude of values whose increments are very close together, rather than a small number of discrete categories. Moreover, the actual interval between different values is meaningful. For example, the difference between a GDP per capita of $25,000 and one of $30,000 is precisely $5,000. Such interval data are perhaps the easiest level of measurement to comprehend because they correspond to what most of us think of as real numbers.

That is, they are measured in terms of some quantity, such as dollars in your or Uncle Sam's pocket, the percentage of people living in poverty, or the number of votes that a candidate receives.

There is also a **distinction between interval data and ratio data**. This distinction is critical for mathematics. However, it is not very important for political science research because almost every imaginable interval scale is also a ratio scale. Indeed, it is hard to think of an interval scale that is not a ratio one, with temperature being one of the few examples that comes to mind.

Technically, a ratio scale is an interval scale that has a real or nonarbitrary zero point. For example, GDP per capita is a ratio scale because, as anyone who has maxed out their credit card knows, zero dollars is definitely a definable quantity. When the zero point is not arbitrary, ratios between two numbers can be easily calculated. For example, the U.S.'s 2007 GDP per capita of $45,489 is almost double Portugal's $22,815. Thus, the relative, as well as the absolute, difference between two cases can be measured precisely for a ratio scale.

EXERCISES

1. Compare two American states on one of the indicators available on the StateMaster website (www.statemaster. com). Which state is better in terms of this indicator? Present two bar graphs of the data, one that is distorted and one that is not. Which one would the Governor of your state emphasize?
2. Compare two developed democracies in terms of their economic growth rates for 1990–2004, using the data in Table 2.12 in Chapter 2. Present the data in two alternative pictographs, one which is accurate and one which greatly overstates the degree of difference between the two countries. Which graph would each nation probably publicize?
3. Find data on the change in income inequality in America during the George W. Bush administration. Did income inequality increase, decrease, or stay the same? What does this imply about the distortion in Kevin Phillips' data in Part A of Table 6.1?

4. The following table reports the number of people in the 2008 NES survey and in a survey conducted in March 2010 who wanted to cut or to increase government spending and services. Based on these numbers, use percentages and percentage point differences to indicate how conservative or liberal Americans were at each point in time. Then use percentage point differences and percentage changes to show how public opinion changed over this year and a half.

	NES 2008 Survey	March 2010 survey
Cut services	251	500
Increase services	434	400

5. What is the level of measurement for each of the following scales? Which ones would allow us to say that one case's value is exactly twice as great as another's?

   (a) A five-point scale that goes from greatly cutting government services to greatly increasing them.
   (b) A thermometer measured in degrees Fahrenheit?
   (c) A person's family income in dollars.
   (d) A person's family income in six categories that range from very poor to very rich.
   (e) A typology of people's religions.
   (f) The poverty rates of a group of nations.
   (g) The state in which someone resides.
   (h) The position that someone takes on abortion.
   (i) The number of miles between two cities.

Chapter 7

Summary Statistics for an Entire Distribution: Moving Beyond Data Arrays and Graphs

The data arrays and graphs discussed in Chapter 2 provide appropriate and valuable methods for presenting information about a variable when the number of cases is small. While graphs especially are visually attractive and easy to understand, these very advantages are also associated with two distinct limitations. First, once the size of the analysis expands beyond a handful of cases, these forms of presentations become cluttered and confusing. Second, they are much more appropriate for comparing the values of a few individual cases than for describing the full distribution of an interval variable[1] in the accessible manner that a frequency table does for categoric data. As a result, statisticians have developed a variety of summary statistics that describe such distributions concisely, while permitting the relative ranking of the individual cases to be assessed as well. Summary statistics are also important because they are essential for understanding the inferential statistics that will be discussed in Chapter 8.

---

[1] See the section of "Levels of Measurement" in Chapter 6.

Sections 7.1 and 7.2 of this chapter examine the two most important types of summary statistics which measure the average or central tendency of an item and its degree of variability. Section 7.3 applies these concepts for distinguishing among some of the principle forms that distributions can have.

7.1 MEASURES OF CENTRAL TENDENCY

Measures of central tendency are quite familiar to most of us, if not by that name, then by the more commonplace term of average. This discussion of averages in social statistics covers three major topics. Subsection 7.1.1 describes means and medians, the two measures of central tendency that are often applied to interval data; Subsection 7.1.2 expands this discussion to how the application of such summary statistics is related to the differing levels of measurement that a variable may have; and Subsection 7.1.3 considers the two most prominent uses of measures of central tendencies.

7.1.1 Means and Medians

The idea of an average score that summarizes a distribution should be familiar to every student even if it is not necessarily conceptualized in this way. As Table 7.1 shows, a student will typically take a small number of tests in a class; and her or his grade will be determined by these test scores. The two students in this example each have three test scores — which constitute the distribution in question. Normally, the arithmetic average, which statisticians call the **mean**, is used to summarize or measure the central tendency of a distribution of test scores. It is computed according to the simple formula:

$$\text{Mean} = \Sigma X_i / N,$$

where:
Mean is the mean of X,
X_i is the value of case i for X,
N is the number of cases,
Σ means that all the X_i's must be summed or added together.

Table 7.1: Measures of central tendency for the distribution of test scores for two students.

	Student #A	Student #B
Test #1	90	90
Test #2	80	100
Test #3	<u>100</u>	<u>50</u>
Total Points	270	240
Mean	90	80
Median	90	90

Mean = Total Points/Number of Tests.
  = 270/3 = 90 for Student #A.
  = 240/3 = 80 for Student #B.

Median = value of case in the middle of the distribution (i.e., with an equal number of cases having higher and lower scores).

For example, in Table 7.1, each test is an X_i; and N is three or the number of tests. In this case, Student #A has an average or mean of 90 (with test scores of 90, 80, and 100) and Student #B an 80 (with scores of 90, 100, and 50), indicating that #A should get an A and that #B should get a B. The reason for this difference, even a quick perusal of the individual test results shows, is the tremendous difference in their performance in the third test. Student #A studied extremely hard for the last test, while Student #B partied almost nightly for the last part of the semester.

There is a second measure of central tendency, in addition, which is called the **median**. The median is simply the value of the case in the middle of the distribution — that is, the case that has an equal number of cases having higher and lower scores. In Table 7.1, both students have a median of 90 because each scored higher than 90 on one test and lower than 90 on another test. Table 7.2 presents the more elaborate example of the GDP per capita of developed nations in 2007. In Part A for all 21 countries, the United Kingdom which ranks 11th with a Gross Domestic Product (GDP) per capita of $35,699 represents the middle case since 10 countries have higher scores, while another 10 countries have lower scores. Part B shows how to compute the median for the 20 nations besides the United States. Here, because there are an even number of cases, there are two middle cases: the UK at $35,699 and Belgium at $35,358. In such cases, the median is the arithmetic average of the two middle scores:

$$\text{Median} = (\$35{,}699 + \$35{,}358)/2 = \$35{,}529.$$

In many, if not most, distributions of interval data, the difference between the mean and the median for a variable will be so small that it is really inconsequential. For example, Table 7.6 shows that the means and medians for a variety of political, economic, and social indicators for the developed nations are all quite close to each other. Indeed, this will

Table 7.2: The ranking and median of developed nations on GDP per capita, 2007.

Nations	GDP per capita*
A. All 21 Developed Nations	
Norway	$53,477
United States	$45,489
Ireland	$45,027
Switzerland	$41,101
Netherlands	$39,225
Canada	$38,500
Australia	$37,565
Austria	$37,119
Sweden	$36,603
Denmark	$35,961
United Kingdom	$35,699
Belgium	$35,358
Finland	$34,718
Germany	$34,391
Japan	$33,626
France	$32,686
Spain	$31,586
Italy	$30,381
Greece	$28,423
New Zealand	$27,431
Portugal	$22,815

*Measured in Parity Purchasing Power.
Median = Value of Middle Case (United Kingdom)
= $35,699.

Table 7.2: (*Continued*).

Nations	GDP per capita*
B. 20 Developed Nations Besides United States	
Norway	$53,477
Ireland	$45,027
Switzerland	$41,101
Netherlands	$39,225
Canada	$38,500
Australia	$37,565
Austria	$37,119
Sweden	$36,603
Denmark	$35,961
United Kingdom	$35,699
Belgium	$35,358
Finland	$34,718
Germany	$34,391
Japan	$33,626
France	$32,686
Spain	$31,586
Italy	$30,381
Greece	$28,423
New Zealand	$27,431
Portugal	$22,815

*Measured in Parity Purchasing Power.
Median = Arithmetic Average of Two Middle Cases
   (United Kingdom and Belgium)
   = ($35,699 + $35,358)/2 = $71,057/2
   = $35,529.

generally be the case. In such cases, the mean should be used because, unlike the median, it includes all the values in a distribution.

The values of the mean and median do differ significantly, however, when the distribution for a variable is quite **skewed** in the sense that a few very high values pull the mean up much higher than the median or a few very low scores pull the mean down well below the median. Normally, in these cases, the median is the better measure of central tendency because it represents the case in the middle of the distribution. For example, Table 7.3 gives the mean and median for several variables for the approximately 120 nation states (both developed and developing) in the late-1990s. Here, the mean for GDP

Table 7.3: Measures of central tendency for national conditions (includes both developed and developing countries).

	Mean	Median
GDP per capita (PPP), 1999	$7,077	$3,711
Infant Mortality per 1,000 live births, 1997	43	28
Maternal Mortality per 100,000 live births, mid-1990s	186	63

Table 7.4: Applicability of three measures of central tendency.

	Appropriate levels of measurement
Mean	Interval
Median	Interval
	Ordinal
Mode	Interval
	Ordinal
	Nominal

per capita ($7,077) is almost twice as high as the median ($3,711) because relatively few nations are very wealthy compared to the rest of the world. Thus, the lower median almost certainly provides a better estimate of the level of GDP per capita in the average country because the mean is distorted by the very good conditions that exist in some developed nations. Similarly, a few very high scores pull up the mean for the infant mortality and especially the maternal mortality rates. Again, the median is probably the better measure of central tendency, this time because the mean is distorted by the very bad conditions that exist in some developing nations.

7.1.2 The Level of Measurement and Summary Statistics

As summarized in Table 7.4 the appropriate use of the mean, the median, and the third primary measure of central tendency called the **mode** is limited by the measurement level for the data being analyzed. In particular, because of the way in which they are calculated, these

Table 7.5: Frequency table for Americans' ideological self-identifications, 2008.

Very Liberal	3%
Liberal	10%
Slightly Liberal	15%
Moderate	28%
Slightly Conservative	23%
Conservative	18%
Very Conservative	3%

three measures of central tendency can only be applied to certain types of data. For instance, the mean or arithmetic average requires an interval level of measurement because this is the only one on which mathematical operations, such as those used in computing the arithmetic average, can be performed. Thus, means cannot be computed for either nominal or ordinal items.

The median is the value of the case in the middle of the distribution in the sense that it has an equal number of cases with lower and higher scores. As we have just seen, medians are used as the measure of central tendency for interval variables with skewed distributions that distort the value of the mean. Medians, unlike means, can also be defined for ordinal data. Consequently, they are the primary measure of central tendency applied to ordinal variables. Table 7.5, as an illustration, presents the frequency table for Americans' ideology in 2008 on a seven-point scale from strong liberal to strong conservative. The median falls in the moderate category, even though conservatives outnumber liberals by the considerable margin of 44% to 28% because this category contains the middle case at the 50th percentile on the scale.

The third measure of central tendency is the mode which is simply the value or category that has the most cases in it. In Table 7.5, for example, the mode is the moderate category because the 28% of respondents who picked this category are greater in number than those who selected any other category on the ideology scale. The mode is the only measure of central tendency that can be used with nominal data. It can also be used with ordinal and interval data, but in practice it almost never is because, unlike the mean and median, it does not necessarily locate the center or middle of a scale that goes from low to high. This also underlines the point, incidentally, that summary statistics are generally not used with categoric variables because a frequency count can present an efficient and comprehensive picture of the distribution.

7.1.3 Two Uses of Measures of Central Tendency

Measures of central tendency can be used in two ways. First, they can tell us what the average or typical case is like, as a **summary of the variable** in question. The first two columns in Table 7.6, for example, report the mean and median for seven central political, economic, and social indicators for the 21 industrialized nations for 2003. For all of them, the mean and median are fairly close together, suggesting that the mean provides a good estimate of the average or central tendency since none of the distributions appear to be very skewed.

Turning to the substantive results, these summary statistics indicate that the spending at all governmental levels in the average developed nation accounts for about 46% of GDP. This figure is so high that big government did indeed appear to be commonplace. In terms of economic performance, the developed nations had, on average, a GDP per capita of about $29,000, a long-term growth rate over the past 25 years of 2.5%, and savings rate just over a fifth of their GDP. In the

Table 7.6: Measures of central tendency for developed nations compared to the economic and social performance of the United States.

	Mean	Median	United States
Government Size and Policy			
All Government Spending % GDP, 2003	45.8%	45.6%	37.1%
Economic Performance			
GDP per capita at PPP, 2003	$28,970	$29,627	$37,624
Real GDP Growth, 1980–2004	2.5%	2.3%	3.2%
Gross Savings % GDP, 2003	20.5%	22.2%	13.1%
Social Performance			
Poverty Rate, 2000	10.1%	10.3%	17.1%
Infant Mortality Rate, 2003	4.5	4.3	7.1
Life Expectancy, 2003	79.0	78.6	77.2

sphere of social policy and outcomes, the average developed nation has a 10% poverty rate, a life expectancy of 79, and an infant mortality rate of 4.5 per 1,000 live births.

A second important use of means and medians is as a **benchmark** to rate the performance of individual cases. This is done in the third column of Table 7.6 which gives the values for the United States on the seven indicators. America clearly had a small government as its government-to-GDP ratio of 37% was well below the mean and median. In terms of economic performance, America was well above average for economic growth rate and especially for the GDP per capita. In contrast, the U.S. savings rate was less than two-thirds of the mean and median for the developed world, indicating the consumption-led nature of its economy. Finally, the U.S. was clearly below average on two social outcomes, poverty and infant mortality, but American life expectancy was just about normal for the developed world. In sum, despite some deviations from the general picture, America appears to be marked by small government, strong economic performance, and below average social outcomes in some areas but not in others.

7.2 MEASURES OF VARIABILITY

In addition to their central tendencies, the distributions of variables differ considerably in their variability or how close to the mean and median most of the cases cluster. The four most common measures of variability are the range, standard deviation, variance, and coefficient of variability or CV. The range is simply the difference between the maximum and minimum values; the standard deviation is a measure of how far, on average, cases lie from the mean; the variance is the square of the standard deviation; and the CV is calculated by dividing the standard deviation by the mean. Analysis of variability usually is based on the standard deviation instead of the variance. However, the variance is described here because it is important for measuring the degree of association between two variables — the square of their correlation coefficient is equivalent to the percentage of variance that they share (see Chapter 11).

The next subsection describes what these are for our central political, economic, and social indicators for the developed nations.

This is followed by an illustration of how these summary statistics might be interpreted by using them to test the argument that globalization is forcing convergence in the policies of the industrialized countries.

7.2.1 The Range, Standard Deviation, and Coefficient of Variability

Table 7.7 presents these statistics of variability (with the exception of the variance) for the items concerning the political, economic, and social characteristics of developed nations that were discussed in the previous subsection. The impression given by the first three columns in this table probably is how wide the range is for many of these items, even within just the industrialized world. The GDP per capita of the richest nation, the U.S. at $37,625, is almost double that of the poorest, Portugal at $18,793; and the maximum value is at least twice as high as the minimum for four of the other six indicators included in the table: long-term economic growth, the savings rate, the level of poverty, and

Table 7.7: Measures of variability for data on developed nations.

	Minimum	Maximum	Range	Standard deviation	Mean	CV
Affluence						
GDP per capita at PPP, 2003	$18,793	$37,625	$18,832	$4,582	$28,970	0.16
Government Size and Policy						
All Government Spending % GDP, 2003	33.3%	58.3%	25.0%	7.3%	45.8%	0.16
Economic Performance						
Real GDP Growth, 1980–2004	1.3%	5.1%	3.8%	0.9%	2.5%	0.36
Gross Savings % GDP, 2003	−0.7%	30.4%	31.1%	6.4%	20.5%	0.31
Social Performance						
Poverty Rate, 2003	4.3%	17.1%	12.8%	3.8%	10.2%	0.37
Infant Mortality Rate, 2003	3.0	7.0	4.0	0.9	4.5	0.21
Life Expectancy, 2003	77.2	81.8	4.6	1.2	79.0	0.02

infant mortality. The developed world is only similar on these items in terms of life expectancy which has a narrow range of 77 to 81.

Yet, a somewhat different impression emerges when the standard deviation and CV are applied to give a more systematic and sophisticated measure of how great the variability of these seven items is. As a thumbnail guide, a CV of under 0.10 — that is, the standard deviation is less than 10% of the mean — indicates a low degree of variability; one that is between 0.10 and 0.30 shows moderate variability; and high variability exists only when the CV exceeds 0.30.[2] Applying this criterion, there is only moderate variation among the industrialized nations on over half of these items. For example, the mean and standard deviation for the share of GDP consumed by the spending of all levels of government are 45.8% and 7.3% respectively. That means, on average, one of the 21 countries in this group will have a government spending-to-GDP ratio that is 7.3 percentage points above or below the mean — that is, 53.1% or 38.5%. This certainly seems like a huge difference. Yet, when the CV is computed (7.3%/45.8%), it is only 0.16, indicating that the degree of variability is moderate. The CVs are similarly moderate for GDP per capita (0.16) and infant mortality (0.21); and the variation among these countries in life expectancy is very small as denoted by a minuscule CV of 0.02. In contrast, there is a high degree of variability in the other three indicators — the savings, economic growth, and poverty rates — but even here the CVs of 0.31 to 0.37 are not all that extreme.

7.2.2 Testing for the Predicted Effects of Globalization: An Illustration

The data in the last subsection might be a little confusing. On the one hand, looking at the range suggests that there are large variations among the developed nations. On the other hand, the more sophisticated measures of variability — the standard deviation and CV coefficient — indicate that differences among these countries are

---

[2] John G. Williamson, "Regional Inequality and the Process of National Development: A Description of the Patterns", *Economic Development and Cultural Change*, 8:4 (1965), pp. 3–84.

more moderate. This question has substantive import, furthermore, because of the fears that have arisen in some academic and governmental circles that the economic forces of globalization are forcing all nations into a pattern of *laissez-faire* capitalism, similar to America's, that is producing declining standards of living and governmental welfare services throughout the developed world.[3]

While it is admittedly rather hard to be too sure about what is a big or a small difference, there is a much better way to assess the argument or hypothesis that globalization is forcing the industrialized world into a political and socioeconomic convergence. Rather than judging whether there is still a large degree of variation among these nations, one can test the theory more accurately by examining whether a substantial change in the variability among the developed nations has occurred over the last quarter century when the forces of globalization have supposedly accelerated.

Table 7.8, therefore, compares the summary statistics for the key factor of government size in 1980 and 2003. The globalization hypothesis would make two predictions: (1) that the average ratio of all government spending to GDP should fall significantly; and (2) that

Table 7.8: Summary statistics for all government spending as % of GDP in developed nations.*

	1980**	2003
Mean	44.0%	45.8%
Median	44.1%	45.6%
Minimum	25.4%	33.3%
Maximum	61.9%	58.3%
Range	36.5%	25.0%
Standard Deviation	11.0%	7.3%
CV	0.25	0.16

*New Zealand is excluded because of missing data until quite recently.
**1985–1986 for Ireland, Netherlands, Portugal, and Spain.

---

[3] James H. Mittleman, Ed., *Globalization: Critical Reflections* (Boulder, CO: Lynne Rienner, 1996); Gary Teeple, *Globalization and the Decline of Social Reform* (Atlantic Highlands, NJ: Humanities Press, 1995).

the degree of variability among governments should decline as well. The results in Table 7.8, however, lend only partial support to the thesis that globalization is forcing the convergence of the industrialized nations. Moreover, the nature of this partial support is not really consistent with the overall theory.

The theory that globalization is promoting a convergence of governmental roles and policies in the developed world predicts that the variation in government size should have decreased markedly between 1980 and 2003. This, indeed, turns out to be the case. The range fell by approximately a quarter from 36.5 percentage points to 25 percentage points; and the summary measure of the CV dropped very significantly from 0.25 to 0.16. Yet, a closer examination of the data is totally inconsistent with the thesis that globalization has set off a "race to the bottom" forcing government programs to be slashed. Both the mean and the median for the size of government actually increased slightly from 44% to about 45.5% of GDP. In addition, the minimum size of government rose quite significantly from 25.4% to 33.3% of GDP, more than the decline of the maximum size from 61.9% to 58.3% of GDP.

This example of testing the theory that globalization has created a "race to the bottom" among advanced industrial democracies also illustrates the need to consider carefully what exactly is being argued or predicted before trying to see whether or not it is true. Here, the theory concerns long-term economic and political change. Thus, just looking at one point in time really says nothing about whether change has or has not occurred. Indeed, in looking at the data in Table 7.7, the range for the variables suggested one conclusion, while the CV pointed in the opposite direction. However, even if we could be certain whether the variability among the developed nations was high or low at the beginning of the 21st century, this would really be irrelevant for determining whether globalization had produced a growing convergence among their political economies over the preceding several decades. The data in Table 7.8 indicate that while convergence in government size over the last quarter of a century can clearly be detected among the developed nations, this is just as clearly not the result of a radical down-sizing of their public sectors. However, critics of globalization and even neutral social scientists would probably not be convinced by this one test, especially since the "crisis of the welfare state" is so evident throughout the developed world.[4]

7.3 TYPES OF DISTRIBUTIONS

In Chapter 2, frequency tables were also termed **frequency distributions**; and the values of all 21 nations on a specific variable, such as life expectancy, also constituted a distribution. Technically, distribution means how the cases are divided among the categories of the variable in question. While theoretically there are numerous possible distributions that a variable might have, this section will discuss four principal types (normal, flat, polarized, and skewed) with one of the types — the normal distribution — having two subtypes for the special task of distinguishing between two fundamentally different conditions of public opinion on a specific issue or item. While all these distributions exist in both quantitative and categoric data, the discussion here focus upon categoric data in frequency tables. Table 7.9 summarizes their characteristics, using indicators of Americans' ideologies to provide

Table 7.9: Types of distributions for public opinion data.

Type	Characteristics
Normal Moderate	Normal (bell-shaped) distribution with most people (i.e., the distribution's **mean, median, and mode**) in the middle of ideological spectrum.
Normal Committed	Normal distribution with mean, median, and mode well on either the conservative or liberal side.
Flat	Approximately equal numbers at each point along the liberal-to-conservative scale.
Polarized	Distribution is "bimodal" with many strong conservatives and liberals and few moderates.
Skewed	A very few extreme scores on one end of a scale, while most of the cases are concentrated at the other end of the spectrum.

---

[4]David Macarov, *What the Market Does to People: Privatization, Globalization, and Poverty* (London: Clarity Press, 2003). In contrast, Harold L. Wilensky, *Rich Democracies: Political Economy, Public Policy, and Performance* (Berkeley: University of California Press, 2002) Part II presents detailed data showing that the more alarmist versions of a welfare state crisis appear exaggerated, at least outside the United States.

concrete examples. This table is based on two distinctions. The first is the relative number of people in the middle of the ideological spectrum compared to the extremes; and the second is the relative number of conservatives and liberals.

7.3.1 Normal Distributions

Many variables have a distribution that is close to what is called a **normal** distribution. Most of the cases are concentrated in the middle of the distribution; there are a clearly declining number of cases as one moves from the middle toward either extreme; and the distribution is symmetric in that equal numbers are associated with the two extremes of the distribution.[5] Such a distribution can be represented by a bell curve as illustrated in Figure 7.1. Even when the distribution of public opinion on an issue is fairly normal, the substantive implications of the distribution can differ considerably depending upon whether the middle of the distribution is in the middle of the ideological spectrum or lies significantly toward either the conservative or liberal side. In the first instance, we can consider that public opinion is **normal and moderate**, while in the second, it is **normal and committed** to one ideological position or the other.

Views of the federal government in 2000 provide an example of the first type. Respondents to the National Election Study (NES) survey were asked to rank the federal government on a thermometer that went from zero for strongly dislikes to 50 for neutral to 100 for strongly likes. As the normal curve that is superimposed on the graph in Figure 7.2

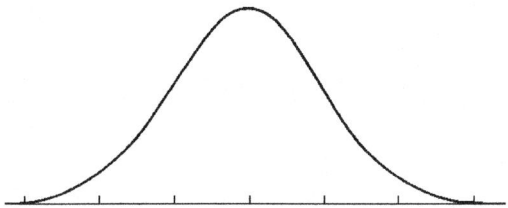

Figure 7.1: Normal curve.
Source: www.psychstat.missouristate.edu/introbook/sbk10m.htm.

---

[5] See Chapter 8 for a more technical description of the normal curve.

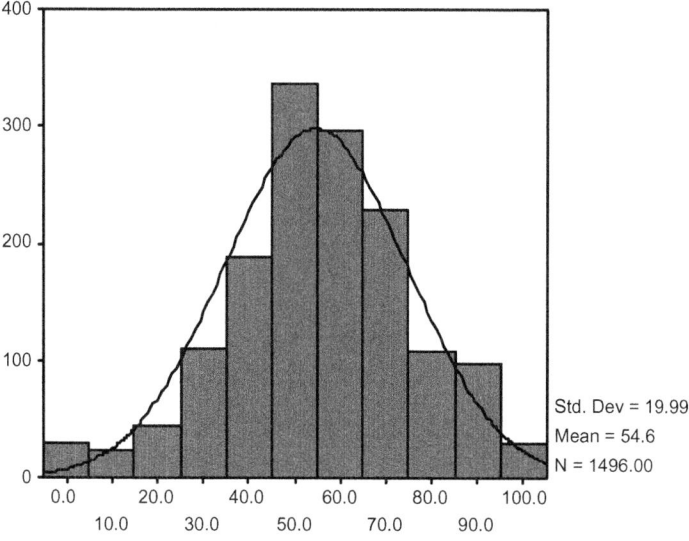

Figure 7.2: Distribution of attitudes about the federal government, 2000.*

*These scores represent a "thermometer" that varies from zero for a very unfavorable attitude to 50 for neutrality to 100 for a very favorable attitude.

shows, Americans' view of the federal government followed a normal moderate pattern in 2000 which was approximately centered on the neutral mark or temperature of 50. Incidentally, this was considerably more favorable than it had been during the 1980s and 1990s. However, the improved image of the federal government obviously did Democrat Al Gore little good or Republican George W. Bush little harm in the presidential election that year.

In contrast, Figure 7.3 indicates that ideological self-identification in 2000 had a fairly normal distribution, but one that was centered on the conservative side of the spectrum. Thus, since the ideological balance is so important in analyzing American politics, it makes sense to distinguish between normal distributions that do or do not favor one side of the liberal-to-conservative spectrum. On a methodological note, in addition, Figure 7.3 shows that a distribution can be displayed as either a bar graph in Part #A or a line graph in Part #B.

Summary Statistics for an Entire Distribution   161

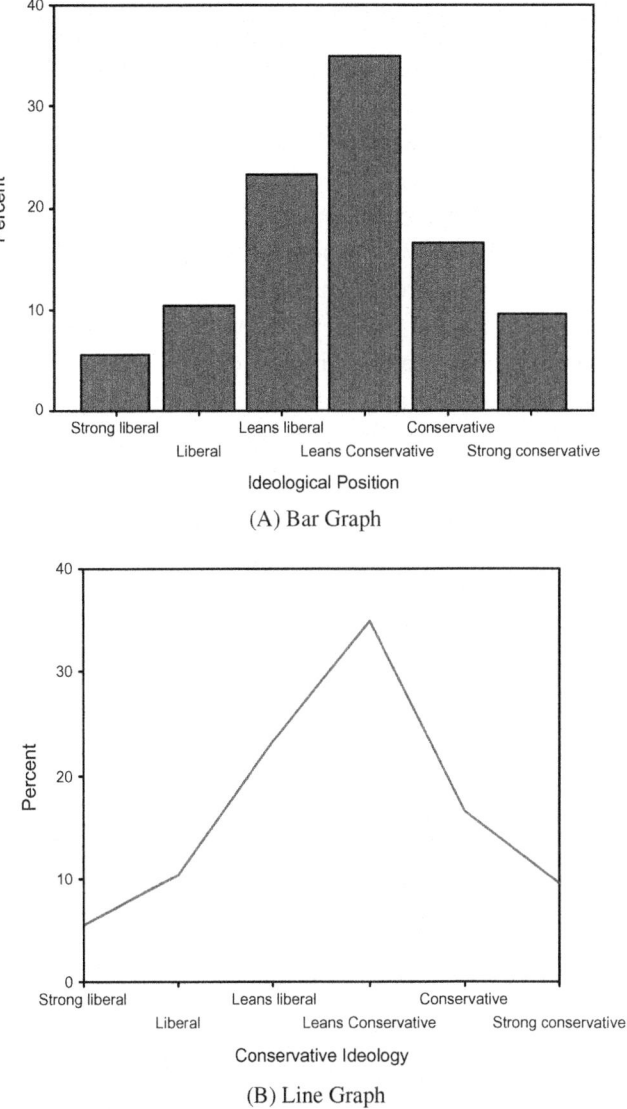

Figure 7.3: Distribution of ideological self-identification, 2000.*

*The "moderate" category is excluded because the pressure on respondents to pick either conservative or liberal in the 2000 NES resulted in an unrealistically very low percentage of moderates that year.

7.3.2 Flat, Polarized, and Skewed Distributions

A third type of distribution that is fairly common might be called a **flat** one. Here, the numbers and percentages of conservatives, moderates, and liberals are all approximately equal, so that a bar graph of the distribution is flat in the sense that the bars for conservatives, moderates, and liberals are all of the same height. A good example, as illustrated in Figure 7.4, was the view of Americans on defense spending in 1988 when approximately a third of the citizenry each wanted to increase, decrease, or not change military expenditures. However, whether this equal division of public opinion reflected satisfaction with the defense build-up over the previous eight years under Ronald Reagan, a desire to switch spending priorities toward domestic issues, or some more convoluted reasoning is hard to say, based on just this distribution itself.

Another type of distribution is a **polarized** one in which there are more cases at the extremes of the distribution than in the middle. Figure 7.5 provides a good example of an issue on which the American public appears to be polarized since respondents to the 2004 NES

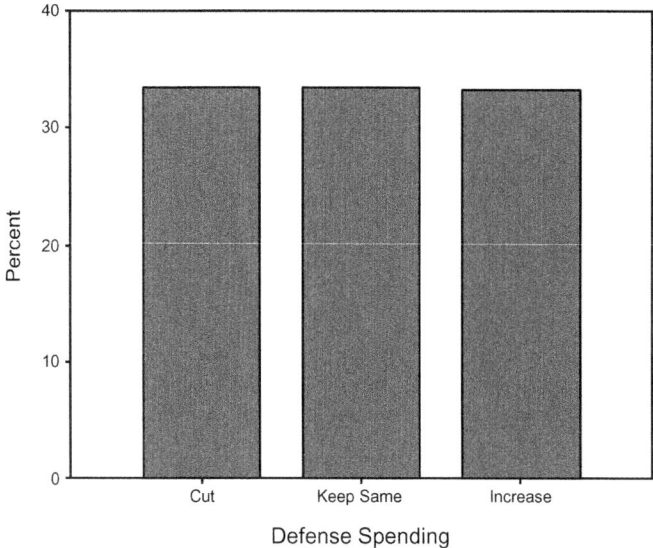

Figure 7.4: Distribution of attitudes about defense spending, 1988.

Summary Statistics for an Entire Distribution 163

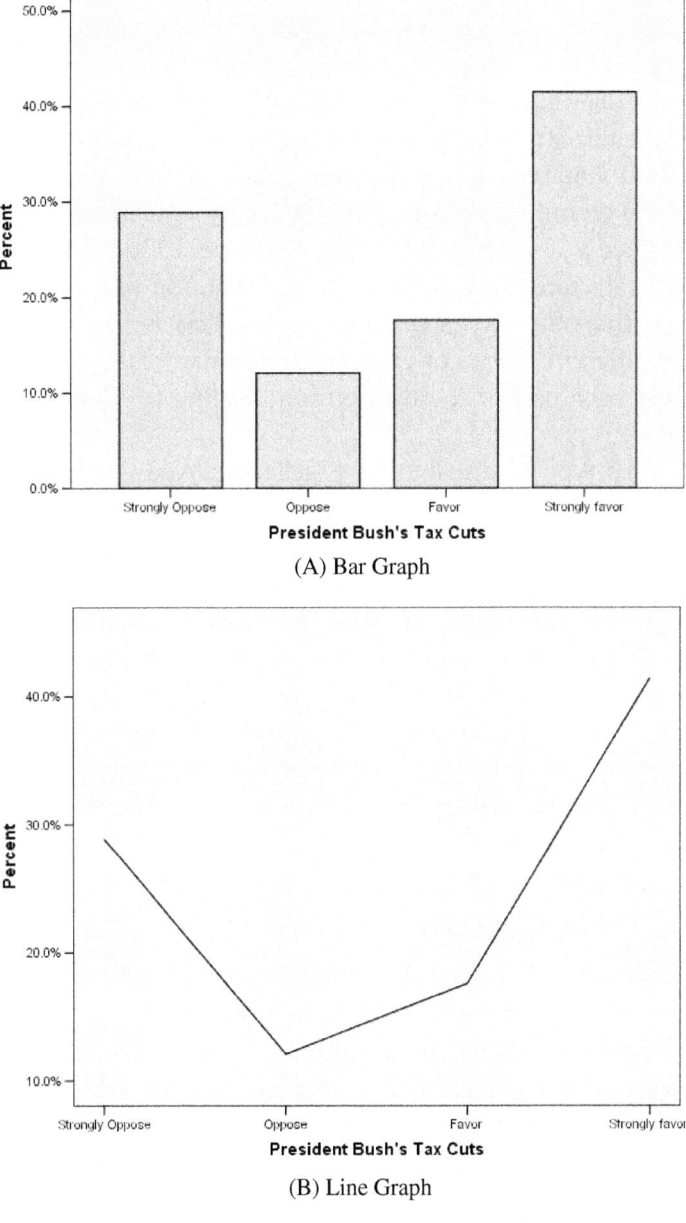

Figure 7.5: Distribution of attitudes about taxes, 2004.

clearly cluster at the extremes of support for or opposition to President Bush's tax cuts. This is not an even division, incidentally, since supporters enjoyed a large lead over opponents (59% to 41%). What makes the distribution polarized, hence, is that considerably more people take the extreme, rather than the moderate, positions.

Methodologically, since the line graph of this distribution in Figure 7.5B resembles a lop-sided U, this type of polarized distribution is also termed a U-shaped curve. This U-shape, in addition, illustrates a special characteristic of the polarized distribution that is not present in any of the other types discussed here. This is that it really has two very different modes or categories with many cases in them. One mode is at each end of the distribution, leading to its description as **bimodal**.

The final type of distribution is called **skewed**. In a skewed distribution, there are a relatively few cases with extreme values at one end of the scale, while most of the cases cluster at the other end of the spectrum. A very good illustration is provided by Americans' feelings toward the military on the 0-to-100 thermometer that are graphed in Figure 7.6. The military is clearly quite popular. Still, a very few people are extremely anti-military. For example, 2% of the respondents gave scores of 19 or less, indicating a decisive dislike for the military. In very sharp contrast, approximately 61% of the population expressed very warm feeling for the military by giving them scores of 80 to 100.

7.3.3 Implications of Different Distributions of Public Opinion

Distinguishing among these different types of public opinion, furthermore, involves more than methodological nit-picking. Political science theories argue that different distributions stimulate very different types of political societies.[6] In particular, when the citizens' attitudes on most issues follow a normal moderate pattern, political competition is likely to be organized around two moderate catch-all parties that compete

---

[6]Peter Mair, *Party System Change: Approaches and Interpretations* (Oxford: Oxford University Press, 1997); Giovanni Sartori, *Parties and Party Systems: A Framework for Analysis* (Cambridge: Cambridge University Press, 1976).

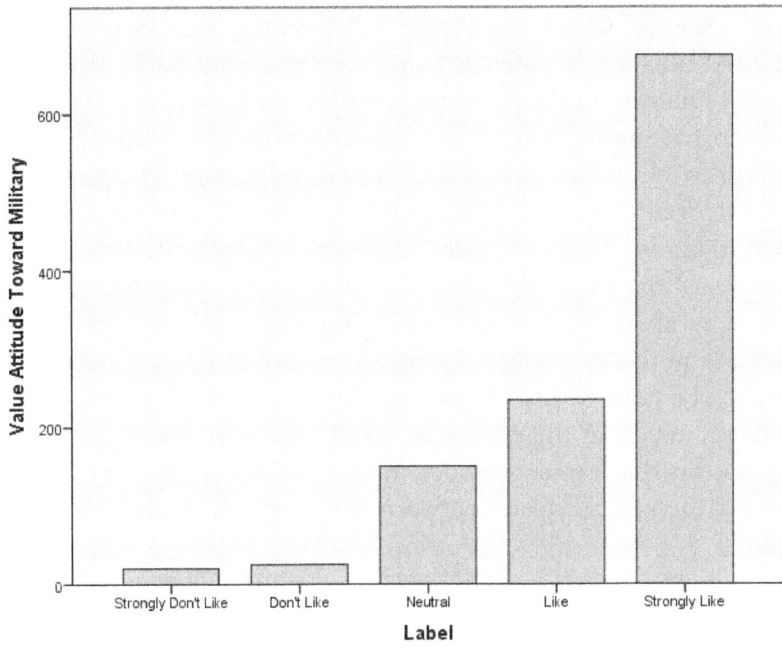

Figure 7.6: Distribution of attitudes about the military, 2004.
*On a thermometer scale of 0 to 100, STRONGLY DON'T LIKE is 0-19; DON'T LIKE is 20-39; NEUTRAL is 40-59; LIKE is 69-79; and STRONGLY LIKE is 80-100.

for the moderate middle or **median voter**. The resulting political life tends to be fairly stable and nonideological; and political change tends to be moderate and incremental. In stark contrast, polarized public create much more conflictual political systems. If most people line up in the same way on the polarizing issues, there is a good basis for two strongly ideological parties. Politics is much more vicious and unstable in the sense that wide policy swings are likely whenever one political party replaces the other in power. If the **issue cleavages are cross-cutting** in the sense that different groups of people hold the extreme positions on various issues, a multiparty system is more likely to emerge, as is political gridlock since no group or party has enough power to force through its specialized agenda.

As argued in Chapter 2, the exact nature of public opinion in the United States is complex and does not neatly fall into any single pattern.[7] Clearly, as Figure 7.5 demonstrated, Americans are polarized on some important issues. Yet, these probably represent a decided minority of the major issues in the U.S. politics today. Many attitudes have more normal distributions. However, relatively few of these probably follow the normal moderate pattern or, alternatively, have the even division of a flat public opinion. Rather, like ideology, public opinion on many issues is normal committed, although the direction of the commitment varies considerably depending upon the issue. The absence of a large and consistent moderate middle may explain why the two major parties are so polarized. In contrast, the absence of a polarized public may explain why both many pundits and seemingly much of the public are irked and disgusted by the strong partisanship that often explodes in our politics as the result of the growing ideological divide between the Democratic and Republican parties.

EXERCISES

1. What do the following measures of central tendency tell us about economic and social conditions in the developed world? Which of them appear to have skewed distributions? Why?

	Mean	Median
Divorces to Marriages, 1996	39.5%	41.0%
Women in Labor Force, 2003	50.9%	52.0%
Poverty Rate, 2000	10.4%	10.4%
High School Enrollment Rate, 2003	92.3%	94.0%
Unemployment Rate 2006	6.3%	5.5%
Savings Rate, 2003	20.3%	22.1%
Births to Women under 20, 1990s	4.2%	3.0%

---

[7] The possible distributions of overall American ideology discussed in Chapter 2 are fundamentally different from the distributions of the views of the U.S. citizens on a single attitude that are graphed in this section. They represented, rather, the nature of American's relative conservatism or liberalism over a wide range of issues. Here, we are looking at how people's attitudes are distributed on a single issue.

2. Use the mean to benchmark the United States and Sweden on the following economic and social indicators. Which ones are consistent with the stereotype that America is more conservative than Sweden and which are not?

	Mean	USA	SWD
Divorces to Marriages, 1996	40%	49%	64%
Women in Labor Force, 2003	51%	60%	63%
Women in Legislature, 2005	25%	15%	45%
Savings Rate, 2003	20%	13%	22%
Unemployment Rate 2006	6%	4%	5%
Births to Women under 20, 1990s	4%	13%	2%
Poverty Rate, 2000	10%	17%	5%
High Tech Share of Manufacturing Exports, 2003	18%	33%	15%

3. Find articles on the Gallup Poll web site (www.gallup.com) that give poll results for political attitudes on three different issues. Present these results in frequency tables and bar graphs. What type of distribution does each item best approximate?
4. There was a strong rise in party polarization in the United States during 2009–2010. Is this what you would have expected given the text's analysis of public opinion in 2008? Why or why not? What happened after the 2008 elections that might have stimulated this polarization?

Chapter

8

An Introduction to Inferential Statistics

Thus far, the analysis in this book has involved what are called **descriptive statistics**. The data on developed democracies described the nature of individual variables and the values of cases on these variables for the entire population of advanced industrial nations. These figures can tell us what Sweden's or America's infant mortality rates are or what the average economic growth and poverty rates in the developed world are.

A much different situation exists for the analysis of the public opinion data in the United States. Here, we can compute the percentage of the respondents who consider themselves conservatives or are conservative on any of numerous specific issues, thereby describing the variables in question. Yet, unlike the analysis of the developed nations, these findings describe the characteristics of about 2,102 nameless and faceless individuals who are manifestly **not the population of the U.S. citizens**. The findings from this sample are relevant or important, therefore, only because we assume that it is **representative of the broader population** from which it was drawn. Even if it is representative, furthermore, it would not be guaranteed (in fact, it would be quite unlikely) that the attitudes of the people in the sample would be exactly the same as those of the full population. For example, if on election eve, a candidate has a lead of 60% to 40% in the polls, we can be quite confident that she or he will win on the morrow. If the lead is 51% to 49%, in contrast, the election is considered a toss-up because the margin of two percentage points is well within what is called **normal sampling error**.

This brings us to the very important subject of **inferential statistics**. This field is based on the question: When you know what exists in a sample, what are the conditions or characteristics of the population likely to be? Indeed, the name "statistics" comes from these studies. Technically, the characteristics of samples are measured by **sample statistics**, while their corresponding measures in a population are termed **population parameters**. For example, Barack Obama was supported by 53.8% of the respondents in the 2008 National Electron Study (NES) survey — the sample statistic — compared to the 52.9% of the total vote that he actually received — the population parameter.

In particular, inferential statistics about a single variable focus upon two central issues concerning the relationship between these figures for a sample and the population which it supposedly represents. First, when you have data on both the sample and the population, as in the example about Barack Obama above, you can determine the probability that the sample really represents the population. Second, when only data from the sample are available, inferential statistics can be used to estimate the likely value of the variable in the population, given its value in the sample. For example, how confident can we be that a candidate is actually ahead if he or she gets 51% or 55% or 60% in a poll? This is by far the most prevalent application of inferential statistics, but understanding the first one is prerequisite to learning how to do this calculation.

This chapter presents an overview of inferential statistics. Section 8.1 discusses sampling because if the sample is not representative of the population, the inferential statistics are meaningless. The discussion then moves on to the central issues concerning a single variable in inferential statistics. Section 8.2 describes the theoretical **sampling distribution** which serves as the basis for making inferences between a sample and the population from which it is drawn. Finally, Section 8.3 discusses two applications of the sampling distribution: (1) how it can be used to estimate the probability that a sample is representative of the full population and (2) how it can be used to estimate **confidence intervals** (C.I.) of the likely mean (average) value for a variable in the population given its mean in the sample.

8.1 SAMPLING

The field of inferential statistics is based on the idea or assumption that it is possible to draw a sample that is so representative of the broader population that the results in the sample will hew very closely to the conditions that actually exist in the population. This is necessitated by the fact that it is often impractical to include an entire population in a study. For example, it would probably be impossible, as well as prohibitively costly, to survey every American citizen about how they plan to vote in the next presidential election. In the economic realm, one can take a sample of a soybean crop to estimate total yield or a sample of a semiconductor batch of production to estimate failure rate. Thus, there are many situations when doing an analysis for the whole population is impractical; so that being able to find a sample that represents the population becomes extremely important.

In theory, there are two general strategies for selecting a representative sample. One is to ensure that the sample includes the major components of the population in something near to the proportions that they exist in the population. For example, a sample from just the citizens of Mississippi in the South, or Massachusetts in the Northeast, or California on the West Coast will almost certainly be unrepresentative of the full American electorate in the political attitudes and voting behaviors of the respondents, given the significant regional variations in political orientations that exist in the United States. Thus, national samples almost always include people from different regions in proportion to their share of national population. The second approach is to select the cases to be included in the sample in a totally random manner. Then, at least according to statistical theory, the laws of probability will almost always result in Southerners, Northerners, etc. being included in the sample proportionately.

Ironically, while the first approach might sound better since the representativeness of the sample is seemingly assured, as opposed to being left to the fate of abstract probability theory, the second approach is, in reality, much sounder. It should not take too much thought to reach this conclusion, if you ask the simple but essential question: What characteristics of citizens need to be taken into account when the sample is drawn? The list would obviously extend far beyond region. We generally assume that a person's income, age, race, gender, religious beliefs, urban or rural place of residence, and many other factors have an impact on his or her political attitudes. Hence, how to ensure the correct proportions of rich and poor, blacks and whites, gays and straights, born again Christians and atheists, etc., assumes mind-boggling (if not impossible) proportions. Thus, the statisticians' assurance that random selection will provide a representative sample, at least with a level of probability that is known, is extremely good news for social science researchers.

8.1.1 Types of Samples

This results in something of a "good news, bad news" situation, though. If the good news is that a random sample can represent the population from which it is drawn, the bad news is that drawing a random sample can be quite problematic in just the situations for which finding an adequate sample is imperative. As summarized in Table 8.1, which lists six major approaches to sampling,[1] a truly **random sample** requires that every case and every possible combination of cases have an equal chance of being included in the sample. This, in turn, requires, first, that there be a list of all possible cases and, second, that random selection techniques be used to draw the sample from this list. This sounds simple and straightforward, at least until we get down to the practical question of what the heck we are actually going to do. For example, the population for a study of the American electorate is, presumably, all adult citizens in the whole U.S. Where could we find

---

[1] The classic treatment of sampling is Leslie Kish, *Survey Sampling* (New York: John Wiley, 1965). See also, Irene Hess, *Sampling for Social Research Surveys* (Ann Arbor: Institute for Social Research, University of Michigan, 1985); Herbert F. Weisberg, Jon A. Krosnick and Bruce D. Bowen, *An Introduction to Survey Research, Polling, and Data Analysis* (Thousand Oaks, CA: Sage, 1996).

Table 8.1: Types of sampling techniques.

Type of sample	Definition	Advantages	Disadvantages
Random	All cases and combinations of cases have equal probability of being included.	Sample representative with known probability.	Hard to achieve: 1. list of full population. 2. randomizing techniques.
Systematic	Every n'th case selected.	Ease of selection.	Not fully random.
Stratified	One or more subgroups sampled separately.	1. Enhance representativeness. 2. Adequate number of cases for subsample.	Magnifies problems of random sampling.
Cluster	Sampled based on geographic units.	Ensure geographic representativeness.	May create problems of representativeness on other important traits.
Quota	Specified numbers of several groups selected.	Make sample like population on some traits.	Nonrandomness makes representativeness of quotas questionable.
Convenience	Select any available respondents.	Ease of selection.	No generalizability whatsoever.

such a list? Every 10 years, the national government goes to huge expense to conduct a census to count every American. It is universally conceded, though, that the census comes up short, thereby creating a political battle over whether estimates of the real population should be used. Similarly, although the scale may not seem so daunting, we cannot be entirely sure about the names of all the citizens of Colorado or Connecticut or of Dallas or Dubuque.

One approach to this inability to define the target population with total accuracy is to substitute an obtainable list of the population that includes almost the total population. While this is probably not feasible at the national or even the state levels, city directories and residential phone books are often used for local studies. For example, while not everyone has a telephone today, telephones are so ubiquitous in American society that the telephone listings can be taken as a good approximation of the actual population.

Finding such a list for a population, though, brings us to a second problem of how we can select a sample from the list in a truly random fashion. Random sampling, as noted above, requires that every case and every combination of cases have an equal chance of being included in the sample. This is equivalent to putting every name in a telephone book or city directory into a hat and pulling out names until a sample of the desired size is obtained — including putting the names that are drawn back into the hat, if all the requisites of statistical theory are to be satisfied. This is far easier said then done. In actuality, this could be accomplished by assigning each name a number, say from 1 to 10,562, and then using a table of random numbers[2] — that is, numbers whose order has been generated randomly — to select the cases for the sample. This is a cumbersome enough procedure to make it impractical in many instances.

Instead, randomness is often approximated by a **systematic sample** which picks the cases for the sample by using a given interval on the list of the population. For example, suppose you wanted to select a sample of 500 from a population of 10,000. This would mean that the sample would be 5% or 1/20th of the population. To use systematic sampling, you would randomly select one of the first 20 names in the population list and then pick every 20th one after that — for example, 14, 34, 54, 74 . . . . This type of sampling is not really random. Every case or person has an equal chance for selection. However, every combination of cases does not, because once the first case is picked, most of the others are eliminated. For example, cases 6 and 44 or most other combinations could not both be picked for the same sample. This departure from randomness is minor enough to be acceptable to most researchers, though, and has become quite common.

---

[2] Many statistics books (but not this one) have an Appendix with a table of random numbers. Statistical packages, such as SPSS, can also be used to generate lists of random numbers.

By the 1990s, though, technology development in the form of random dialing of telephone numbers by machine in what is called **computer-assisted telephone interviewing** or CATI was beginning to make systematic samples based on telephone books obsolete.[3] Random dialing even permitted the creation of state, regional, and national samples based on area codes since random dialing created a random sample for telephones having a particular area code. This gain in the potential randomness of sample selection was more than offset, however, by a down side of this technology — the explosion of telemarketing which has created a corresponding jump in the refusal rates in telephone surveys!

Just as a systematic sample represents a technique for approximating randomness for a full list of a population, three other sampling techniques — cluster, stratified, and quota — were developed to approximate representativeness when the population could not be completely defined by making sure that important groups are proportionately included in the sample, even though this represents a departure from randomness. Cluster and stratified samples can both provide effective methods for overcoming particular sampling problems. Yet, both are also cumbersome and may create new problems with their departures from the requisites of random sampling. In contrast, quota sampling represents a very rough approximation of stratified sampling which is no longer considered adequate.

One method that has been quite useful for state and especially national surveys in which the names of the population cannot be obtained is the **cluster sample**. Here, the sample is based, not on individuals, but on geographic clusters of residences. Usually, this involves a multi-stage sampling process. First, communities (cities or counties) are selected; then, areas within the community are sampled; and, finally, the particular residences or individuals for the sample are chosen. For example, the final units of selection might be every 10th residence (home or apartment) along six blocks of a particular street with different individuals, such as the oldest man or youngest adult woman, being selected in sequential interviews. Given the extreme

---

[3]Weisberg, *et al.*, *op. cit.*, pp. 113–114.

difficulty of identifying the national population, this was once a popular method for national surveys. For example, the NES developed this technique with a great deal of sophistication during the 1950s and 1960s.[4]

One can also try to ensure that the study is inclusive by using **stratified samples**. In a stratified sample, one or more subgroups or strata of the population are sampled separately to ensure that a given number are included in the final sample. This is done for two very different reasons. First, though probably not very often in practice, stratified sampling can be used to make sure that groups of interest are represented proportionately in the population. Thus, if the initial sample clearly under-represents such groups as low-income people or Catholics or Hispanics, this group can be sampled separately to make the final sample more representative. However, randomness by itself should approximate proportionality if fairly large samples are drawn. Consequently, it is probably easier, as well as closer to the requisites of sampling theory, to draw a single large sample rather than to attempt to create several stratified ones.

A second and much different analytic situation probably constitutes the major reason for using stratified samples. In many instances, we would like to examine the opinions and attitudes of a particular subgroup of the population. Yet many of these subgroups — such as business executives, African Americans, or welfare recipients — are such a small proportion of the American population that only a very small number will be included in a national sample. This creates a problem for analyzing their attitudes because there simply are too few cases to provide much confidence in the findings. Hence, oversampling the group of interest provides the best method for subjecting them to analysis.

However, such oversampling poses a new major problem. If, say, African-Americans or business executives are substantially oversampled, the resulting overall sample is clearly no longer representative of America. Thus, the researcher has a new problem of how to restore the representativeness of the full sample. This can be done either by

---

[4] Hess, *op. cit.*

excluding the extra stratified sample from analyses that seek to make generalizations about the population or by **weighting** the responses of different groups in the overall sample, as is done in the 2008 NES survey. Still, either approach can be cumbersome and confusing.

Quota samples can be considered rough-and-ready approximations of stratified sampling which were considered much more valid in the early days of sampling than they are now. A quota sample specifies the number and proportion — that is the quota — of people in the sample having a specific characteristic, such as race, income level, gender, or religion. There are two very fundamental problems with a quota sample. First, as noted earlier, it is probably impossible to specify all the relevant characteristics and create a sample with their desired proportions. Second, unlike a stratified sample, there is no attempt to assure randomness in the selection of the various subgroups in the sample. Thus, the business executives, African-Americans, or born again Christians in the quotas may well not be representative of their groups. For example, most of the African-Americans might be business executives; or most of the business executives might be Hollywood movie producers. Consequently, with the development of technology that allows more sophisticated sampling, quota samples have lost almost all, if not all, of their respectability.

There is, finally, no respectability whatsoever in a **convenience sample**. A convenience sample, as its name indicates, is not really a sample of any larger population but is created, instead, by the ease of obtaining subjects. For example, the survey takers could be sent to busy street corners and sample anyone who is willing to stop and talk with them. The only reason, really, even to mention convenience samples is that they point to the questionable nature of some types of studies that might appear less problematic than they really are. For example, a considerable amount of research is based on surveys of college students taking specific classes. This represents the convenience of having a captive audience and raises the question about what the broader population is that is being sampled. In addition, many surveys now get a fairly high rate (25% or more) of refusals, which suggests that the participants may represent something of a convenience sample whose representativeness of the broader population is open to question.

This is particularly a problem when mail questionnaires are used, for which the rate of return is very often quite low (25% to 33% or less).[5] Even more questionably, the increasingly popular web polls on the internet are totally convenience samples whose participants are extremely unlikely to be representative of the general public.

To sum, studies of public opinion must be based on representative samples for all but the very smallest of political units. Statistical theory tells us that a random sample can represent a larger population, even one as large as the entire American public, quite well. Yet, the ability to draw random samples from large communities is somewhat circumscribed. Consequently, most such samples can only approximate the requisite of sampling theory. Over time, technological developments have allowed these approximations to improve dramatically. Still, it is good to keep in mind that even under the best of circumstances, the messy real world departs from the abstract world of statistical theory.

8.1.2 Two Cautionary Tales of Mis-Called Elections

It is almost obligatory to include the embarrassing fiasco of the *Literary Digest*'s poll for the 1936 presidential election as a warning about how disaster can strike when the procedures for random sampling are violated. In short, the *Literary Digest*, which had conducted fairly accurate polls for several preceding presidential elections, created a huge sample in 1936 that was clearly biased toward oversampling the wealthy. The results of this poll indicated that Democratic President Franklin Roosevelt, who was just concluding his first term in office, would lose in a landslide to Republican challenger Alf Landon, presumably reflecting widespread dissatisfaction with his New Deal programs. Instead, on election eve, it was Roosevelt who was returned to the White House in a landslide. The general moral of this tale is that rich folks and poor folks have different political allegiances and that, especially during the Great Depression of the 1930s, there were many more poor folks than rich folks in the United States. Thus, a biased sample doomed the poll's results.

---

[5] Don A. Dill, *Mail and Telephone Surveys: A Total Design Method* (New York: John Wiley, 1978) discusses the response rates for mail and telephone surveys.

A closer look at this bit of trivia in the history of public opinion polling raises the two more subtle points that poor polling can work due to idiosyncratic contextual factors but that such polling techniques which were once fairly accurate can then fail miserably when these conditions change. The *Literary Digest* used two sources to create its sample in 1936: people included in telephone books and on lists of automobile owners. This produced a sample of approximately 10 million people — compared, for example, to the 2,102 in the 2008 NES poll. The sample was polled by mail; and over two million responses were received, producing what might quite well have been the largest presidential poll ever. The results, however, were anything but representative or accurate. In the sample, Landon won easily with 57% of the vote, but, at the polls, Roosevelt won an even more sweeping victory of 61%. Clearly, the *Literary Digest* had goofed big time!

The obvious explanation is that the biased or unrepresentative sample produced totally unrepresentative results. This raises the question, however, of why the *Literary Digest*'s poll was so wrong in 1936 when similar polls based on smaller samples had correctly predicted the presidential victories of Warren Harding in 1920, Calvin Coolidge in 1924, Herbert Hoover in 1928, and Roosevelt in 1932. The answer, which takes a bit of retrospective analysis, is that the political battle lines for voting changed dramatically in America in 1936 from previous patterns. In the late 19th and early 20th centuries, the basic political division in the U.S. followed sectional or geographic lines with the Northeast and Midwest supporting Republicans and the South and the West supporting Democrats. The privations of the Great Depression and the revolution in government policy represented by the New Deal, however, created a new "politics of rich and poor" in the 1930s which dominated America's partisanship for several generations.[6] The lesson here is that a clearly unrepresentative sample can produce accurate results if its bias does not include politically relevant factors, as occurred for the *Literary Digest*'s polls from 1920 to 1932. If conditions change

---

[6]See Gary Miller and Norman Schofield, "Activists and Partisan Realignment in the United States", *American Political Science Review*, 97 (2003), pp. 245–260 for an overview of this realignment in voting cleavage.

and the bias does become relevant, as happened to the *Literary Digest* in 1936, the poll's results will become embarrassingly wrong.

There is a second and much less told story about polling for the 1936 election which makes the same point. In 1936, an emerging pollster, George Gallup, literally bet his business on the accuracy of his poll results by selling them with a money-back guarantee if his prediction of the presidential race proved to be wrong. Gallup used a quota sample that included income levels and urban versus rural residence. Unlike the gross bias toward the wealthy in the *Literary Digest* poll, this turned out to produce a fairly representative sample.[7]

As discussed in the previous subsection, however, quota samples are not really random ones. Thus, using them has some dangers. In fact, Gallup continued to use quota samples through the 1940s, successfully for the 1940 and 1944 presidential elections but erroneously in 1948 when incumbent Democrat Harry Truman narrowly beat Republican challenger Thomas Dewey — so narrowly in fact that on the day following the election Truman happily held up a newspaper that had gone to press with the banner headline "Dewey Wins". There were several reasons for mispredicting this race, as Gallup and many other pollsters did: the extremely narrow margin, their stopping of polling in early October, and the fact that the undecideds disproportionately voted for Truman. Yet, Gallup was also undercut by his quota sample which was based on 1940 census data. By 1948, the dislocations of World War II had made America significantly more urban than it had been at the beginning of the decade. Thus, Gallup's sample was more rural and less urban than the U.S. as a whole, which was politically relevant because urban areas were disproportionately Democratic.[8] Again, therefore, an approximation to a random sample, albeit a far better one than that employed by the *Literary Digest*, became fallacious when its method for approximating randomness turned politically relevant.

---

[7] Theodore Caplow, Louis Hicks and Ben J. Wattenberg, *The First Measured Century: An Illustrated Guide to Trends in America, 1900–2000* (Washington, DC: American Enterprise Institute, 2000).

[8] Earl R. Babbie, *The Practice of Social* Research, 7th Edn. (Belmont, CA: Wadsworth, 1995), pp. 188–190.

8.2 THE SAMPLING DISTRIBUTION

Inferential or inductive statistics are used to draw conclusions about the relationship between a sample and the population from which the sample is drawn. Usually, these inferences concern what the population mean is in relation to the sample mean. In particular, the most frequent application of inferential statistics is to **estimate the range of values within which a population mean lies, given the value of the mean for a random sample taken from the population**. For example, if you listen closely when poll results are being reported, you will often hear the announcer say that a candidate's support in a sample, say 53%, will be within 3 percentage points of her or his support in the population 95% of the time. This is what is called a **Confidence Interval or C.I.** It is computed from a special probability distribution called the **sampling distribution** which statisticians have derived to estimate how close a sample mean should be to the mean in the population from which the sample was drawn.

In inductive statistics, we assume that a single sample is just one of an infinite number of samples of a given size N that could be drawn from the population in question. Perhaps, the hardest thing to understand initially in inferential statistics is this idea of a sampling distribution, rather than how it is used. In inferential statistics, we are really dealing with three distributions — (1) the distribution of a variable in the population, (2) the distribution of the same variable in a sample drawn from the population, and (3) the hypothetical distribution of sample means for that variable which would result if an infinite number of samples of size N were taken. By convention, Roman letters are used to denote the characteristics of samples, while Greek letters denote the characteristics of populations. Figure 8.1 then summarizes the terminology used for these three distributions. A sample, for example, has a mean of $\bar{x}$ and a standard deviation of s; and for a population, the mean is μ and the standard deviation is σ. While such distributions have many characteristics, basic inductive statistics are primarily concerned with just their means and standard deviations.

The only one of these distributions that we will probably be able to know with complete certainty in almost all circumstances, incidentally, is the one for the sample. The distribution of the population is normally

Type of Distribution Characteristics	SAMPLE	POPULATION	SAMPLING
Mean	$\bar{x}$	μ	μ
Standard Deviation	s	σ	$\sigma/\sqrt{N}$
Variance	s^2	σ^2	σ^2/N
Size	N	N	Infinite

Figure 8.1: The three distributions involved in inferential statistics.

simply estimated based on what was observed in the sample. Indeed, samples are usually used because it is impossible to get data on all the members of the population. Finally, the distribution of sample means is a totally hypothetical one, based on abstract statistical theory.

The sampling distribution is the presumed distribution of the sample means ($\bar{x}$'s) from an infinite number of samples of the same size. Luckily, statisticians have computed a probability distribution for this based on what is called the **central-limit theorem**:

> If repeated random samples of size N are drawn from any population (of whatever form) having a mean of μ and a variance of σ^2, then as N becomes large, the sampling distribution of sample means approaches normality with a mean of μ and variance of σ^2/N.[9]

According to the central limit theorem, therefore, once the sample size N becomes fairly large (100 or greater), the mean of the hypothetical distribution of sample means will approximate μ (the population mean). In addition, its standard deviation, which is called the **standard error of the mean** or **S.E.$_m$**, will approximate: $\sigma/\sqrt{N}$ — that is, the square root of the variance σ^2/N or the population standard deviation divided by the square root of the sample size.

---

[9] Hubert M. Blalock, Jr., *Social Statistics*, 2nd Edn. (New York: McGraw-Hill, 1972), p. 181.

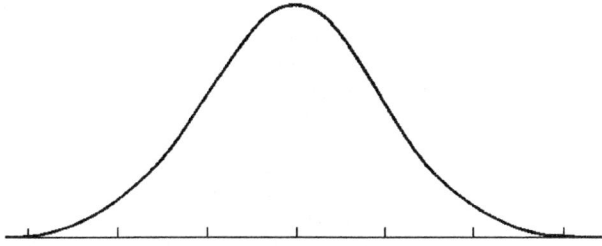

Figure 8.2: Normal curve.
Source: www.psychstat.missouristate.edu/introbook/sbk10m.htm.

8.2.1 The Normal Distribution and Z Scores

The sampling distribution is a **normal distribution** in which the largest number of cases cluster around the mean and then decline symmetrically, the further away from a mean that a score lies. This distribution has a bell shape; and the mean, median, and mode are all exactly the same and lie in the middle of the distribution, as indicated in Figure 8.2. Normal curves are important for descriptive research because many variables used in social science analysis have normal distributions. Thus, understanding this bell-shaped pattern can provide important insights about a wide variety of substantive subjects. For statistical analysis, though, probably the most important characteristic of a normal curve is that **a given proportion of the cases fall within specific standard deviations of the mean**. For example, 34.13% of the cases are one standard deviation above (or below) the mean; and 47.73% are two standard deviations above (or below) the mean as graphed in Figure 8.3.

Because of this, normal distributions can be converted into **standardized** or **Z** distributions where each case's score (**Z score**) represents how many standard deviations from the mean it is. This is done by applying the following simple formula to each case in the distribution:

$$Z_i = (X_i - \bar{x})/s,$$

where:

Z_i is the Z score for a particular case on variable X;
X_i is the original score for a particular case on variable X;

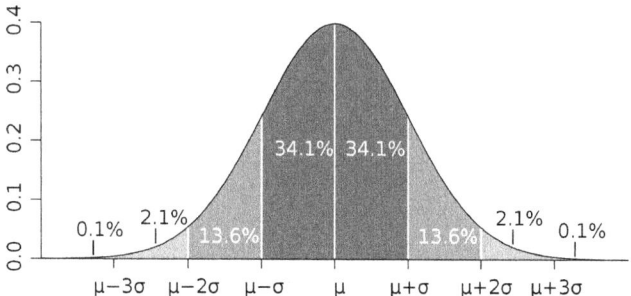

Figure 8.3: Percentage of cases within one or two standard deviations of the mean in a normal distribution.
Source: "Images for a Normal Curve". Available at www.wikipedia.org.

$\bar{x}$ is the mean of X; and
s is the standard deviation of X.

In this standardized distribution, the mean is $\bar{x}$; and the standard deviation is one by simple arithmetic.

For example, Table 8.2 presents data on transforming the distribution of 2007 GDP per capita in the developed world into a set of Z or standardized scores. Part A gives the mean of $36,056 and standard deviation of $6,711 for this variable, which are necessary for calculating the Z scores for the 21 countries in the table. Part B then shows the results for the two steps in the calculation. The first column is the value of each nation on GDP per capita. The first step is to calculate the difference between a country's actual GDP per capita (X_i) and the mean ($\bar{x}$) for the entire developed world of $36,056. Thus, for the United States:

$$(X_i - \bar{x}) = \$45{,}489 - \$36{,}056 = \$9{,}433.$$

These results for all the countries are reported in the second column under DIFFMEAN which is short for "difference from the mean". The second step then is to divide this difference by the standard deviation of $6,711. For example, for the United States:

$$Z_i = \text{DIFFMEAN}/s = \$9{,}433/\$6{,}711 = 1.41.$$

These Z values are printed out in the third column under the title ZGDP. Looking at the whole distribution, there are nine positive and

Table 8.2: Transforming 2007 GDP per capita into Z scores.

A. Descriptive Statistics for GDP per capita, 2007

Minimum	$22,815
Maximum	$53,477
Mean	$36,056
Standard Deviation	$6,711

B. Elements in this Transformation

NATIONS	GDPPC07	DIFFMEAN	ZGDP
Australia	$37,565	$1,509	0.22
Austria	$37,119	$1,063	0.16
Belgium	$35,358	−$698	−0.10
Canada	$38,500	$2,444	0.36
Denmark	$35,961	−$95	−0.01
Finland	$34,718	−$1,338	−0.20
France	$32,686	−$3,370	−0.50
Germany	$34,391	−$1,665	−0.25
Greece	$28,423	−$7,633	−1.14
Ireland	$45,027	$8,971	1.34
Italy	$30,381	−$5,675	−0.85
Japan	$33,626	−$2,430	−0.36
Netherlands	$39,225	$3,169	0.47
New Zealand	$27,431	−$8,625	−1.29
Norway	$53,477	$17,421	2.60
Portugal	$22,815	−1,3241	−1.97
Spain	$31,586	−$4,470	−0.67
Sweden	$36,603	$547	0.08
Switzerland	$41,101	$5,045	0.75
United Kingdom	$35,699	−$357	−0.05
United States	$45,489	$9,433	1.41

C. Descriptive Statistics for ZGDP, 2007

Minimum	−1.97
Maximum	2.60
Mean	0.0000
Standard Deviation	0.9999

12 negative Z scores. Part C of the table, though, demonstrates that the positive and negative Z scores are indeed exactly balanced since the mean for the Z distribution is 0.0000 with a standard deviation of 0.99999.

Table 8.3: Percentage of cases a given number of standard deviations above or below the mean in a normal distribution.

Number of standard deviations above or below mean (Z score)	Percentage of cases falling between score and mean
0.0	0.0%
0.1	3.98%
0.2	7.93%
0.5	19.15%
0.67	24.86%
0.75	27.34%
1.0	34.13%
1.25	39.44%
1.50	43.32%
1.65	45.05%
1.75	45.99%
1.96	47.50%
2.0	47.73%
2.01	47.78%
2.50	49.38%
2.58	49.51%
3.0	49.865%
3.5	49.97674%
4.0	49.99683%
5.0	49.99997133%

Source: Adapted from Hubert M. Blalock, Jr., *Social Statistics* (New York: McGraw-Hill, 1972), p. 558, which presents a much more detailed table.

Once the Z score for an individual case is obtained, a table of Z scores that is included in most statistics books can be used to determine what proportion of all cases fall between the mean and the score of the case in question. Table 8.3, for example, provides one such abbreviated list. Note that because the normal curve is perfectly symmetrical, only positive values for Z are given because the percentages for negative Z's are exactly the same. For example, 34.13% of the cases fall between the mean and a Z score of -1.00; and 45.05% of the cases fall between the mean and a Z score of 1.65. Since half or 50.00% of the cases have scores above (or below) the mean, one can subtract this probability from 50.00 to see what proportion of the cases have higher positive or lower negative Z scores than the one in question. For example, 4.95% of the cases have Z scores higher than 1.65; and, slightly more complexly, 15.87% of the cases have Z scores lower than one of -1.00 because there are 34.13% (between -1 and the mean) plus 50% (above the mean) of the cases with higher values for a total of 84.13%. In essence, therefore, this determines a score's percentile.

The perceptive student might well question the point of going through all these exercises with normal curves, Z scores, and percentiles. After all, for one thing, using Z scores to compute percentiles would appear to be a needlessly convoluted operation because, if you have the data to compute the Z scores, you should be able to calculate percentiles directly. The answer is that these characteristics are not that important for dealing with empirical distributions. However, when we move on to theoretical probability distributions and inferential statistics, Z scores become the key factor in calculating C.I. and levels of statistical significance.

The concept of probability distributions forms the basis for inferential statistics, which might make them threatening to some students. However, these distributions also underlie many of the games of chance purveyed by gambling casinos, thus making them far more interesting to gamblers. A probability is simply the likelihood that one in a set of outcomes will occur. For example, there is a 0.5 probability that a flipped coin will come up heads and a 0.167 one that a rolled die will come up six. A probability distribution, then, is simply the distribution of probabilities for all possible outcomes — which obviously have to equal 1.00 or 100%. Thus, when rolling one die, there is a distribution of six outcomes each with a probability of $1/6$ or 0.167. If two or three dice are used, the distribution becomes more complex, but the basic principle stays the same. Table 8.4, for example, shows the probability distributions for one, two, and three dice.

What is vitally important about these probability distributions is that they are derived theoretically or deductively, not empirically. This is fundamentally different from the empirically derived distributions for people's family income or presidential preferences in the United States, which are based on responses to survey or census questionnaires. Here, the probability distributions for dice come from the assumption that all outcomes are equally likely, not from observing and recording

Table 8.4: Probabilities of rolling particular scores with one, two, or three dice.

	1 Die	2 Dice	3 Dice
1	1/6 = 0.1667		
2	1/6 = 0.1667	1/36 = 0.0278	
3	1/6 = 0.1667	2/36 = 0.0556	1/216 = 0.0046
4	1/6 = 0.1667	3/36 = 0.0833	3/216 = 0.0139
5	1/6 = 0.1667	4/36 = 0.1111	3/216 = 0.0139
6	1/6 = 0.1667	5/36 = 0.1389	10/216 = 0.0463
7		6/36 = 0.1667	15/216 = 0.0694
8		5/36 = 0.1389	21/216 = 0.0972
9		4/36 = 0.1111	25/216 = 0.1157
10		3/36 = 0.0833	30/216 = 0.1389
11		2/36 = 0.0556	30/216 = 0.1389
12		1/36 = 0.0278	25/216 = 0.1157
13			21/216 = 0.0972
14			15/216 = 0.0694
15			10/216 = 0.0463
16			3/216 = 0.0139
17			3/216 = 0.0139
18			1/216 = 0.0046

what happens when dice are actually rolled in the real world. When real events diverge dramatically from this, we assume that something is wrong rather than that probability theory has erred. For example, if a gambler rolls 10 straight 7's, most people would assume that he or she was cheating, perhaps by shaving the dice, rather than being extremely lucky. At least with dice, though, the basis for the probability calculation should be clear. When we move on to some of the theoretical probability distributions used in political science statistics, though, the derivation is not so clear, forcing us to take the statistical theory somewhat on faith.

8.3 TWO APPLICATIONS OF THE SAMPLING DISTRIBUTION

The two most important applications of the sampling distribution are to estimate whether a sample is representative of a broader population and to estimate the likely population mean given the mean in the sample.

The second one is by far the major usage. Here, however, we shall start with the first because it uses the basic Z formula for the sampling distribution, while the second involves a manipulation of this formula.

8.3.1 The Probability that a Sample Comes from a Population

The sampling distribution, according to statistical theory in the central limit theorem, is normal with a known mean and standard deviation. These characteristics, in turn, allow the simple calculation of how close the sample and population means should be with a given probability. This is done by applying the formula for Z scores to the sampling distribution. As noted in the last section, the formula for Z is:

$$Z_i = (X_i - \bar{x})/s.$$

For the sampling distribution:

X_i (the score of an individual case) is $\bar{x}$ (the mean of a particular sample);
$\bar{x}$ (the mean of the distribution) is μ (the population mean); and
s (the standard deviation of the distribution) is $\sigma/\sqrt{N}$ (the standard deviation of the population divided by the square root of the sample size).

These figures can then be plugged into the Z formula to calculate the probability that a given sample came randomly from a population:

$$Z = (\bar{x} - \mu)/(\sigma/\sqrt{N}).$$

What Z really represents here, hence, is the probability that a sample has been drawn randomly from some larger population with the **null hypothesis** of **no difference** being that the population and sample means are equal. Based on the formula, this probability is determined by three factors. First, the larger the difference between the sample and population means ($\bar{x}-\mu$), which forms the numerator in the formula for Z, the greater is the likelihood that the sample is not representative — which is so obvious that it hardly bears stating. Second, any specific ($\bar{x} - \mu$) will be less significant the greater the standard deviation of the population (σ) is. Technically, this is because higher σ's increase the size of the denominator, but the substantive reason is probably more important: the smaller ($\bar{x} - \mu$) is relative to σ, the less likely it is to represent a significant difference.

Third, larger samples will give higher Z scores since the larger N is, the smaller the standard error of $\sigma/\sqrt{N}$ will be. It certainly makes intuitive sense that the larger the sample, the more confidence that can be placed in the sample results. However, it is a surprising fact of statistical theory that, when samples and populations are not very small, sample size alone — not the ratio of the sample size to the population — effects statistical significance. For example, a sample of 1,000 is as representative of a population of 100,000 as it is of a population of 100,000,000.

When the mean and standard deviation of both the population and sample are known, this formula for Z can be applied to test the **null hypothesis** that the two means are equal which indicates whether or not the sample can be considered representative of the population. This application of the sampling distribution is not that common in practice because, if the characteristics of the whole population are known, it makes little sense to examine a sample! Sometimes, though, a researcher may test to see whether a sample is not representative because it possesses some special characteristics of its own. As an illustration, let us consider the infant mortality rates in 2003 of the four Scandinavian countries — Denmark, Finland, Norway, and Sweden — compared to the average for all the developed world. Given their reputation for well developed welfare states, we might predict that the Scandinavian nations would stand out for having low levels of infant mortality. If they do, in fact, have lower than average infant mortality, a policy analyst might examine their healthcare systems more closely to try to discover the sources of their success.

The first step in doing this is to calculate the mean and standard deviation for infant mortality both for the population of all 21 advanced industrial societies and for the sample of four Scandinavian countries. Table 8.5 provides these summary statistics. The average infant mortality rate is 4.45 for the entire developed world and 3.50 for the sample of four Scandinavian countries; and the standard deviations

Table 8.5: Summary statistics for infant mortality rates, 2003.

A. All 21 Developed Nations

Minimum	3.0
Maximum	7.0
Mean	4.45
Standard Deviation	0.943

B. Four Scandinavian Countries

Minimum	3.1
Maximum	4.4
Mean	3.50
Standard Deviation	0.616

are 0.943 for the population and 0.616 for the sample. Thus, as anticipated, infant mortality is clearly lower in Scandinavia than in the developed world as a whole. Whether this difference is large enough to reject the null hypothesis that infant mortality in Scandinavia is not different from the one for all developed countries is another question. To answer it, we must put the relevant figures from Table 8.5 into the Z formula.

$$Z = (\bar{x} - \mu)/(\sigma/\sqrt{N})$$
$$= (3.50 - 4.45)/(0.943/\sqrt{4})$$
$$= -0.95/(0.943/2)$$
$$= -0.95/0.4715$$
$$= -2.01.$$

Once this value of Z is calculated, you need to consult a Z table, such as the abbreviated one in Table 8.3 or the much more elaborate ones included in many statistics books. This would indicate how many of the cases in the sampling distribution — potential sample means — would be expected to have more extreme values than the mean from the actual sample. If, for example, only 1% of the cases lie outside the Z score, we would conclude that the null hypothesis of no difference between the sample and population means probably is not tenable. That is, the sample is not representative of the population because it differs from the population in some systematic fashion.

This is what is meant by **statistical significance**: the probability that the null hypothesis is true. When this probability is low, the null hypothesis is rejected; and the conclusion is made that a "statistically significant relationship exists". Here, this relationship would be that Scandinavian countries have atypically low infant mortality rates. Conventionally, the 5% level is chosen to mark statistical significance; and this is called the 0.05 significance level. Thus, the lower the significance level, the greater the significance. For instance, the 0.01 significance level is more significant than the 0.05 one.

In applying a Z test, either a **one-tailed** or **two-tailed** distribution can be used. In a two-tailed test, no prediction is made about the direction of deviation from the mean; so that both positive and negative higher scores are included in the significance calculation. For example, 47.5% of the cases lie between a Z score of 1.96 and the mean; so that in a two-tailed test, the 2.5% of the cases beyond both the $+1.96$ and -1.96 Z values are included to give a 0.05 significance level. In a one-tailed test, the direction, either above the mean (positive) or below the mean (negative), is predicted. Consequently, the 0.05 level of significance is attained when 45% of the cases lie between the mean and the Z score in question which occurs when $Z = +1.65$ or -1.65. When using the one-tailed criterion, hence, you must not only look at the size of Z, but also make sure that its sign, $+$ or $-$, is in the predicted direction.

For the example of infant mortality in Scandinavia, the Z table (see Table 8.3) shows that approximately 0.4778 or 47.78% of the cases lie between this Z score of -2.01 and the mean. Thus, it is highly improbable that Scandinavia is representative of all developed nations in terms of the level of infant mortality. Rather these four countries have atypically low infant mortality. Since we started with the expectation that their infant mortality would be lower than normal, a one-tailed test is appropriate, but even the more stringent criterion of a two-tailed test indicates a statistically significant difference:

0.0212 or 2.1% level for a one-tailed test: $(0.5000 - 0.4778)$; and
0.0424 or 4.2% level for a two-tailed test: $2 \times (0.5000 - 0.4778)$.

8.3.2 Confidence Intervals

The preceding section showed how to calculate the probability that a given sample represents a population when we know both the population and sample distributions. Most of the time, however, we are primarily interested in estimating population parameters from sample characteristics. This requires treating the difference between the sample mean and the population mean $(\bar{x} - \mu)$ **as the unknown** in the equation. Since there can only be one unknown quantity if the equation is to remain solvable, this means that a value for Z must be specified. To do this, we pick a level of acceptable statistical significance — typically, a Z of 1.96 to represent the 0.05 level for a two-tailed test — and manipulate the equation to calculate other unknowns.

This revised formula is then used to calculate the **sampling error** or C.I. This is the expected difference between the sample mean and the true population mean at given levels of probability and statistical significance. For example, setting Z equal to 1.96 produces a C.I. of how close the population mean will be to the sample mean that holds true 95% of the time or is significant at the 0.05 level. In many national surveys, for instance, the poll proportion is within 3% or percentage points of the true population mean 95% of the time.

Thus, the equation has to be rearranged to solve for the C.I.

$$\text{C.I.} = (\bar{x} - \mu).$$

Substituting 1.96 for Z and manipulating the previous equations through simple algebra then produces:

$$1.96 = \text{C.I.}/(\sigma/\sqrt{N})$$
$$\text{C.I.} = 1.96 \times (\sigma/\sqrt{N}).$$

For example, suppose we tried to estimate the average infant mortality rate among the developed nations from the data on just the sample of four Scandinavian countries. To get the C.I., we simply substitute in the requisite values:

$$\text{C.I.} = 1.96 \times (\sigma/\sqrt{N})$$
$$= 1.96 \times (0.943/\sqrt{4})$$

$$= 1.96 \times (0.943/2)$$
$$= 1.96 \times 0.4715$$
$$= 0.92.$$

Since the mean of the sample was 3.50, we would then estimate that the true population mean for infant mortality was:

$$\text{C.I. for } \bar{x} - \mu = 3.50 \pm 0.92$$
$$= 2.58 \text{ to } 4.42.$$

Of course, because Scandinavia has lower than normal infant mortality rates, the estimate of the average for the population of all developed nations is somewhat biased in a low direction. In particular, the upper limit of the C.I. for the population mean of 4.42 is slightly below the actual one of 4.45.

Probably, the primary use of C.I. in political science is to estimate what proportion of a population a particular attitude has given the results in a survey. This involves two important modifications to the formula and calculations in this section. First, the basic formula must be changed because the population parameters (μ and σ) are not known. Second, another change must be made because the calculations involve percentages, not absolute numbers like infant mortality rates. Neither of these modifications is particularly daunting, either mathematically or conceptually. Still, they are cumbersome and lengthy enough, so they are not presented in the main text.[10] As a quick example for campaign polls, if we assume that the population's mean is the 50% needed for victory, the population standard deviation σ works out to be 0.5. Thus, if a candidate receives 55% support in a survey of 1,600 citizens, the calculation of the C.I. is quite easy:

$$\text{C.I.} = Z \times (\sigma/\sqrt{N})$$
$$\text{C.I.} = 1.96 \times (0.5/\sqrt{1,600})$$
$$= 1.96 \times (0.5/40)$$

---

[10] See *Ibid.*, Chapter 12.

$$= 1.96 \times 0.0125$$
$$= 0.0245 = 2.45\%.$$

Consequently, 95% of the time (as represented by the Z of 1.96), the population mean should be within 2.45% or percentage points of 55%, that is, between 52.55% and 57.45%.

EXERCISES

1. Suppose you were asked to conduct a survey of the citizens of the largest city in your state. Discuss the type of sample you would use and how you would administer the questions. Would you have a truly random sample? If not, how could you conclude that your sample is representative of the city's population?
2. The website of Real Clear Politics (www.realclearpolitics.com) posts poll results for many races. Find one that reports at least five polls during a one-month period. How close are these results? Do the different polling organizations generally agree or are there substantial differences among them? What does this suggest about the validity of their sampling procedures?
3. Find a description of the research design for the 2008 NES survey. This is available at: www.icpsr.umich.edu/icpsrweb/SETUPS2008/. Once you get to the website, double click on SURVEY RESEARCH METHODS. Briefly describe the sampling technique and how the survey was administered. Then discuss how adequate this approach is for providing data that are representative of the American citizenry.
4. A candidate in a congressional campaign was supported by 52% of the registered voters in a sample of 900. Calculate a C.I. that should be true 95% of the time, assuming that $\sigma = 0.5$. Does that suggest that you should conclude that the candidate holds a majority in the population? Given the formula for a C.I., what could you do to reduce its size?

Part III

Discovering Relationships for Nominal and Ordinal Data

Chapter 9

Crosstabulation: Why Do Americans Vote Democratic or Republican?

The frequency tables discussed in Chapter 2 describe the state of public opinion in the United States on individual issues and allow us to make a judgment about whether Americans are conservative or liberal on a given issue. They do not, however, tell us anything about the **relationship** between citizens' views on issues and their partisan loyalties or between an individual's partisanship and his or her personal characteristics, which are normally considered to influence attitudes about politics. Measuring the degree of relationship or **association** between two variables, therefore, is necessary if we are to answer such important questions as: Are conservatives on cultural, economic, and security issues also more likely to be Republicans, as is generally assumed? Do some issues influence voting more than others? Are the rich and more traditionally-oriented more conservative and Republican in their political views than other Americans? Do wealth and traditional values influence people's positions on some issues, but not others? Since social science theory and analysis are concerned with **explanation** much more than simple description, techniques to measure the strength of a relationship between two variables assume a very important role in political science research methodology.

Crosstabulation tables or crosstabs are the principal techniques used to describe direct or bivariate relationships between two categoric variables at the nominal and ordinal levels of measurement. This chapter begins by describing this technique and the tables and statistics associated with it, using the relationship between views on abortion and presidential vote in 2008 as an illustration. The second part then shows how to test the socioeconomic model of voting developed in Chapter 3 with crosstabulation results.

9.1 CROSSTABULATION TABLES: THE BASICS

When statistical relationships are described for categoric variables, that is, variables which have a small number of categories with a substantial number of cases in most of them, the data are usually presented in the form of a crosstabulation table. Tables 9.1 and 9.2 describe the relationship between attitudes about abortion and voting for Barack Obama in the 2008 presidential election. In this relationship, a person's position on abortion forms the explanatory or independent variable; and her or his vote for Obama (as opposed to John McCain) is the dependent variable because, we assume, ideology makes someone more or less likely to vote Democratic, depending upon whether a person is a conservative or a liberal. In short, ideology is the **cause**, and voting decision is the **effect** — one's vote is dependent upon one's ideology.

This overview of crosstabulation is presented in four stages. The first describes the basic components of a crosstabulation table; the second shows how percentages can be used to depict the relationship between the two variables under analysis; and the third and fourth stages discuss summary statistics that have been developed to measure the strength

Table 9.1: Crosstabulation of Obama vote by abortion attitudes (number of respondents).

Obama vote	Abortion position			
	Pro-life	Intermediate	Pro-choice	TOTAL
McCain	190	70	89	349
Obama	117	58	230	405
TOTAL	307	128	319	754

Table 9.2: Crosstabulation of Obama vote by abortion attitudes (percentages and correlation coefficient).

Obama vote	Abortion position			
	Pro-life	Intermediate	Pro-choice	TOTAL
McCain	190	70	89	349
	62%	55%	28%	46%
Obama	117	58	230	405
	38%	45%	72%	54%
TOTAL	307	128	319	754
	% Col = 100%	% Col = 100%	% Col = 100%	% Col = 100%
	% Row = 41%	% Row = 17%	% Row = 42%	% Row = 100%

Note: Percentage Comparison, Obama: 72% − 38% = 34% or percentage points.
Ordinal Correlation Gamma = 0.49 Approximate Sig. = 0.004.

of association between the two items and the statistical significance of this correlation.

9.1.1 Setting Up a Crosstabulation

By convention, the explanatory or independent variable is placed in the columns of the table, while the dependent variable is placed in the rows. For the crosstabulation in Tables 9.1 and 9.2, the independent variable is support for abortion which contains three categories (pro-life, intermediate, and pro-choice); and the dependent variable is presidential vote, which has two categories (voted for McCain and voted for Obama). Thus, in Table 9.1, there are five columns and four rows. The top row and left column are composed of labels for the individual categories of the two variables. The next two rows and three columns contain the data on the number of cases falling into each combination of categories.[1] Finally, the right column and bottom row are the total or sum of each category down a particular column or across a particular row.

The interior of this table is formed by the six **cells** which represent the number of cases having a specific **joint frequency**. These are called

---

[1] Because this crosstabulation is the result of a "weighted" analysis, the frequencies were estimated using the same technique described in Footnote 4 of Chapter 2.

cells because they are surrounded by four unbroken lines, suggesting jail cells. A joint frequency is how many people share two of the characteristics in the crosstabulation. For example, the number of pro-choice respondents who voted for Barack Obama represents the joint frequency of a category of abortion attitudes (pro-choice) and a category of presidential vote (Obama) because only people who have *both* of these characteristics are so classified.

The interior of the table is ringed or enclosed by the labels at the top and left and by the column and row TOTALs. These last two are called the **marginals** and are the row at the bottom of the table and the column at the far right. They are called marginals because they are at the margins of the table. The two marginals represent the **totals** for each column and row within the table, that is, the number of cases having a particular value for either the independent or dependent variable. The column marginals in the bottom row, thus, form a frequency distribution for the independent variable; and the row marginals in the last column are a frequency distribution for the dependent variable.

For nominal variables, it makes no difference whatsoever how the categories are placed in the table. Obviously, the situation is quite different for ordinal variables, such as the two in Table 9.1. Support for abortion has to follow an order from pro-life (low) to intermediate to pro-choice (high). Likewise, Obama vote has to follow an order from McCain (low) to Obama (high). By convention, the categories and values of an ordinal independent variable are arranged in ascending order from low to high as you go from the first to the last column in the crosstab. In Table 9.1, hence, "Pro-life" is in the first column following the labels, "Intermediates" is in the second, "Pro-choice" is in the third, and the marginal TOTAL is in the last column.

Also by convention, the categories and values of an ordinal dependent variable are arranged in ascending order from low to high as you go down the table. For example, in Table 9.1, "McCain voters" are in the first row under the labels, "Obama voters" are in the second, and the marginal TOTAL is in the bottom row. The reason for this is that we add down columns in almost all arithmetic operations. Thus, it makes sense to start with the category having the low value at the top and end with the category having the high value at the bottom, right before we give the sum or the total.

Table 9.1 contains just the actual or raw numbers of respondents to provide a first step in understanding a crosstabulation. Each of the six cells represents one of the possible joint frequencies from abortion and presidential vote. For example, 230 respondents to the 2008 National Election Study (NES) survey both were pro-choice *and* reported voting for Barack Obama, while 190 were pro-life and voted for John McCain. The marginals are the sums or totals of the number of cases in all the categories in a column or row. The marginal at the bottom of the first column, for instance, shows that there are 307 pro-lifers among these respondents (190 McCain voters + 117 Obama voters); and the marginal at the end of the second row shows that there are 405 people who voted for Obama (117 pro-lifers + 58 intermediates + 230 pro-choicers). These marginals, therefore, are really frequency counts for abortion and presidential vote, but they can differ somewhat from the frequency counts for the whole sample because the crosstabulation excludes as missing data anyone who did not *both* vote and state their position on abortion.

9.1.2 Showing the Relationship with Percentages

The purpose of crosstabulation is to see if a relationship exists between two items. Often this relationship can be specified deductively as a **hypothesis**. Here, the obvious hypothesis would be that people who are pro-choice on abortion should be much more likely than other Americans, especially those who are pro-life, to vote for Obama. Even the raw data in Table 9.1 confirm this expectation quite strongly. While Obama was supported by pro-choice supporters by approximately two-and-a-half-to-one (230 to 89), McCain handily carried those who took a pro-life position (190 to 117), as well as narrowly winning among the intermediates (70 to 58). Such relatively crude estimates, however, certainly suggest the value of a more comprehensible comparison than is provided by these raw numbers.

As for the frequency tables discussed in Chapter 2, **percentages** provide a standardized measure that is easy to compare and interpret, as is illustrated by Table 9.2 which provides the crosstabulation table for the relationship between abortion attitudes and Obama vote, with the relevant percentages added to the cells and marginals. For the six cells within the table, the columns for **the three categories of the independent variable abortion are percentagized** — that is, they add up to 100%, as indicated by the column marginals in the bottom row. In addition, the very bottom row of COLUMN MARGINALS reports two sets of percentages. The top one is the sum of the column percentages, which is 100%, unless there is a rounding error. The bottom is the row percentage which is the number of cases in that category of the independent variable divided by the total N. In Table 9.2, for example, the row percentages tell us that 41% of the respondents were pro-life, 17% were intermediate, and 42% were pro-choice.

Within the table, the column percentages can be compared to estimate the strength of the relationship. On the one hand, 72% of pro-choicers voted for Obama versus only 28% for McCain. In contrast, pro-lifers favored McCain 62% to 38%. This form of percentagizing is used because the hypothesized relationship between the two variables predicts, in essence, that the distribution of the dependent variable (presidential vote) will be different for the various categories or values of the independent variable (abortion). In particular, the normal hypothesis would be that pro-choice supporters should vote disproportionately for Obama, while pro-life advocates should be especially supportive of McCain.

Whether or not this is true can easily be seen by comparing the column percentages across one of the relevant rows in the table. As a rough convention, **compare the first and the last columns in the bottom row**, unless there is a strong substantive reason for making another comparison.[2] In Table 9.2, the percentage comparison for Obama voters in the bottom row is calculated by subtracting the 38%

---

[2] In particular, if the percentage of cases in the bottom row is considerably smaller than in the top row, it is probably better to use the top row for the percentage comparison. In addition, if either the dependent or independent variable is a nominal one, the logic for ordinal variables used here does not apply; and you should make percentage comparisons using categories based on substantive interest.

of votes that Obama received from pro-lifers on abortion (the first column) from the 72% he garnered from pro-choicers (the last column) for a total of 34% or percentage points, as reported by the first line under the table.

Percentage Comparison, Obama: 72% − 38% = 34%.

In terms of the substantive interpretation of the percentage comparison in Table 9.2, a rough scale for using the size of the percentage comparison to estimate the strength of the relationship is presented in Table 9.3. According to this scale, when the percentage comparison is over 30 percentage points, we can conclude that the relationship between the two variables in the table is strong. Therefore, this table indicates that abortion's impact on voting for president in 2008 was strong.

In sum, to use percentage comparisons in a crosstabulation, first **percentagize down the columns** or categories of the independent variable and then **compare across the rows** or categories of the dependent variable. If the independent variable has no influence on the dependent one, the percentages will be exactly the same across the row — creating what is called a **null relationship**. For example, if abortion had no impact whatsoever upon presidential vote in 2008, exactly the same percentage (54%) of pro-life, intermediate, and pro-choice people would have voted for Obama. In contrast, the greater the difference or percentage comparison is, the stronger is the association between the two items in question.

Table 9.3: Approximate strength of correlations and percentage comparisons.

Strength of relationship	Correlation coefficient	Percentage comparison
No Associations	0.00–0.14	0%–10%
Weak Association	0.15–0.25	11%–20%
Moderate	0.26–0.40	21%–30%
Strong Association	0.41–1.00	31%–100%

9.1.3 Correlation Coefficients for the Strength of Association

The **strength** of a relationship tells us how closely two variables are linked together. The strength of an association is measured by standardized **correlation coefficients**. They have a **minimum of zero for a null relationship** in which, as we have seen, the percentages are exactly the same in all the columns across a row in the crosstab. The highest possible value for a correlation coefficient is **one for a perfect relationship** in which the value or category of the dependent variable can be predicted exactly from the value of the independent variable. For a perfect relationship to exist in a crosstabulation, therefore, all the cases in each category of the independent variable must fall into a single category of the dependent item. In Tables 9.1 and 9.2, for instance, this would occur if all pro-choicers (100%) voted for Obama, all pro-lifers for McCain, and all intermediates for either candidate (it would not matter which one).

A number of correlation coefficients have been developed for nominal and ordinal data. They differ in exactly what characteristics of the relationship that they measure and, consequently, have differing strengths and weaknesses. To keep things from getting too confusing, **Gamma** will always be used in this text when both of the variables in a crosstabulation are **ordinal** ones; and **Lambda** will be used when one or both are **nominal**.[3] Table 9.3 contains a scale for estimating the strength of correlation coefficients, as well as percentage comparisons. In general, these are: 0.00 to 0.14 no association; 0.15 to 0.25 weak association; 0.26 to 0.40 moderate association; and over 0.40 strong association.

Gamma is the appropriate correlation coefficient for this relationship because both abortion attitudes and Obama vote have ordinal values. Here, the Gamma for the crosstab is reported in the second and bottom line under Table 9.2. Its value of +0.49 indicates a strong positive association between holding pro-choice beliefs and

---

[3] For a more technical treatment of these two correlation coefficients, see Hubert M. Blalock, Jr., *Social Statistics*, 2nd Edn. (New York: McGraw-Hill, 1972), pp. 424–426 for Gamma and pp. 302–303 for Lambda.

voting for Barack Obama, confirming the impression that resulted from just eyeballing the data in Table 9.1. Thus, even though there are "exceptions to the rule", such as the 38% of pro-lifers who voted for Obama, a voter's beliefs about abortion evidently played a key role in her or his decision about how to cast their presidential ballot in 2008.

Since both of the variables in Tables 9.1 and 9.2 are ordinal ones, the correlation coefficient between them can be either positive or negative. For a **specific hypothesis, the direction of the relationship is determined by the actual variables in the crosstab**. In the relationship between abortion and presidential vote, for example, the liberal pro-choice position would be predicted to have a positive association with voting for the Democratic candidate Barack Obama.

There are two easy ways to determine whether the relationship in a crosstab is positive or negative. The first and easiest is to look at the **sign of Gamma**. In Table 9.2, Gamma indeed is positive, as expected. Second, one can examine the **trend in percentages as you move across the bottom row** (excluding the marginals) in the table. If the percentages consistently go up, the relationship is positive; while if they consistently go down, it is negative. In Table 9.2, where Obama vote is in the bottom row of the table, the percentages certainly go up as one goes from the first column or low value of the independent variable (pro-life at 38%) through the middle value (intermediate at 45%) to the high value (pro-choice at 72%), confirming that a liberal position on abortion does indeed have a positive impact on Obama vote. To apply this test, however, you must remember to always use the bottom row.

9.1.4 Statistical Significance

Another approach to assessing whether the independent variable influences the dependent variable in a crosstab is to calculate the **statistical significance** of the relationship. Technically, statistical significance is the probability that the observed relationship in a sample occurred by random chance due to sampling error when the members of the sample were selected.[4] Putting this in terms of making an inference from a

---

[4] For a more detailed discussion of sampling error and how large it is likely to be, see the discussion of inferential statistics in Chapter 8.

sample to its population, statistical significance is the probability that there really is no association whatsoever between two variables in a population given the strength of the correlation between them in a representative sample. Thus, this represents the **probability that the null hypothesis of "no difference" among the categories of the independent variable holds true**. For example, how probable is it that the correlation in the population is zero if a Gamma in the sample is 0.05 or 0.20 or 0.45 or 0.80?

When this probability is quite low, the degree of association is considered to be **statistically significant** in the sense that we can assume that there is a real relationship between the two variables. Conventionally, a probability of 5% or less, what is termed the 0.05 level, is used to reject the null hypothesis that there really is no association between the two variables in the population, given the strength of the correlation between them in the sample. The probability that the null hypothesis is true is determined by a **test statistic**, like Z (see Chapter 8), which has a known distribution that can be used to give a precise estimate of how likely some outcome is. Because the population parameters are not usually known, Z (which requires knowing them) is not used that much in political science statistics. Rather, the major test statistics are F, t, and chi square.

Unlike asking whether a correlation coefficient is weak, moderate, or strong, we usually just indicate whether or not a relationship is statistically significant at a given level or probability, such as the 0.05 or 0.10 level. Thus, variations in the size of significance statistics are the opposite of those for correlation coefficients. That is, while higher correlation coefficients denote stronger relationships, smaller significance figures mean that a relationship is more significant.

The statistical significance of a correlation coefficient, like Gamma or Lambda, is influenced by two factors. First, the strength of the correlation itself is obviously key based on the assumption that stronger correlations should be more significant. That is, they are less likely to reflect random chance in sample selection rather than real association. Second, the size of the sample or number of cases included in the analysis is also important because more confidence can be placed in the results of a larger, rather than a smaller, sample. Because of the way in which statistical significance is calculated, therefore, the large size of the NES sample means that marginal associations can be statistically significant. For example, even the very weak Gamma of 0.12 between family income and conservative ideological self-identification in Table 9.5 is extremely significant at the 0.004 level. In such situations, however, the strength of the relationship is clearly more important. Thus, we should not pay much attention to a weak association, even if it is statistically significant.

There is no direct measure of statistical significance for either Gamma or Lambda, but statisticians have developed estimates which are termed the "approximate significance" of these correlation coefficients. The approximate significance for the crosstab of Obama vote by support for abortion is reported after Gamma on the bottom line underneath Table 9.2. Since the Gamma of 0.49 is strong; and the sample size (754) is fairly large, the relationship should be very highly significant. In fact, the level of significance reported is 0.00. This represents, incidentally, a rounding off of the real significance measure which must have been 0.004 or less. That is, the probability that the observed pattern of pro-choicers voting disproportionately for Obama and pro-lifers disproportionately for McCain occurred by random chance in picking the sample, rather than because ideology is really related to voting in the United States, is a minuscule 0.4% or less. Certainly, we can be confident that **ideology matters**.

9.2 TESTING THE SOCIOECONOMIC MODEL OF VOTING

The socioeconomic model of voting, which was developed in Chapter 3, posits a multi-stage process. In the first two stages, people with high socioeconomic status (SES) and with traditional values are hypothesized to be more likely than other Americans to be conservative ideologically; and, in the final stage, conservatives are presumed to have a strong tendency to be Republicans. Here, we shall see how crosstabulation analysis can be used to test this theoretical model. The first subsection presents the results of a correlation matrix summarizing the impact of a variety of political attitudes on presidential vote in 2008 and confirms the importance of ideology for voting behavior.

The second subsection then moves one step back in the model to explain Americans' ideologies using indicators of SES and traditional values as the explanatory factors. As will be seen, these results are somewhat weaker and more nuanced than for the relationship between ideology and partisanship.

9.2.1 Correlation Matrices: Testing the Impact of Ideology on Voting

The socioeconomic model of voting predicts that ideology should have a strong impact on voting in America, with conservatives favoring Republicans and liberals Democrats. The example of crosstabulation in the last section supported this theory since liberals on abortion strongly supported Obama, while McCain carried abortion conservatives by a large margin. There is no guarantee, of course, that this will hold true for many specific issues, though. For example, the skeptical could claim that only one variable is not sufficient to establish the linkage between ideology and partisanship, especially since there are at least three distinct issue areas (cultural, economic, and security) in contemporary American politics.

We could explore the impact of ideology on voting by computing and presenting numerous crosstabulation tables for the various indicators of ideological beliefs. One problem with this would be that the presentation of 10 or more crosstabs would take up quite a few pages of text. Since the correlation coefficient really summarizes the strength of the relationship in a crosstab (which is usually the principal information in which an analyst is interested), therefore, it makes sense (and saves considerable space) to present just the correlations when looking at more than a few relationships.

This is done in the **correlation matrix** in Table 9.4 which reports the Gammas for the correlations between Obama vote and 18 indicators of a person's ideology, including the correlation with abortion attitudes from Table 9.2. There are two columns in this table. The first gives the predicted direction of the relationship between an issue position and support for President Obama, based on the assumption that liberals should support and conservatives should oppose him. For example, a self-identified conservative should be less likely to be an Obama voter

Table 9.4: Correlations of issue positions with Bush vote.

	Predicted association with Obama vote	Gamma with Obama vote*
Overall Ideology		
Conservative	−	−0.77
Economic Issues		
More Government Services	+	0.57
Government Health Insurance	+	0.58
Environmental Protection	+	0.48
More Public School Spending	+	0.20
More Poor Spending	+	0.24
More Welfare Spending	+	0.13
More Child Care Spending	+	0.27
Cultural Issues		
Support Gay Marriage	+	0.55
Supports Gays in Military	+	0.38
Want More Gun Control	+	0.48
Pro-Choice on Abortion	+	0.49
Security Issues		
Approves War on Terror	−	−0.70
Approves Iraq War	−	−0.83
Approves Afghan War	−	−0.73
More Defense Spending	−	−0.44
More Crime Spending	−	−0.28
Support Death Penalty	−	−0.39

*All these gammas are statistically significant at the 0.004 level.

than other Americans, while someone who wants more government services should be more likely. The second column then gives the actual Gamma from the crosstabulation. For example, there is a correlation of −0.77 between Obama vote and conservative self-identification.

This form of presentation has the advantage of presenting a large amount of information concisely. For example, it is easy to see that all these items have correlations with voting which are in the predicted direction and are quite significant statistically. The disadvantage is that, unless the reader is fairly familiar with correlation coefficients, the results are not as easy to discern as in a full crosstabulation where the percentages can usually be interpreted even by the uninitiated.

Substantively, the correlations in Table 9.4 demonstrate that ideology does indeed exert a strong impact on voting but also that the strength of the individual relationships vary quite considerably. Conservative self-identification has an extremely strong association with presidential vote with a Gamma of -0.77. That is, conservatives tended to vote against and liberals for Barack Obama. With the partial exception of economic issues, furthermore, all three issue dimensions exerted a strong influence over voting in 2008.

In the economic realm, there was a clear division between philosophical divisions about the role of government and opinions about government spending in specific social welfare areas. The first three items under economic issues reflect general support for an activist government, including more government services and spending, government health insurance, and environmental protection. All of these items would be expected to be positively related to voting for Barack Obama and, indeed, they are with strong correlations of between 0.48 and 0.58. In contrast, support for increasing spending in four specific areas (for public schools, aiding the poor, welfare, and child care) are only weakly correlated with supporting Obama at the polls with Gammas between 0.13 and 0.27 (although all of these are statistically significant at the 0.004 level). Americans were fairly liberal on all these issues (see Table 2.4 in Chapter 2), suggesting that the effects of the Great Recession might have lessened the normal conservative–liberal divide on specific programs.

Four cultural issues were included in Table 9.4: support for gay marriage, more gays serving in the military, more gun control, and abortion rights. Since all of these are liberal positions, the variables would be expected to have positive correlations with Obama vote. This turns out to be the case, as they have strong or almost strong Gammas of 0.38 to 0.55 with casting ballots for Barack Obama. In relative terms, they are about equal in strength to the influence of the items concerning general philosophy about the role of government. Given the centrality of economic issues in the 2008 election,[5] these

---

[5] John Heilemann and Mark Halperin, *Game Change: Obama and the Clintons, McCain and Palin, and the Race of a Lifetime* (New York: HarperCollins, 2010).

strong correlations imply a continuing importance of cultural issues for voting.

The last area of national security produced by far the strongest Gammas in Table 9.4 with the exception of ideological self-identification. In particular, approval of the wars on terror in Iraq and Afghanistan influenced presidential voting very greatly, despite the fact that the first was popular and the second and third were not (see Table 2.6 in Chapter 2). These are all conservative attitudes; and their negative correlations were in the -0.70 to -0.83 range. There was also a strong negative Gamma of -0.44 between support for increased defense spending and Obama vote. In contrast, conservative concerns with domestic security, as indicated by support for more crime spending and for the death penalty, were only moderately correlated with voting against Obama. Consequently, America's wars appear to have been the most polarizing issue in the 2008 presidential race.

9.2.2 The Weaker Impact of SES and Traditional Values on Ideology

The lore of American politics, as long as almost anyone who is now alive can remember, is that the wealthy and businesspeople are conservative and vote Republican, and that the poor and workers are liberal and vote Democratic. More recently, the culture wars that emerged between conservatives and liberals in the 1980s[6] added a second important partisan cleavage that pits the holders of traditional values against the proponents of modernism and secularism. This subsection, hence, seeks to test the initial stage of the socioeconomic model of voting by examining the impact of affluence and traditional orientations upon ideology. Family income is used to measure SES; and traditional values are indicated by whether or not someone considers themselves a born again Christian.

Tables 9.5 to 9.6 present the crosstabs for the relationship of conservative ideology to having a high family income and being a born again Christian. Both of these relationships would be predicted to be

---

[6]James Davison Hunter, *Culture Wars: The Struggle to Define America* (New York: Basic Books, 1991).

Table 9.5: Crosstabulation of conservative by family income.

Ideology	Family income			
	Under $30,000	$30,000 to $75,000	Over $75,000	Total
Liberal	30%	28%	26%	28%
Moderate	30%	32%	21%	28%
Conservative	40%	40%	53%	44%
TOTAL	100%	100%	100%	100%

Note: Percent Comparison, Conservative:
53% − 40% = 13% or percentage points.
Gamma = 0.12   Approximate Sig. = 0.004.

Table 9.6: Crosstabulation of conservative by born again Christian.

Ideology	Born again Christian		
	No	Yes	Total
Liberal	32%	20%	28%
Moderate	31%	25%	28%
Conservative	37%	55%	44%
TOTAL	100%	100%	100%

Note: Percent Comparison, Conservative:
55% − 37% = 18% or percentage points.
Gamma = 0.31   Approximate Sig. = 0.004.

positive. This, indeed, turns out to be the case. In terms of strength, though, they vary considerably. Religiosity does have a moderate Gamma of 0.31 with conservatism. For example, 55% of the born again Christians are conservatives compared to 37% of those who are not. The association between affluence and conservatism is surprisingly limited, however, as the Gamma of 0.12 suggests that there is hardly any association between these two variables, although the relationship is statistically significant. Thus, at least at the time of the 2008 presidential election, traditional values appear to be replacing social class as the most important cleavage in the U.S. politics. These results also suggest that the initial stages in the socioeconomic model of voting are markedly weaker than the final one. That is, while ideology has a strong impact on partisanship, the linkage of background factors to ideology is considerably looser.

Table 9.7: Crosstabulation of conservative ideology by region.

	Region				
Ideology	Northeast	South	Interior West	West Coast	Total
Liberal	30%	23%	23%	41%	28%
Moderate	30%	30%	27%	25%	28%
Conservative	40%	47%	50%	34%	44%
TOTAL	100%	99%	100%	100%	100%

Lambda = 0.02 $\sqrt{\text{Lambda}}$ = 0.14   Approximate Sig. = 0.004.

Furthermore, to introduce an example using a nominal independent variable, regional variations in ideology are surprisingly muted. The now famous divide between Red States (Republican) and Blue States (Democratic)[7] suggests that there should be substantial regional variation in ideology. To test this supposition, Table 9.7 presents this relationship with America being divided into four regions: the Northeast, South, Interior West, and West Coast. The South and Interior West are generally considered the conservative heartland of the U.S., while the Northeast and West Coast are seen as more liberal.

The data in Table 9.7 are consistent with this image or stereotype. The Interior West and the South have significantly more conservatives (50% and 47%) than do the Northeast and the West Coast (40% and 34%); and the West Coast is the only region where there are more liberals (41%) than conservatives (34%). However, the overall strength of association between region and ideology is very weak. The Lambda for this nominal relationship is only 0.02. This correlation coefficient probably understates the strength of the relationship, though, because Lambda is really equivalent to the square of other correlation coefficients.[8] Thus, the square root ($\sqrt{\ }$) of Lambda should be used to estimate the strength in terms of the scale in Table 9.3. This is still

---

[7] For example, see Pew Foundation, *The 2005 Political Typology* (Washington, DC: The Pew Foundation, 2005).

[8] Lambda measures the percentage improvement in correct predictions of the value of the dependent variable that results from knowing the value of the independent variable. This is equivalent to the "percentage of explained variance" which is represented by the square of the correlation coefficient, Pearson's r, in regression (see the section on "Scatterplots and Regression Analysis: The Basics" in Chapter 11).

only 0.14 which denotes a weak association at most. Overall, therefore, these statistics indicate that, while regional differences in ideology can certainly be discerned, they are relatively weak and far less than the prevailing stereotype of a polarization between red states and blue states would imply.

We can also use crosstabulations to test a theory about how SES and traditional values differ somewhat in shaping public opinion. While both high SES and strong religiosity should make people more conservative, their impacts could well vary by issue area. In particular, religiosity should have a stronger influence than SES over people's attitudes about cultural issues since religion is especially relevant for establishing morality. Conversely, SES would be expected to be more important than religiosity in determining how Americans divide over "the politics of rich and poor".

Table 9.8 contains a correlation matrix in which high family income and being a born again Christian are used to explain attitudes about government services and abortion. Since liberals support both of these issues, we would expect all of these Gammas to be negative. These data generally support the theory but suggest a caveat as well. The data on economic issues follow expectations, although the correlation between family income and wanting more government services is surprisingly low. There was a low (almost moderate) negative relationship between family income and support for an expansive government (Gamma = −0.23), while religiosity had no association with attitudes about this economic issue (Gamma = −0.03). Also, as

Table 9.8: Correlations between demographic factors and indicators of economic and cultural liberalism.*

	High family income	Born again Christian
Want More Government Services	−0.23***	−0.03
Pro-Choice on Abortion	0.07**	−0.41***

*All correlation coefficients are Gammas.
**Statistically significant at 0.05 level.
***Statistically significant at 0.004 level.

expected, religiosity had a strong negative correlation with support for abortion rights (Gamma = −0.41), while there was little association between family income and abortion attitudes (Gamma = 0.07). What does depart from the socioeconomic model here, though, is that people with high income were actually slightly more liberal, not more conservative, than other Americans on abortion.

EXERCISES

1. Interpret the following crosstabulation table. First, discuss the theoretical model implied by the table. What are the independent and dependent variables? What is the logical hypothesis that would link them? Second, use the statistical results in the table to test this hypothesis. What is the direction of the relationship? Is it the one that you predicted? How strong is the relationship according to the three measures discussed in this text? Are these results what you would expect since the survey was taken while George Bush was still President? Why or why not?

Presidential vote	Bailout of Financial Industry		
	Wrong	Right	Total
McCain	56%	38%	45%
Obama	44%	62%	55%
TOTAL	100%	100%	100%

    Gamma = 0.35   Approximate Sig. = 0.004

2. Analyze the following correlation matrix for how attitudes on economic issues were related to voting for President Bush in 2004. What would be the hypothesis for each relationship? Is the correlation in the predicted direction? How strong is the association? Compare these results to the correlations between views on economic issues and Obama vote in 2008 in Table 9.4. What is

one major difference between these two sets of results? Why do you think this is so?

	Gamma with Bush vote*
More Government Services	−0.57
Government Health Insurance	−0.48
Pro-Tax Cuts	0.87
More Public School Spending	−0.69
More Poor Spending	−0.58
More Welfare Spending	−0.42

*Statistically significant at the 0.0004 level.

3. Conceptually, economic and culture issues seem quite different. Yet, we would probably expect that people who are conservative in one area would be conservative in the other. Use the following crosstab to examine how strongly attitudes in these two areas are related to each other in the contemporary United States. Which is an economic issue; and which is a cultural one? What are the conservative positions on each? Is the actual relationship in the predicted direction? How strong is it?

Government services	Abortion			
	Pro-life	Intermediate	Pro-choice	Total
Less	35%	30%	21%	28%
Same	24%	26%	21%	23%
More	41%	44%	58%	49%
TOTAL	100%	100%	100%	100%

Gamma = 0.23   Approximate Sig. = 0.004

Chapter

10

Multivariate Tables: More Nuanced Explanations for Conservative Attitudes and Behavior

The crosstabulations discussed in Chapter 9 provide an important first step in charting the causes and consequences of Americans' ideological positions. A more advanced sorting out of real causal influence can be done by applying **multivariate table analysis** to trace the relationships among three or more variables. In essence, this technique assesses whether a bivariate relationship between two variables (X and Y) might be affected by some third item (Z) which is termed the **control variable**. Separate crosstabulations are run between the independent and dependent variables for each category of the control variable. The results from these **subtables** are then compared to the original relationship; and different sets of findings imply various causal sequences among the control, independent, and dependent variables.

This chapter provides an overview of multivariate table analysis, illustrating the technique by showing how it can provide more complex or nuanced explanations of why the people in the 2008 National Election Study (NES) survey were conservative or liberal or why they voted for Barack Obama or John McCain than was possible with just the simple or bivariate crosstabulations discussed in Chapter 9. Section 10.1 describes the technique in detail. Sections 10.2 and 10.3 discuss the major types of relationships that can emerge when a control variable is added to a simple crosstabulation. Finally, Section 10.4 provides an overview of this technique.

10.1 MULTIVARIATE TABLES: THE TECHNIQUE

As an illustrative example, this section considers how controlling a person's gender affects the relationship between support for abortion and conservative ideology. Normally, a fairly strong negative relationship between abortion advocacy and conservative ideology would be expected because liberals are associated with a pro-choice position and conservatives with a pro-life one. In addition, gender might well shape the association between attitudes about abortion and ideology since abortion is widely viewed as the central issue of the Feminist Movement. This raises the question of how much of the simple or direct association between abortion and ideology might be affected by whether a person is a woman or a man.

An advanced technique called multivariate table analysis can be applied to sort out the relationships among three (and sometimes more) variables, such as gender, support for abortion, and conservatism. This technique begins with the simple or direct crosstabulation that shows the association between abortion views and ideology, which presumably will show that pro-choicers tend to be liberals and pro-lifers conservatives by considerable margins. Separate crosstabulations of ideology by position on abortion are then calculated for men and women. Finally, these two **subtables** are compared to the original crosstabulation and to each other in order to see whether and how controlling for gender affects the original relationship between stance on abortion and partisanship.

Table 10.1 presents the multivariate table to test the relationship between abortion attitudes and ideology in 2008 controlling for gender. The overall table has three components or subtables. The first presents the relationship between support for abortion and conservatism for all Americans. Clearly, this is a marked relationship in the predicted direction since advocates of a pro-life position were

Table 10.1: Multivariate table for the impact of support for abortion on conservative ideology controlling for gender.

All Americans

Ideology	Abortion position			
	Pro-life	Intermediate	Pro-choice	Total
Liberal	12%	23%	41%	26%
Moderate	28%	25%	21%	28%
Conservative	60%	52%	38%	46%
TOTAL	100%	100%	100%	100%

Gamma = −0.45   Approx. Sig. = 0.004

Subgroups

A. Men

Ideology	Abortion position			
	Pro-life	Intermediate	Pro-choice	Total
Liberal	13%	25%	29%	21%
Moderate	29%	22%	34%	29%
Conservative	58%	53%	37%	50%
TOTAL	100%	100%	100%	100%

Gamma = −0.27   Approx. Sig. = 0.004

B. Women

Ideology	Abortion position			
	Pro-life	Intermediate	Pro-choice	Total
Liberal	10%	20%	50%	30%
Moderate	28%	29%	29%	28%
Conservative	62%	51%	21%	42%
TOTAL	100%	100%	100%	100%

Gamma = −0.59   Approx. Sig. = 0.004

much more likely (60% to 38%) than pro-choice supporters to be conservatives. Overall, the correlation (Gamma) of −0.45 denotes a strong relationship, confirming our original hypothesis.

This **initial table for the full or entire sample** is then followed by two tables which **divide the sample into two groups** — the first or top one is for men; and the second or bottom one is for women. Note that, in at least one important regard, multivariate table analysis does not involve any new statistics beyond those used in simple crosstabulations. Both these subtables contain column percentages, row and column marginals, Gamma correlation coefficients, and estimates of statistical significance, just like the simple crosstabulations that were described in Chapter 9, but no new statistics are presented. Rather, in multivariate table analysis, you just need to compare these statistics for several crosstabulations.

The most important facet of interpreting a multivariate table rests in the comparison of the strength and direction of the relationship in the original table for all the cases with the results for the two or more subsets of cases defined by the values of the control variable. If all these relationships are the same, the control variable has no effect on the original relationship and, consequently, can be dropped from the analysis. Conversely, if the nature of the relationship in one or more of the subtables differs significantly from the original crosstabulation, the control variable is vital for understanding the nature of the original relationship. Furthermore, the pattern in which the crosstabulations within a multivariate table differ determines the type of multivariate relationship that exists, as will be described in the next two sections.

The middle crosstab in Table 10.1 for men shows that the negative relationship between support for abortion and conservatism is somewhat weaker for them than it is for all Americans. Among this group, 58% of the pro-lifers and 37% of the pro-choicers identified themselves as conservatives, creating a Gamma of -0.27 which is markedly below the one of -0.45 in the original table. For women, in contrast, the relationship between abortion attitudes and ideology is markedly stronger than for the population as a whole. The Gamma is -0.59, as 62% of pro-life women but only 21% of pro-choice ones called themselves conservative. Thus, the issue of abortion appears to be more important to women than to men because it affects their ideological identification to a considerably greater extent.

To sum, this multivariate table tells us several things. First, there is a fairly strong tendency for support for abortion to be negatively correlated with conservatism, as would certainly be expected. Second, introducing gender as an explicit control variable shows that this relationship is decidedly stronger for women than for men. That is, this issue is more important for determining women's overall ideology than men's.

10.2 REVEALING AND REPLICATING RELATIONSHIPS

This section discusses two of the major types of relationships that can emerge in multivariate table analysis. It begins by defining and giving examples of these two possible outcomes of introducing a control variable. A substantive illustration is then provided by showing how these two effects indicate whether or not a particular issue affects the votes of one group more than another.

10.2.1 Revealing Relationships

The results from the multivariate table in Table 10.1 represent one type of effect that occurs when a control variable is applied to a simple or direct relationship. In essence, we start with a relationship between an independent variable X (support for abortion) and a dependent variable Y (identifying with a conservative ideology) and see what happens when a control variable Z (gender) is introduced.

What happens in this particular case is that a **conditional relationship** emerges. Views about abortion affect the ideology of women more strongly than the ideology of men. For example, the difference in the Gammas for the two groups (-0.59 and -0.27) is 0.32, which is triple the absolute difference of 0.10 that is the commonly accepted standard for judging whether or not two such correlations differ significantly in their strength. That is, as depicted schematically in Figure 10.1, a person's gender creates a condition which determines the strength of the association between support for abortion and conservatism —

Figure 10.1: Arrow diagram for revealing effect for attitudes about abortion's (X) impact on ideology (Y) controlling for gender (Z).

strong for women but only moderate for men. This might also be called the **revealing effect** in multivariate table analysis because the condition of the control variable reveals or defines situations in which the nature and the strength of the relationship between the independent and dependent variables differ.[1] Thus, you need to know what the condition of the control variable or Z is to anticipate how strongly X and Y will be related.

10.2.2 Replicating Relationships

The revealing effect is only one of several possible outcomes in multivariate table analysis — and one of the most dramatic at that. The least dramatic but one of the most common is what is called the **replicating effect** which occurs when the control variable has no effect on the bivariate relationship. Such an outcome is represented in Table 10.2 for the relationship between support for increasing government services and conservative ideology controlling for gender. We would expect that there should be a negative association here since conservatives prefer small government. The top table for the whole population demonstrates that this is certainly true, as indicated by the strong Gamma of -0.50. For example, 74% of the people who want to cut government called themselves conservatives, in very sharp contrast to the only 31% of supporters for expanding government who were conservative ideologically.

Unlike abortion which is widely assumed to be more important for women than for men, there is little reason to suppose that men and women would react much differently to this issue regarding the role of the government. Indeed, the relationship between views about government services and ideology is almost exactly the same for women and for men. The Gamma for women is -0.51, while the one for men is -0.49; and both are almost exactly equal to the one for the total

---

[1] The idea of labeling the different effects in multivariate tables with names alliterating with the letter r is taken from Dickinson McGaw and George Watson, *Political and Social Inquiry* (New York: John Wiley, 1976), pp. 437–444. The names that they used for specific effects differ somewhat from the ones used here, though.

Table 10.2: Multivariate table for the impact of support for more government services on conservatism controlling for gender.

All Americans

Ideology	Government services			
	Cut	Keep same	Increase	Total
Liberal	9%	23%	38%	27%
Moderate	17%	38%	31%	28%
Conservative	74%	39%	31%	45%
TOTAL	100%	100%	100%	100%

Gamma = −0.50   Approx. Sig. = 0.004

Subgroups

A. Men

Ideology	Government services			
	Cut	Keep same	Increase	Total
Liberal	8%	24%	33%	22%
Moderate	16%	33%	33%	28%
Conservative	76%	43%	34%	50%
TOTAL	100%	100%	100%	100%

Gamma = −0.49   Approx. Sig. = 0.004

B. Women

Ideology	Government services			
	Cut	Keep same	Increase	Total
Liberal	11%	22%	43%	30%
Moderate	17%	43%	29%	29%
Conservative	72%	35%	28%	41%
TOTAL	100%	100%	100%	100%

Gamma = −0.51   Approx. Sig. = 0.004

population (−0.50) Hence, the two subtables replicate the original crosstabulation. As sketched in Figure 10.2, therefore, the control variable (Z) has no effect upon the relationship between the independent variable (X) and the dependent one (Y). In this instance, consequently, the control variable can simply be ignored.

Figure 10.2: Arrow diagram for replicating effect for support for more government service's (X) impact on ideology (Y) controlling for gender (Z).

10.2.3 Do Issues Influence One Group More than Another?

One important application of the difference between revealing and replicating relationships is to explore whether a particular issue is more important to one group than another in terms of how it affects their voting. For example, let us consider the positive relationship between support for increasing government services and voting for Barack Obama. This is an economic issue that is presumably important to both the poor and the rich. The poor should be motivated to vote for Democrats because they can benefit from that party's program of expanding government services, while the rich should vote for Republicans because they can benefit from the lower taxes that a decrease in government services would allow. Both these tendencies are widely assumed to be at work in most American elections. However, if one is notably stronger than the other, this should be quite significant politically because it would favor one or the other of our major parties.

Table 10.3 presents the multivariate table that allows us to compare the relative strength of how the rich and the poor respond to the issue of government services. The top crosstabulation for all Americans shows that views on government services had a strong association with presidential voting in 2008 in the hypothesized positive direction. Barack Obama received 71% of the ballots cast by those who wanted more spending and services by the federal government but only 21% of the votes from those who wanted less. This created a very strong Gamma of 0.65.

There is no *a priori* or logical reason to expect that the issue of the general size and role of government would be more important to the rich or poor since, as argued above, both have a material stake in this issue. The statistics in Table 10.3 are quite clear cut on this

Table 10.3: Multivariate table for the impact of support for more government services on Obama vote controlling for family income.

All Americans

Presidential vote	Government services			
	Cut	Keep same	Increase	Total
McCain	79%	45%	29%	48%
Obama	21%	55%	71%	52%
TOTAL	100%	100%	100%	100%

Gamma = 0.65   Approx. Sig. = 0.004

Subgroups

A. Family Income Under $30,000

Presidential vote	Government services			
	Cut	Keep same	Increase	Total
McCain	47%	52%	29%	37%
Obama	53%	48%	71%	63%
TOTAL	100%	100%	100%	100%

Gamma = 0.34   Approx. Sig. = 0.004

B. Family Income Over $30,000

Presidential vote	Government services			
	Cut	Keep same	Increase	Total
McCain	85%	44%	28%	53%
Obama	15%	56%	72%	47%
TOTAL	100%	100%	100%	100%

Gamma = 0.72   Approx. Sig. = 0.004

question, however. Views on government services influenced the votes of wealthier Americans considerably more than those of their less affluent compatriots. For example, the correlation coefficient Gamma is much higher for the subsample of those whose family income exceeded $30,000 than for the subsample of those with family incomes below that figure (0.72 to 0.34). This should be good news for Republicans since it implies that their constituents are more turned on than a key group of the Democrats' supporters by a central issue in American politics.

10.3 REMOVING AND REDUCING RELATIONSHIPS

This section discusses removing and reducing relationships, the two other principal types of effects that might be produced by multivariate table analysis discussed in this chapter. These two effects are somewhat more complex than the revealing and replicating relationships described in the last section. The nature of the removing relationship differs fundamentally depending upon whether the control variable is antecedent to or intervening between the two items in the initial analysis. Reducing relationships, for their part, involve more complex causal connections among the control, independent, and dependent variables.

10.3.1 Removing Relationships

Perhaps the most dramatic effect of introducing a control variable in multivariate table analysis is what is called a **removing relationship**. For this to occur, there has to be a significant direct association between the independent and dependent variables (X and Y) in the original crosstabulation. When the control variable (Z) is introduced, however, the correlation between X and Y vanishes or falls below the line for no association in all of the subtables defined by the categories of Z. Thus, this is termed a removing relationship because adding the control variable removes the direct or observed association between X and Y.

While the theoretical literature posits many such causal situations, a complete removing relationship is very hard to find in the relationships involving presidential voting and ideology. First, as we saw in Chapter 9, the indicators of socioeconomic status (SES) and traditional roles only have weak-to-moderate correlations with ideology and voting. Thus, using them as controls cannot explain the entire association that, for example, ideology and partisanship have with each other. Second, almost all political attitudes are influenced by several factors, rather than simply being the result of a single causal impact. Thus, controlling only one of these influences will not entirely eradicate the effects of the other independent variables.

Consequently, the illustration of a removing relationship used here turns to hypothetical data and a fanciful comparison of competing theories not directly related to politics, at least before the emergence of the culture wars in the United States. The importance of not just accepting a direct correlation but searching for a removing relationship is suggested by an example in which the initial association is obviously ridiculous. This involves the seemingly scientific question of how babies are born. In the days before sex education and Marilyn Manson, mothers used to tell their young children, when they asked about where babies came from, that storks brought their younger brothers and sisters in order to preserve an "age of innocence". If one wanted to conduct a normal social science test of this theory, it would seem easy to correlate the number of storks and the births rates in various countries around the world.

As the hypothetical data in multivariate Table 10.4 indicate, the bivariate crosstabulation would strongly support this hypothesis. Of the 80 nations with large stork populations, 65% have high birth rates, compared to just 40% of the 120 countries where storks are hard to find, producing a fairly strong relationship with a Gamma of 0.47. Perhaps the heated debate between Surgeon General Joycelyn Elders and the Christian Coalition in the early 1990s over how best to attack teenage pregnancy (sex education vs. abstinence education) was totally irrelevant! To protect young girls, all we need to do is have a 365-day hunting season for storks.

Luckily for those who believe in the validity of scientific explanations of human reproduction, it is easy to find a control variable that removes the initial or direct stork–baby correlation. Storks like it hot; and evidently so do lovers, both young and old. Thus, both birth rates and stork populations are much higher near the equator than in arctic climes. Consequently, in the two subtables for countries that are, respectively, close to and far away from the equator, there is absolutely no association between the number of storks and the number of babies.

The interpretation of such a removing effect depends critically upon the presumed causal sequence between the control and independent variables, as indicated by the two arrow diagrams in Figure 10.3. If the control variable Z can be seen as the cause of both X and Y, the association between the independent and dependent variables is

Table 10.4: Multivariate table for the hypothetical impact of stork population on birth rate controlling geography.

All Nations

Birth rate	Storks		
	Few	Many	Total
Low	72 (60%)	28 (35%)	100 (50%)
High	48 (40%)	52 (65%)	100 (50%)
TOTAL	120	80	200

Gamma = 0.47   Approx. Sig. = 0.000

Subgroups

A. Near Equator

Birth rate	Storks		
	Few	Many	Total
Low	8 (20%)	12 (20%)	20 (20%)
High	32 (80%)	48 (80%)	80 (80%)
TOTAL	40	60	100

Gamma = 0.00   Approx. Sig. = 0.98

B. Far From Equator

Birth rate	Storks		
	Few	Many	Total
Low	64 (80%)	16 (80%)	80 (80%)
High	16 (20%)	4 (20%)	20 (20%)
TOTAL	80	20	100

Gamma = 0.00   Approx. Sig. = 0.98

termed **spurious**. That is, there is no real association between the two items, but one appears in the direct or bivariate crosstabulation because the control variable is related to each of them. A different pattern exists when Z is assumed to be an intervening variable between X and Y. In this case, the intervening control variable provides an **interpretation** or **explanation** for the observed relationship between X and Y.

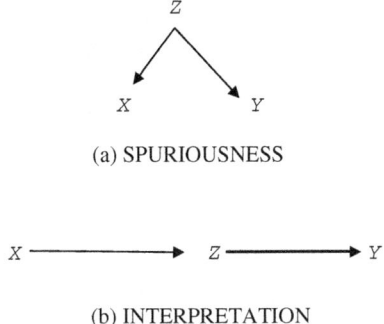

Figure 10.3: Arrow diagrams for the two types of removing effects.

The example of storks and babies is clearly the first type of a **spurious** association. Certainly, storks are not really connected with the process of how babies are born, even though at first glance lots of storks can be found where there are lots of babies. Thus, you should now be able to appreciate the old social science saying "**correlation does not necessarily prove or mean causation**". In many instances, though, spurious associations are far more sensible. For example, suppose that there are strong correlations both between high family income and opposition to more government services and between wanting more services and voting for Obama. In such a case, controlling for position on government services might well remove the observed association between family income and presidential vote. Here, however, we would not say that the relationship between high income and voting against Obama is ridiculous. Rather, the control factor is an intervening variable between the independent and dependent variables which provides an **interpretation** of the initial relationship.

10.3.2 Reducing Relationships

While a full removing relationship is quite hard to find in the linkages among the variables that we have been analyzing, what might be termed **partial removing relationships** are fairly common. In fact, they constitute a fourth possible outcome of introducing a control variable that is called the **reducing effect**. A reducing effect occurs when the correlations in the subtables are substantially lower than the

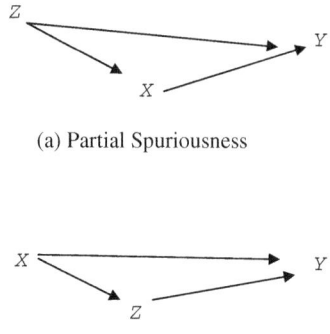

(a) Partial Spuriousness

(b) Partial Interpretation

Figure 10.4: Arrow diagram for reducing effect for relationships among three variables.

original bivariate association but are still above zero. As illustrated by Figure 10.4, both X and Z are really independent variables that exert separate effects upon Y. In addition, there is a significant relationship between them. Thus, such a multivariate relationship reflects partial or reduced spuriousness (if Z causes X) or interpretation (if X causes Z). In a reducing relationship, both X and Z exercise independent effects on Y. Thus, X and Z are interrelated independent variables for explaining the dependent variable Y. Because of the interrelationship between X and Z, their impact on Y overlaps. Consequently, controlling for Z removes the overlapping influence and, thus, reduces the original or uncontrolled correlation between X and Y.

This logic in multivariate table analysis can be applied to the question of whether specific issues influence voting beyond the effect exercised by general ideology. As sketched in Figure 10.5, voters' attitudes on specific issues, such as supporting abortion or increased spending for homeland security, contribute to their general ideology or overall attraction to conservatism or liberalism (Path A in Figure 10.5). In turn, a person's overall ideology is generally a strong determinant of her or his support of Democrats or Republicans at the polls (Path C). What remains a somewhat open question, though, is whether attitudes on a specific issue have any independent impact on voting (Path B) once the effect of general ideology is taken into account. This can be determined by a multivariate table in which the relationship between

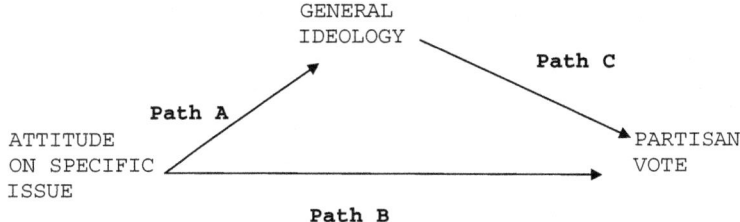

Figure 10.5: Model of relationships among attitudes about a specific issue, general ideology, and partisanship in voting.

position on a specific issue and presidential vote is controlled for general ideology. Since ideology is the intervening variable, this is a case of interpretation. If attitudes about the issue in question are just part of a larger ideological syndrome, controlling ideology should produce a removing relationship. In contrast, if the issue influences voting over and beyond the effects of ideology, a reducing relationship will emerge.

Table 10.5 presents the multivariate table for the relationships of support for gay marriage with Obama vote controlling for whether or not a respondent is a conservative. This table depicts a reducing relationship. As would well be expected, the initial correlation between support for gay marriage and Obama vote is a strongly positive one with a Gamma of 0.56. When the NES sample is broken up into two groups with conservatives in one and liberals and moderates in the other, the correlations in the subsamples drop considerably by almost 0.20 to 0.38 for conservatives and 0.37 for moderates and liberals. Clearly, therefore, attitudes about gay marriage *per se* influenced voting in the 2008 presidential elections beyond the tendency for conservatives to support McCain and liberals to vote for Obama. This suggests that, despite the current stereotype of partisan and ideological polarization in the United States, a considerable degree of issue complexity still remains.

10.4 AN OVERVIEW OF THE EFFECTS OF MULTIVARIATE TABLES

Multivariate table analysis, to sum, takes an original crosstabulation showing the impact of an independent variable X on a dependent variable Y and separates or breaks it down into individual subtables, one

Table 10.5: Multivariate table for the impact of support for gay marriage on Obama vote controlling for conservatism.

All Americans

Presidential vote	Gay marriage			
	Oppose	Civil unions	Support	Total
McCain	63%	56%	21%	46%
Obama	37%	44%	79%	54%
TOTAL	100%	100%	100%	100%

Gamma = 0.56   Approx. Sig. = 0.004

Subgroups

A. Liberals and Moderates

Presidential vote	Gay marriage			
	Oppose	Civil unions	Support	Total
McCain	36%	26%	16%	23%
Obama	64%	74%	84%	77%
TOTAL	100%	100%	100%	100%

Gamma = 0.37   Approx. Sig. = 0.004

B. Conservatives

Presidential vote	Gay marriage			
	Oppose	Civil unions	Support	Total
McCain	79%	84%	39%	74%
Obama	21%	16%	61%	26%
TOTAL	100%	100%	100%	100%

Gamma = 0.38   Approx. Sig. = 0.004

for each category of a control variable Z. Thus, the **control variable is physically held constant** so we can see what happens under each specified condition. As summarized in Table 10.6, the second and third sections of this chapter outlined the most prominent types of relationships that can emerge in such an analysis. As the table shows, each type of relationship represents a different causal sequence among Z, X, and Y; and, quite importantly, each is defined by a specific pattern of Gammas in the original table as compared to the two subtables.

Table 10.6: Summary of control effects.*

Effect	Causal interpretation	Pattern of correlations
Replicating	Z does not affect $X - Y$ association	Gamma = Gamma$_1$ = Gamma$_2$
Revealing	$X - Y$ association varies according to value of Z	Gamma$_1 \neq$ Gamma$_2$
Removing	Z explains all $X - Y$ association: SPURIOUS: $Z \longrightarrow X$ Interpretation: $X \longrightarrow Z$	Gamma > Gamma$_1$ = Gamma$_2$ = 0
Reducing	X and Z are inter-related independent variables	Gamma > Gamma$_1$ = Gamma$_2$ > 0

*Assumes control variable has two subcategories.
Z is the control variable; X is the independent variable; and Y is the dependent variable.
Gamma is the Gamma for the original bivariate table; and Gamma$_1$ and Gamma$_2$ are the Gamma's in the two subtables.

In the **replicating effect**, the control variable has no effect on the relationship between X and Y. Thus, the Gammas in both the subtables are the same as the original one. In the **revealing effect**, the nature of the relationship between X and Y differs, depending on what the value of Z is. Therefore, the Gammas in the two subtables must differ significantly. In a **removing relationship**, the control variable accounts for the direct association between X and Y. The initial relationship must be significant but in the control tables the value of Gamma approaches zero. The interpretation of a removing relationship is quite different, furthermore, depending on whether Z is assumed to cause X (spuriousness) or whether X is assumed to cause Z (interpretation). A **reducing relationship** can be thought of as being halfway between the replicating and removing ones in that the Gammas in the subtables are significantly below the original one for the full sample but still above zero, as well as being equal to each other. The causal interpretation here is that X and Z are interdependent factors that both influence Y.

Multivariate table analysis possesses both significant advantages and disadvantages. On the decidedly positive side, it allows more sophisticated analysis than can be accomplished with simple crosstabulation, in the sense that the initial association between two variables may well be altered dramatically after the effects of a third or control variable are taken into account. In addition, applying multivariate table analysis forces us to be explicit and systematic in our theories and in the causal models or sequences that they lay out.

However, there are also two distinct disadvantages to this approach. First, it does not permit the measurement of the combined impact of two explanatory factors upon a dependent variable. For example, family income has a weak relationship with conservative ideology, while religiosity shares a moderate relationship with it (see Tables 9.5 and 9.6 in Chapter 9). It would certainly be valuable to know how strong their combined impact is. Unlike multiple regression (see Chapter 12) and logistic regression (Chapter 13), however, multivariate table analysis cannot determine this. Second, while it is possible to add fourth or fifth variables to a multivariate table analysis, this is not very practical for two technical reasons. The number of subtables becomes so large that a coherent interpretation is difficult; and the number of cases in each subtable can easily drop below the level (50 to 100) where much confidence or statistical significance can be put in the results. In sum, multivariate table analysis can provide valuable information, but it also suffers from important limitations.

EXERCISES

1. Interpret the following multivariate table: (1) Briefly discuss the original bivariate table showing the relationship between X and Y: What hypothesis is being tested? How strongly is it supported? (2) Discuss the control variable Z: What is it? Why might it be expected to affect the nature of the association between X and Y? (3) Discuss the strength of the relationship in each subtable; (4) Indicate which type of causal situation the multivariate table depicts: (a) replicating, (b) reducing, (c) removing (spurious correlation or interpretation), or (d) revealing. Does adding the control variable alter the interpretation in the original bivariate crosstabulation? Do these results suggest that the issue in question is more important to either of the two groups? If so, which group it is? Is this, what you would logically expect?

MULTIVARIATE TABLE FOR THE IMPACT OF SUPPORT FOR GAY MARRIAGE ON OBAMA VOTE CONTROLLING FOR WHETHER SOMEBODY IS A BORN AGAIN CHRISTIAN.

All Americans

Presidential vote	Gay marriage			
	Not allow	Civil Un.	Allow	Total
McCain	63%	56%	21%	45%
Obama	37%	44%	79%	55%
TOTAL	100%	100%	100%	100%

Gamma = 0.59   Approx. Sig. = 0.004

Subgroups

A. Not a Born Again Christian

Presidential vote	Gay marriage			
	Not allow	Civil Un.	Allow	Total
McCain	56%	54%	21%	41%
Obama	44%	46%	79%	59%
TOTAL	100%	100%	100%	100%

Gamma = 0.40   Approx. Sig. = 0.004

B. Born Again Christian

Presidential vote	Gay Marriage			
	Not allow	Civil Un.	Allow	Total
McCain	66%	64%	25%	59%
Obama	34%	37%	75%	41%
TOTAL	100%	100%	100%	100%

Gamma = 0.49   Approx. Sig. = 0.004

2. Suppose you wanted to see whether attitudes about the military affected the votes of people with traditional values more than those of other Americans. Design a multivariate table that would do this. Then present two sets of hypothetical results: one that supports this hypothesis and one that does not.
3. Design a multivariate table that shows a removing relationship when some demographic factor is used as the control variable for the association between a political attitude and voting for Barack Obama in 2008. What is the original hypothesis? What happens when the control variable is added? Present hypothetical data for the table.

Part IV

Discovering Relationships for Interval Data

Chapter 11

Regression Analysis: International Patterns and Benchmarks for American Performance

This chapter discusses the most widely used technique for measuring the relationship between two variables at the interval level of measurement, such as Gross Domestic Product (GDP) per capita or the infant mortality rate. This is known as the **regression and correlation analysis**, along with the graphical presentation of these results in a **scatterplot**. Two stages of the analysis will be presented. The first examines relationships among the economic, political, and social indicators discussed in Chapter 2. This raises such questions as: Do countries that are richer have higher levels of investment, lower levels of infant mortality, and so forth? Do countries with larger governments have poorer growth records, longer life expectancies, etc.

Note that the first set of questions concerns the effects of national **resource bases**, while the second concerns the effects of national **policies**. Especially when objective resource conditions are being modeled, such analysis allows us to establish empirically international **benchmarks** that depict how well a country is doing taking its resource base into account. Thus, a second stage of analysis is to evaluate the performance of individual nations in terms of whether their economic and social outcomes are better or worse than would be predicted for them based on such factors as their relative affluence.

Basically, these analyses will ask what the principal determinants of the economic and social performance of developed nations are. Since conservatives and liberals differ drastically on this question, the empirical results should tell us which view, if either, of how the world works is more realistic. For **economic performance**, conservatives provide the prevailing theory with their hypothesis:

> The free operation of markets promotes efficiency; therefore, the larger the government and the greater the state intervention in the economy which big government brings, the worse its economic performance will be.

For **social performance**, in contrast, it is the liberal hypothesis that is the most prevalent:

> State assistance is necessary to prevent the normal operations of capitalism from producing an unacceptably high level of social inequality and distress; therefore, the more comprehensive the welfare state, the more equitable social outcomes will be.

Finally, note also the problem that we face if both the prevailing hypotheses — conservative on economic performance and liberal on social performance — turn out to be true. What promotes economic progress retards social progress!

This chapter begins with a description of how to interpret scatterplots and the basic correlation and regression statistics. Once we have learned how to understand and use these statistical results, Section 11.2 then applies regression analysis to the substantive question of how well the conservative and liberal hypotheses about the effects of government size apply to the advanced industrial nations in today's world. The final two parts then turn to more technical subjects about this statistical technique. Section 11.3 shows how regression can be used as a benchmarking tool to assess how well individual countries are performing; and Section 11.4 discusses several assumptions underlying regression analysis.

11.1 SCATTERPLOTS AND REGRESSION ANALYSIS: THE BASICS

The basic logic of regression analysis is that, if a relationship exists between two variables, the values of the dependent variable or the effect should vary in a systematic manner according to the different scores on the independent variable or the cause. In regression analysis, **scatterplots** are used to provide a summary picture of the relationship between two interval-level variables. A scatterplot plots each case on a two-dimensional graph according to its values on the dependent and independent variables. A statistical technique called **regression analysis** can then be applied to describe the relationship that best charts the pattern of the scatterplot. The **correlation coefficient** r tells us how strong this relationship is and whether it is positive or negative. In addition, **the regression coefficient** b provides a precise measure of how much change in the dependent variable is produced by a given increase in the independent variable. Finally, several methods of calculating the **statistical significance** of the relationship or the probability that it occurred by random chance are available.

11.1.1 Constructing a Scatterplot

As an example of a scatterplot, let us consider the relationship between GNP growth and the size of government. Conservatives predict that there should be a strong negative one, while liberals question the *laissez-faire* assumption that big government stifles economic performance. To keep the presentation of the scatterplot simple, we will start with just five countries that seem very appropriate for this analysis. Two, the Netherlands and Sweden are considered models of a highly developed welfare state. In contrast, the United States under President Ronald Reagan and the United Kingdom under Prime Minister Margaret Thatcher had conservative governments during the 1980s which enacted *laissez-faire* reforms, creating what many considered to be the antithesis of a welfare state. Finally, Japan appeared to be an emerging economic superpower, at least during the 1970s and 1980s; so, it is also included in the analysis. Since the major political changes in America

Table 11.1: National profiles of government size and economic growth for five sample nations, 1980s.

Country	All government spending % GDP, 1980	GNP growth, 1980–1989
Sweden	62%	1.8%
Netherlands	61%	1.7%
United Kingdom	45%	2.6%
United States	34%	3.3%
Japan	31%	4.0%

and Britain during the Reagan and Thatcher administrations occurred in the 1980s, this analysis begins with that decade.

Table 11.1 presents the raw data for these nations on the spending of all levels of government as a percentage of GDP in 1980 (to indicate the size of government) and average annual economic growth during 1980–1989 (to indicate economic performance). Note that government size is measured at the beginning of the period under consideration because the nature of government in a particular year can only affect economic growth after that point in time. The five countries are listed in descending order of government size. As would be expected, the two welfare states have by far the largest governments that spent slightly over 60% of their GDP, almost twice as much as the United States at 34% and Japan at 31%. The U.S. then lives up to its stereotype for small government, but the low level of public spending in Japan might be surprising to those who are not fairly familiar with that nation's political economy, given Japan's well-deserved reputation for substantial state intervention in the economy.[1] Finally, the UK is in the middle at 45% — which is high enough to suggest that early in Thatcher's administration, the UK government was not all that "lean and mean".

Turning to the second column on GNP growth rate, the conservative prediction that larger governments would turn in worse economic performances is very strongly supported by even the most cursory

---

[1] Ezra F. Vogel, *Japan as Number One: Lessons for America* (Cambridge: Harvard University Press, 1979).

eyeballing of the data. As one reads down the table from row to row going from larger governments to smaller ones, the economic growth rates go up with the exception of a very slight reversal between Sweden at 1.8% and the Netherlands at 1.7%. The two smallest governments, Japan and the U.S., grew markedly faster than the others, at 4.0% and 3.3%, about twice as fast as the two large welfare states. In addition, Britain with its medium-sized government had an average growth rate of 2.6% which was in the middle between the big governments and the small governments.

This relationship between government size and economic performance for the five nations under analysis can be presented graphically in a **scatterplot** which presents the data in a two-dimensional graph where Y represents the vertical axis and X represents the horizontal axis. Since we normally assume that government size should influence overall economic growth, it is the independent variable; and GNP growth is the dependent one. Conventionally, **dependent variables are denoted by** Y and plotted along the vertical axis of the graph, while **independent variables are denoted by** X and plotted along the horizontal axis. The scatterplot in Figure 11.1, then, consists of five dots — each one representing a case or country — placing it in the graph in terms of its economic growth rate and size of government. For example, the United States had a growth rate of 3.3% and a government spending/GDP ratio of 34%. Thus, its dot is placed at the spot in the graph which corresponds to the intersection of 3.3 on the vertical Y-axis and 34 on the horizontal X-axis.

In the scatterplot in Figure 11.1, this produces a pattern in which the dots follow a downward slope from left to right. That is, the further to the right a country is on the horizontal axis, the lower is its position on the vertical axis. Or, in terms of the actual variables, the higher its government spending is relative to GDP, the lower its economic growth rate will be. A downward sloping pattern indicates a negative relationship in which higher values on the independent variable produce lower values or scores on the dependent variable. The data in this figure, therefore, definitely correspond to the conservative prediction that larger government should bring deteriorating economic performance.

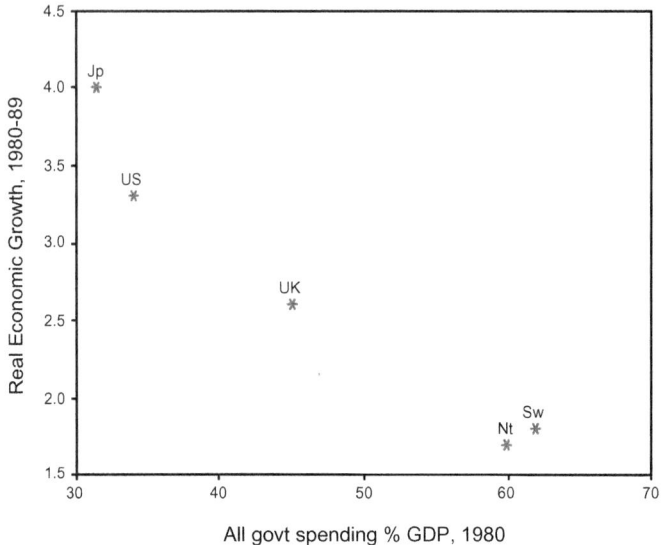

Figure 11.1: Scatterplot of government size and economic performance for five sample nations, 1980s.

11.1.2 The Regression Line as a Summary of the Scatterplot

Regression analysis provides a precise estimation of what the nature of the relationship depicted by a scatterplot is. In essence, regression calculates the straight line that best describes the pattern of dots in the scatterplot. The **regression line** for the scatterplot in Figure 11.1 is drawn in Figure 11.2; and the associated regression statistics are presented under the figure. As would be expected from eyeballing the individual dots, this line slopes downward and to the right. For reasons that we thankfully do not have to pursue here, the regression line is defined by drawing it so that **the sum of the squared vertical distance of all the dots from the regression line is minimized**. This is why, incidentally, regression is often called **Ordinary Least Squares** because its model is based on minimizing the squared deviations from the regression line.

Technically, it plots a straight line satisfying the equation:

$$Y = a + bX.$$

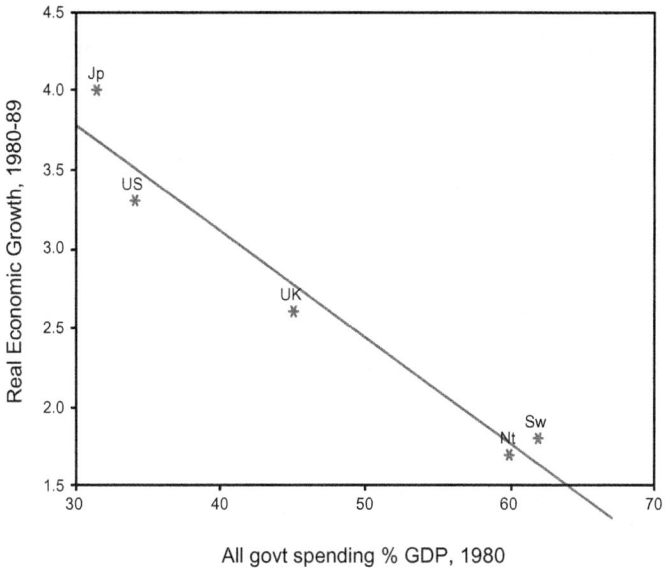

$$Y = a + bX$$

$$Y = 5.82 - 0.068X$$

$$r = -0.97$$
$$r^2 = 0.95$$
$$F = 53.76$$
$$\text{Sig.} = 0.005$$

$$b = -0.068$$
$$\text{S.E.} = 0.009$$
$$t = -7.339$$
$$\text{Sig.} = 0.005$$

Figure 11.2: Regression line for plot of the relationship between government size and economic growth for five sample nations, 1980s.

The coefficient a is the **intercept**, that is, the value of Y when X equals zero. The coefficient b is called the raw or **unstandardized** regression coefficient. This measures the **slope** of the relationship which is the change in Y caused by an increase of one unit in X. If you remember simple algebra, these interpretations of *a* and *b* are obvious. When X is zero, bX must equal zero; so $Y = a$. Similarly, since *b* is a constant, its value represents how much of a change in Y is produced by a one-unit increase in X, whether it is from 1 to 2 or 37 to 38 or 676 to 677.

The regression coefficient can be meaningful and important since *b* or the slope gives an estimate of how much change in Y results when X increases by one unit. In this case, the statistics at the bottom of Figure 11.2 show that the slope coefficient is -0.068. This tells us that for every one percentage point increase in government's share of GDP (whether it is from 36% to 37% or from 51% to 52%), the real economic growth rate goes down by 0.068 percentage points. Note that the slope is negative because larger governments have lower growth rates.

The slope, therefore, can provide valuable information about a relationship. Several conditions must be met, however, for the slope coefficient *b* to have much meaning. First, both the independent and dependent variables must be measured on scales that are readily interpretable, such as dollars or percentages. If one of the variables, such as the Gini Index of income inequality, does not have such a metric, the slope is hard to interpret because it is not intuitively obvious what an increase of one (or any other) unit of this scale connotes. Second, the correlation for the relationship must be quite strong, as we shall see that it is here. If X does not have a strong impact on Y, it makes little sense to ask how much Y will change when X increases or decreases by a given amount.

The intercept or *a* tells us what the value of Y will be when X is zero. In this case, a straight-line projection based on the existing data for the five countries included in the analysis suggests that any country that had abolished its government during the 1980s — that is, had a government spending-to-GDP ratio of 0% — would have recorded the sterling growth rate of 5.82%. However, few people would entertain such an extreme vision; and the resulting anarchy would probably not be conducive to a strong economy. Thus, the information contained in the intercept coefficient is meaningless for understanding how government size influences economic performance. In any event, *a* seldom enters into the substantive interpretation of regression results in political science, although it is necessary for a full specification of the regression equation.

11.1.3 The Strength of Association

Probably, the most important part of a regression analysis is the estimation of how strong the relationship between the two variables is. This is calculated from a measurement of how closely the dots in the scatterplot cluster around the regression line. The correlation coefficient **Pearson's** r (or r) measures this association. Like almost all other correlation coefficients, it possesses a standardized scale of zero to one. When all the dots fall exactly on the regression line, there is a perfect relationship in that the value of Y can be predicted exactly from the value of X. Thus, r will equal 1 or -1 depending on the direction of the relationship between X and Y: that is, whether the regression line goes up or down. Conversely, r equals zero when X and Y are totally unrelated. In this case, the dots will fall randomly throughout the scatterplot around a straight line at the mean of Y, like the flat line on a heart monitor after the patient dies. As a thumbnail sketch for evaluating the strength of r, Table 11.2 presents an approximation of how strong particular correlations are considered to be: 0.00–0.14 no association; 0.15–0.25 weak association; 0.26–0.40 moderate association; and over 0.40 strong association. This is the same scale, incidentally, that is used for Gamma and Lambda (see Table 10.3 in Chapter 10).

The correlation coefficient r reported at the bottom of Figure 11.2 is extremely high and negative at -0.97, indicating that the tendency

Table 11.2: Estimating the strength of the correlation coefficient Pearson's r.*

0.00–0.14	No association
0.15–0.25	Weak association
0.26–0.40	Moderate association
0.41–1.0	Strong association

*This same scale applies to both positive and negative correlations. That is, an r of -0.60 is stronger or higher than one of $+0.45$.

for larger governments to depress economic growth is an extremely strong one, just as the Reaganauts and Thatcherites claimed! The square of the correlation coefficient r^2 is also presented because it has an interpretation that is easy to understand. Fairly simple algebra shows that r^2 represents the **percentage of variance** in Y that is explained by X, which is equivalent to the predictive power of the independent variable. Thus, r^2 is called the **Coefficient of Determination**.[2] The r^2 of 0.95 (the square of any negative number is positive) here, thus, shows that 95% of the variance or difference in scores among the five countries in GNP growth is accounted for by the differences in their size of government. Thus, government size can be said to have 95% predictive power over economic growth, which certainly is extremely strong. The degree of support here for the basic assumptions of Reaganomics, therefore, is striking.

11.1.4 Statistical Significance

Finally, the **statistical significance** of the relationship can be computed. In a nontechnical sense, a measure of statistical significance estimates the probability that something would happen by random chance. For a relationship between two variables, measures of statistical significance estimate the probability that an association as strong as the one observed would have occurred by random chance due to sampling error. Or, in terms of making an inference from a sample to a population, it is the probability that the association between the two variables in the population is zero, given the size of the correlation between them in the sample. Conventionally, whenever this probability is 5% — or 0.05 in the manner in which it is presented in Figure 11.2 — or less, the relationship is considered to be so improbable that it can be termed **statistically significant**. Thus, in interpreting the bottom line in significance measures, all you have to do is see **whether the**

---

[2] Variance, in nontechnical language, is simply the tendency of different cases to have different scores. Technically, the variance for a variable is the square of its standard deviation. That is, $v = s^2$. For the demonstration that r^2 represents the percentage of explained variance, see Hubert M. Blalock, Jr., *Social Statistics*, 2nd Edn. (New York: McGraw-Hill, 1972), pp. 389–393.

significance is 0.05 or less, which can be done with a very quick glance!

This probability in a measure of statistical significance is determined by two things. First, obviously, is the strength of the correlation since the stronger the correlation the less likely that it could have occurred by happenstance. Second, the number of cases in the analysis is also important since the greater the number of cases, the more confidence can be put in the results. The relationship between government size and economic performance modeled in Figure 11.2 rates very differently on these two criteria. The correlation or r of -0.97 is extremely strong, while the number of cases in the analysis (five) is extremely small.

The statistical significance of the correlation coefficient r and slope coefficient b are calculated from separate statistics, but in simple regression where there is just one independent variable, both estimation techniques produce the same results. The **significance of r is determined by the test statistic F** which is based on the ratio of the "explained variance" (r^2) to the unexplained variance ($1 - r^2$). In contrast, the **significance of b is determined by the test statistic t which is the ratio of b to its standard error**. The standard error represents the confidence interval for the value of the slope (see the section on Confidence Intervals in Chapter 8).[3] Both F and t are **test statistics** which have known distributions given the numbers of cases and of independent variables that determine their statistical significance.[4] While their values are quite different in Table 11.2 ($F = 0.53.76$ and $t = -7.339$), they both indicate that the relationship is statistically significant at the 0.005 level. That is, the probability that the pattern of association between the two variables in the scatterplot occurred by random chance is less than 1%, or 0.5% to be precise.

---

[3] *Ibid.*, pp. 400–405 describes the standard error of the slope in more technical detail.
[4] Technically, the significance of a given F or t is determined by their degrees of freedom or the number of nonarbitrary values that can be assigned to the cases in a distribution. Here, the degrees of freedom equal $N - 1$ since arbitrary values can be assigned to all but the last case which has to be given an equalizing value to produce the mean in question.

11.2 A CLOSER LOOK AT THE CONSERVATIVE AND LIBERAL HYPOTHESES REGARDING GOVERNMENT SIZE AND NATIONAL PERFORMANCE

Now that we have gone over the basics of scatterplots and regression, this section applies the technique to assess the conservative and liberal hypotheses about how the size of a state should affect its economic and social performance. The first subsection takes a more detailed look at the conservative hypothesis that larger governments will have worse economic records; and the second provides some data to test the liberal theory that larger governments should be able to provide their citizens with better social outcomes. In both these subsections, only a preliminary test of the direct impact of government size on economic and social performance is presented because, as we shall see in the Chapter 12, a complete evaluation involves testing the more complex models with multiple regression.

11.2.1 Do Larger Governments Depress Economic Performance?

Because the sample of five nations is so small and was not really selected on a random basis, the representativeness of the regression results in Figure 11.2 might be open to question. Figure 11.3, therefore, presents the scatterplot and regression coefficients for this relationship for the entire group of advanced industrial nations with the five original countries indicated by abbreviations. This scatterplot does, in fact, turn out to be fairly similar to the one for just the five sample countries, although the strength of the association is markedly weaker. The regression line follows the same pattern, although its slope and intercept are slightly lower. For example, b tells us that a one percentage point increase in the budget/GDP ratio will depress growth by 0.03 percentage points. The negative relationship is nowhere nearly as strong as for the five sample countries, although it is still fairly high at -0.51, which is statistically significant at the 0.022 level. Thus, the selection of the five nations for the initial scatterplot and regression analysis did not lead to any great distortion of the very strong negative relationship that

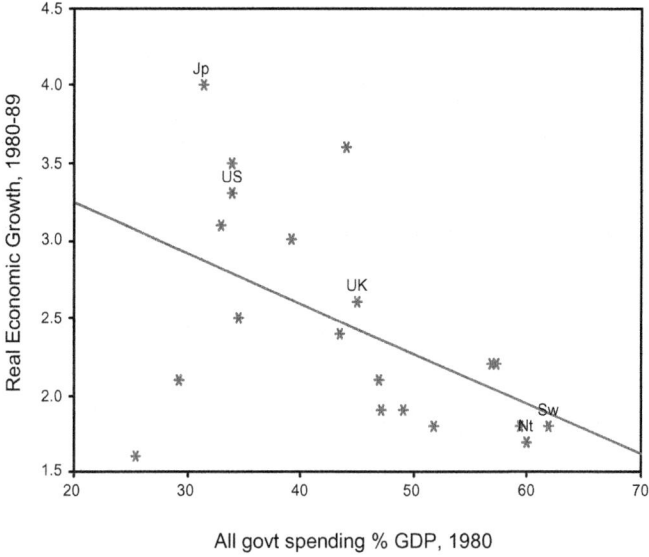

$$Y = 3.89 - 0.03X$$

$$r = -0.51$$
$$r^2 = 0.26$$
$$b = -0.03$$
$$\text{Sig.} = 0.022$$

Figure 11.3: Regression line for the plot of the relationship between government size and economic growth for all developed nations, 1980s.

existed between government size and economic performance during the 1980s.

Furthermore, this strong linkage between large government and poor economic performance is not just peculiar to the 1980s. Table 11.3 gives the correlations between economic growth and government size for several time periods over the last half century. The first two rows present the data for 1965–1980 and 1980–1989, respectively. For 1965–1980, the correlation between government size and economic growth of −0.75 is considerably stronger than it was for the 1980s (−0.51). In terms of explained variance as measured by r^2, government size had more than double the explanatory

Table 11.3: Correlation between government size and economic growth rate by time periods.

	r	r^2	Sig.
Economic growth, 1965–1980 with Government/GDP, 1970	−0.75	0.56	0.001
Economic growth, 1980–1989 with Government/GDP, 1980	−0.51	0.26	0.005
Economic growth, 1990–2004 with Government/GDP, 1990	−0.11	0.01	0.65
Economic growth, 1990–2004 with change in Government/GDP, 1990–1997	−0.55	0.30	0.01

power for 1965–1980 (56%) than it did for 1980–1989 (26%). Thus, the negative impact of large government on economic performance certainly predated the Reagan revolution.

When we turn to the more recent period of 1990–2004 in the third row in the table, however, the picture changes considerably. During 1990–2004, there was almost no association between government size and economic growth, as their r is a minuscule −0.11. Seemingly, then, the economic penalty for large government was almost completely mitigated after 1990. Yet, a further search finds significant evidence linking government size to economic performance over that 15-year period, which is consistent with the conservatives' suspicion of large government. It turns out that what was important for economic vitality after 1990 was not the absolute size of government but, instead, the change in the size of government. Indeed, the final row in Table 11.3 shows that the correlation between the percentage change in the size of government and average annual growth during 1990–2004 is a very high −0.55. This strong negative correlation between change in government size and economic growth, therefore, saves the conservative hypothesis that big government hurts the economy for the period after 1990.

Yet, not all the data support the conservative critique of government's impact on the economy. Conservatives decry big government and predict that it will bring disastrous economic consequences for several reasons. Government regulations, for example, greatly increase

Table 11.4: Correlation between government size and savings rate for all developed nations, 1980–2000

Savings % GDP	Government/GDP ratio			
	1980	1990	1997	2003
1980	−0.13			
1989		0.06		
1999			−0.04	
2003				0.02

the cost of doing business; and private entrepreneurs must waste time dealing with bureaucrats rather than applying their economic skills. One of the most serious conservative concerns is that the costs of big government drain money out of the productive activities of the private sector to finance the very state bureaucracies that undercut economic efficiency and promote well intentioned, but economically inefficient, programs of redistribution. This argument, hence, hypothesizes that big government will be associated with low levels of savings and investment.

Table 11.4 on the correlation between government size and the savings rate at four points in time over the last two decades (1980, 1990, 1997, and 2004), however, decisively refutes this hypothesis. Substantively, there simply is no such relationship since all four r's are close to zero! Thus, while the conservatives are right about big government stifling growth, they are wrong, at least in this one instance, about why this is so.

Methodologically, this is an example of a **correlation matrix** which contains the correlations between two sets of variables that are listed in the columns and rows of the table or matrix. For example, in Table 11.4, the dates that the government/GDP ratio was measured (1980, 1990, 1997, and 1999) form the columns of the table, while the dates that the savings rate was measured (1980, 1989, 1999, and 2003) form the rows. The only correlations listed in the table fall on the main diagonal because government size and savings rate are correlated with each other only for the same year. For example, the first figure in the upper left of the table shows that there was an r of -0.13 between these two variables in 1980, while the last figure at the lower right indicates that their correlation was 0.02 in 2003.

11.2.2 Do Larger Governments Bring Better Social Outcomes?

Liberals argue that achieving social equity is a very important goal which justifies government welfare and redistributive policies. This brings us to the empirical question of whether government size is associated with good social outcomes. Figures 11.4 and 11.5 test this hypothesis by presenting the scatterplots for the impact of government size on the infant mortality and poverty rates for all the developed nations at the beginning of the 21st century. These data provide marked empirical support for the liberal hypothesis. Government size has strong correlations in the expected negative direction with both of these indicators of social outcomes. Government size has a correlation

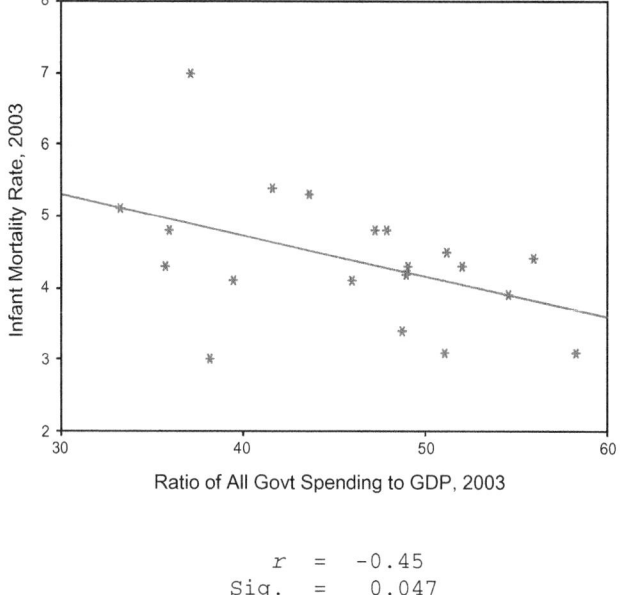

$r = -0.45$
$\text{Sig.} = 0.047$

Figure 11.4: Impact of government size on infant mortality for all developed nations, 2003.

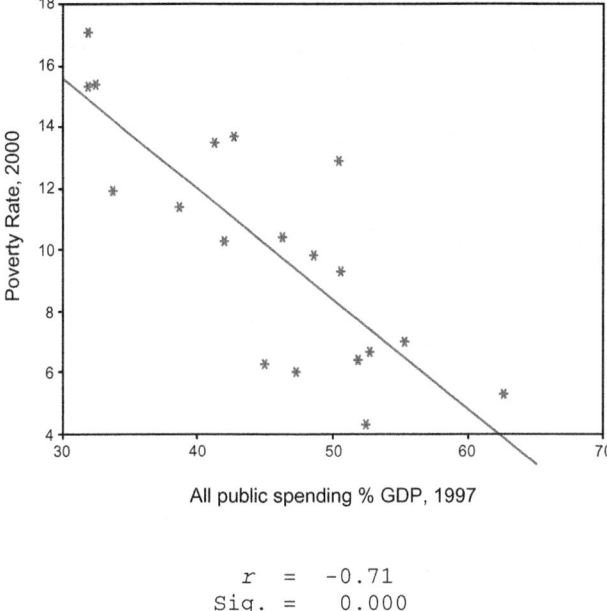

```
    r   =  -0.71
    Sig. =   0.000
```

Figure 11.5: Impact of government size on poverty rate for all developed nations, 2000.

of -0.45 with infant mortality; and its r with the poverty rate is an extremely high -0.71.

11.2.3 The Paradox of Large Government

The conservative and liberal hypotheses about the effects of large government can be considered paradoxical in the sense that conservatives predict that larger governments will have worse economic performance, while liberals postulate that they will promote better social outcomes. This leaves us in something of a policy quandary if both these theories turn out to be true. The techniques of regression, correlation, and scatterplots allow us to measure how strong the relationship is between two variables. Thus, they were applied in this chapter to test whether big government is, indeed, associated with bad economic and good social performance for the 21 advanced industrial nations. Although there were a few significant exceptions in the findings, the statistical results do support both hypotheses. Nations with larger governments do have lower rates of growth, but they also have better outcomes in terms of several important social indicators. These findings, however, are only preliminary since they might well change when more complex theoretical models are evaluated.

11.3 USING REGRESSION ANALYSIS FOR BENCHMARKING

Another important application of regression results is to use **residuals analysis** to establish **benchmarks** for evaluating national performance on specific dependent variables, such as economic growth or infant mortality rate. Technically, a **residual** is the difference between the score predicted for a case (country) by the regression equation and the actual value that is observed. This **predicted value** is often considered a **benchmark of normal achievement** when the independent or explanatory variable is a measure of natural resources or wealth, such as GDP per capita.

In Chapter 7, means and medians were used as the benchmark; and nations were considered to be overachievers or underachievers simply on the basis of whether they had values above or below average on the socioeconomic indicator in question. A more sophisticated approach to benchmarking, though, seeks to control for the resources available to a nation in evaluating how well it is doing on the very reasonable assumption that social and economic performance should be better in wealthier nations or states. For example, the United States would be expected to have a much lower infant mortality rate than India or even Greece. This can be done by using a measure of wealth, such as GDP per capita, to explain social and economic outcomes in nations or states. The distance above or below the regression line that an individual state or country falls, therefore, indicates how well or poorly it is doing given its own resource base. For example, countries that have better than predicted records on economic or social indicators can be considered overachievers. Conversely, those whose records are worse than predicted are underachievers. Of course, the measure of wealth must have a fairly strong correlation with the socioeconomic indicator in question, or else there would be little point in doing the residuals

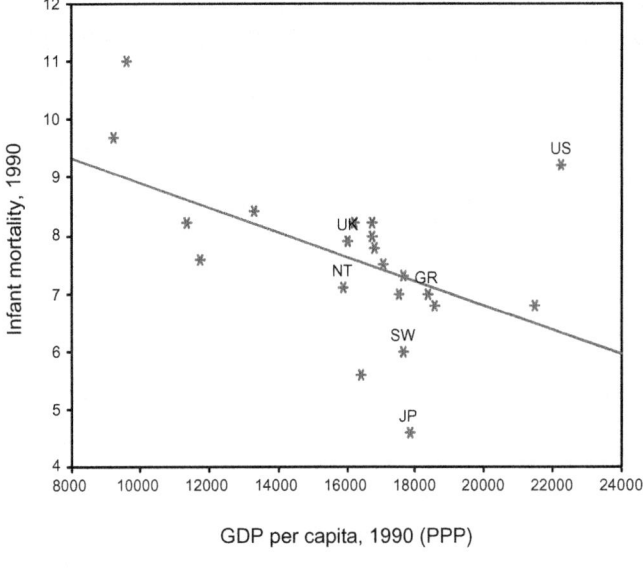

Figure 11.6: Impact of GDP per capita on infant mortality rate for all developed nations, 1990.

analysis because the residual from the regression equation would differ little from the difference from the mean.[5]

Assessing how well-developed nations were doing in terms of reducing infant mortality in 1990[6] provides an excellent illustration. The scatterplot and regression statistics in Figure 11.6 show that

---

[5] For a more detailed description and illustrative application of this technique for measuring overachievers and underachievers on policy outcomes, see Steve Chan and Cal Clark, *Flexibility, Foresight, and Fortuna in Taiwan's Development: Navigating between Scylla and Charybdis* (London: Routledge, 1992), Chapter 4.

[6] This analysis is done for 1990 because later the impact of GDP per capita on infant mortality had become too weak (as indicated, for example, by an r of -0.22 in 1997) to make this benchmarking technique meaningful.

national wealth did indeed have a fairly strong impact on the infant mortality rate in 1990, as indicated by a correlation coefficient of -0.51 and a downward sloping regression line. The predicted value of the dependent variable Y, the infant mortality rate, is calculated for each country by substituting its score on an independent variable X, GDP per capita, in the regression equation:

$$Y \text{ (Infant Mort)} = 11.01 - 0.00021 X \text{ (GDP p.c.)}.$$

Since the GDP per capita for America in 1990 was $22,266, this regression equation predicts that the U.S. should have had an infant mortality rate of 6.3:

$$\begin{aligned} Y &= 11.01 - (0.00021 \times 22{,}266) \\ &= 11.01 - (4.69) \\ &= 6.32 \text{ or } 6.3. \end{aligned}$$

This predicted infant mortality rate of 6.3, hence, constitutes a benchmark of what would normally be expected of a country with the same level of affluence as America's. In actuality, America's infant mortality rate was 9.2 or almost 50% higher than the predicted level. This can be seen in America's position well above the regression line in Figure 11.6.

More inclusively, Table 11.5 lists the residuals for all the developed nations. Both the scatterplot and the residuals data show the United States as standing out as the worst underachiever among the industrialized nations in terms of its infant mortality rate — that is, being the furthest above the regression line in Figure 11.6 and having by far the highest positive residual in Table 11.5. The U.S.'s *laissez-faire* political economy, therefore, does appear to exact a significant cost in terms of poorer-than-expected social outcomes. In contrast, Sweden, the Netherlands, and Finland with their well-developed welfare states ranked among the top five overachievers. This might suggest that there is a trade-off between the conservative goal of rapid growth through *laissez-faire* and the liberal one of improving social conditions by the actions of a welfare state. However, the greatest overachiever on infant mortality was Japan which has a very small

Table 11.5: Residuals analysis for infant mortality explained by GDP per capita for the developed nations.

	Infant mortality rate	Predicted value by regression	Residual
Japan	4.6	7.3	−2.7
Finland	5.6	7.5	−1.9
Sweden	6.0	7.3	−1.3
Spain	7.6	8.5	−0.9
Netherlands	7.1	7.7	−0.6
Ireland	8.2	8.6	−0.4
Norway	7.0	7.3	−0.3
Canada	6.8	7.1	−0.3
Germany	7.0	7.1	−0.1
France	7.3	7.3	0.0
Denmark	7.5	7.4	0.1
New Zealand	8.4	8.2	0.2
United Kingdom	7.9	7.6	0.3
Switzerland	6.8	6.5	0.3
Austria	7.8	7.5	0.3
Belgium	8.0	7.5	0.5
Italy	8.2	7.6	0.6
Greece	9.7	9.1	0.6
Australia	8.2	7.5	0.7
Portugal	11.0	9.0	2.0
United States	9.2	6.3	2.9

state, indicating that something else besides the support of a strong welfare state — presumably the habits of a well-educated population and the influence of Japan's distinct culture — can produce better health care outcomes.

11.4 ASSUMPTIONS OF REGRESSION ANALYSIS

Regression analysis is based on several assumptions that must always be kept in mind. First, both the independent and dependent variables must be at the interval level of measurement. In a few instances, though, political scientists have argued that ordinal data approximate interval measurement so that regression techniques can be applied to them.[7] This is usually done because when we move on to the multivariate statistics that estimate the impact of a group of explanatory factors, regression is a far more powerful technique than the crosstabulations that are usually applied to ordinal data (see Chapters 9 and 10). While statisticians rightfully have conniptions over this, it is probably not too dangerous to use some basic results, such as the combined impact of the independent variables and their relative influence on the dependent variable, if they are treated with caution. Still, some important elements in regression analysis can only be applied when interval data are used. Regression coefficients are only meaningful for variables whose values can be interpreted in real world terms (i.e., money, votes, etc.); and scatterplots form coherent patterns only when almost all the cases have different values on the two variables being correlated. Furthermore, the development of logistic regression (see Chapter 13) has provided an alternative technique that is far sounder and more justified methodologically.

Second, it is assumed that values of X are independent of other influences on Y. If they are not, the direct correlation between two variables may well overstate the degree to which one influences the other. For example, government size has strong correlations of -0.45 with infant mortality and -0.71 with poverty level among the developed nations (see Figures 11.4 and 11.5). That is, as liberals would predict, infant mortality and poverty are lower in countries that have larger governments. Yet, both these social outcomes might well be better in wealthier nations than in poorer ones. Thus, until we control for national wealth with a technique like multiple regression, there is always the possibility that the association that seems to be there "ain't necessarily so". Thus, if you suspect that other confounding factors exist, multivariate analysis should be applied to measure the relationship between X and Y after other potential independent variables are controlled (see Chapter 12 on multiple regression).

Third, as the term linear regression implies, it is assumed that a linear relationship exists between the independent and dependent

---

[7] For example, Warren E. Miller and J. Merrill Shanks, *The New American Voter* (Cambridge: Harvard University Press, 1996) make this argument in one of the most influential analyses of public opinion in the United States.

variables. That is, as X increases in value, Y will either increase (positive association) or decrease (negative or inverse association) at a steady rate. However, this is not always the case. In particular, three forms of the relationship between X and Y are fairly common. First, as we have assumed so far in this chapter, a change in X may produce a linear change in Y. For example, each 1% increase of investment as a share of GDP might raise the growth of GDP by an additional 0.3%.

Alternatively, the effects of X may diminish after it reaches a certain value. For example, whereas increases in GDP per capita have a significant positive impact upon the quality of life among the people of the poorest countries by increasing food consumption and life expectancy or by decreasing fertility and infant mortality, this impact declines precipitously among the most affluent countries. This diminishing effect can be modeled by what is called a log transformation or replacing the actual value of the independent variable (X) with its logarithm because the values of the logarithms increase much more slowly than the absolute numbers on which they are based:

$$Y = a + b \, \text{LOG}(X).$$

Figure 11.7 shows that such an effect existed among the advanced industrial nations in terms of their infant mortality rates in 1980, when the wealth gap among them was considerably greater than it is today. The scatterplot at the top of the figure shows that several of the poorer countries had substantially higher infant mortality rates than the rest of the nations included in the analysis. At the bottom of the table, the statistics for the linear and logistic regression models indicate that the log model has somewhat more predictive power (38% to 30%), although even the linear relationship is fairly strong itself as indicated by a r of -0.54.

In addition, the direction of a relationship may change at different values of the independent variable. Consider the normal relationship between income inequality and development level. Income inequality is usually relatively low in the poorest nations, in part because there is so little money to go around. As development and industrialization occur, income inequality tends to increase as the benefits of industrialization are tightly concentrated. After a point, however, economic development becomes so pervasive that more and more people see their

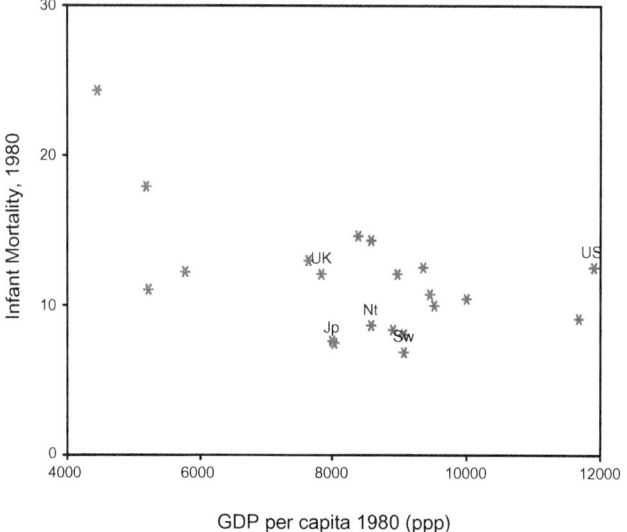

$Y = 21.09 - 0.0011X$

$r = -0.54$ $r^2 = 0.30$ Sig. = 0.011

(A) Linear Regression Model

$Y = 97.66 - 9.56(\log)X$

$r = -0.61$ $r^2 = 0.38$ Sig. = 0.003

(B) Logistic Regression Model

Figure 11.7: Scatterplot of infant mortality by GDP per capita, 1980.

incomes climb, thus decreasing inequality.[8] This scenario implies the graph in Figure 11.8 of the relationship between income inequality (Y) and GNP per capita (X) which are predicted here to have an "inverted U-shaped" relationship. For such a case, the normal correlation and regression coefficients will be close to zero, reflecting the absence

---

[8] Simon Kuznets, "Economic Growth and Income Inequality", *American Economic Review*, 45 (March 1955), pp. 1–28.

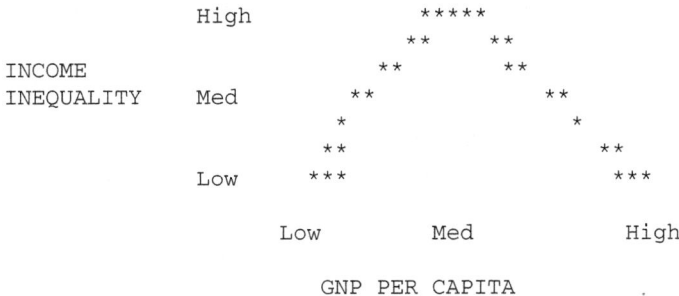

Figure 11.8: Generally assumed relationship between economic development level and income inequality.

of a linear association. However, a strong **curvilinear relationship** clearly exists. This can be analyzed by applying a nonlinear equation to explain the relationship in what is called polynomial regression. Thus, the equation for such a **changed-direction** relationship is a quadratic equation (which is an example of multiple regression):

$$Y = a + b_1 X + b_2 X^2.$$

Furthermore, this underlines the importance of inspecting the full shape of a relationship in a scatterplot rather than just relying upon the summary coefficients, which may well be misleading if all the assumptions on which linear regression are based do not, in fact, hold.

The scatterplots and regression equations in Figure 11.9 demonstrate that such a situation exists in the relationship between wealth and income inequality among the developed nations. If a quadratic equation is used to explain income inequality in the 1990s, Figure 11.9 demonstrates that the r of 0.49 and r^2 of 0.24 are, respectively, twice and five times as high for the correlations in a linear regression. An inspection of the scatterplot for the quadratic relationship, however, shows that the actual shape of the relationship, a U-shaped one, is the inverse of the one in Figure 11.8. That is, the poorest countries in the developed world have such high development levels that they are at fairly high levels of inequality worldwide, which puts them somewhere near the middle of the X axis on Figure 11.8. Greater wealth in the developed world, hence, is associated with decreasing inequality as predicted by the right side of Figure 11.8. However, in a relationship

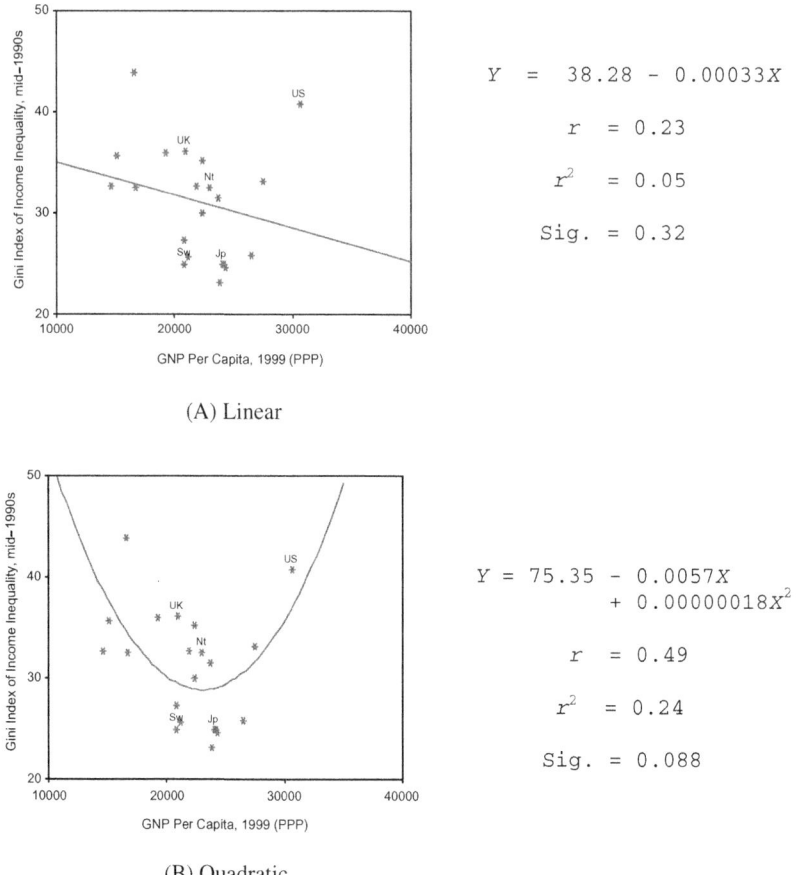

Figure 11.9: Models of GNP p.c.'s impact on income inequality for all developed nations, mid-1990s.

not included there, inequality evidently jumps again among the very richest nations in the world.

A fourth and final methodological question concerns the applicability of statistical significance in regression results. Measures of statistical significance are very widely used in the reporting of political science research. They are also somewhat abused in the sense of being applied in many situations where they really are not warranted. This is because, technically, measures of statistical significance are only appropriate when the data being analyzed come from a representative sample of some larger population. Thus, the statistical significance of a correlation or a relationship is the probability that an association as strong as the one observed in the sample could occur by random chance if there were no relationship at all in the population from which the sample was drawn — that is, if there were a correlation of 0.00 denoting a null relationship in the larger population.

For the regressions in this chapter, both those for the illustrative sample and those for the whole advanced industrial world, there really is no representative or random sample. The five countries in the regression analysis in Figure 11.2 are a sample of the theoretical population of the 21 industrialized and developed nations in the world at the beginning of the 21st century. They were chosen to represent key characteristics of the independent and dependent variables. However, as discussed in much more detail in Chapter 8, this is a far more problematic technique than selecting a random sample because there is no real guarantee that the cases actually conform to the selection criteria. Moreover, it would make little sense to take an extremely small sample from a population which itself has only a small number of cases. If regression analysis is applied to all 21 developed nations, in addition, there is no sample because they constitute the population. Still, many political scientists report the statistical significance of findings for which they are not technically appropriate to give an idea of how strong a correlation is relative to the number of cases in the analysis. Theoretically, this is sometimes justified by the argument that an actual population, such as the 21 developed democracies, can be conceptualized as just one of an infinite number of populations that might hypothetically exist. Thus, the significance measures that are reported in these regressions should be considered primarily illustrative of the technique and somewhat problematic in their substantive interpretation.

Even when all 21 developed nations are used in a regression analysis, the number of cases is quite small by statistical standards. Thus, even fairly strong correlations may not be statistically significant. For example, the strong r of -0.45 between government size and infant mortality in 2003 is only significant at the 0.047 level (see Figure 11.4), raising a very difficult question of whether strength or significance should be emphasized in such a situation.

EXERCISES

1. Interpret the following set of regression statistics for the relationship between the size of government and life expectancy in 2003. Which is the dependent variable? Which is the independent variable? Would the conservative or liberal hypothesis be more relevant here? What would it predict about the interrelationship between these two variables? Discuss what the regression statistics show about this relationship. Is it positive or negative? Is this the direction predicted by your hypothesis? How strong is the relationship? Is it statistically significant? How much change in the dependent variable does a one unit increase in the independent variable produce?

Life Expectancy and the Government/GDP Ratio, 2003

$r = -0.26$
$r^2 = 0.07$
$b = -0.044$
$a = 81.09$
Sig. $= 0.27$

2. Use the following correlation matrix to test the conservative and liberal hypotheses about the effects of having a large or liberal government. What is the hypothesis for each relationship? Is the correlation in the predicted direction? How strong is the association? What do these findings imply overall about the validity of the conservative and liberal theories?

	2003 Ratio of Government Spending to GDP
High School Enrollment rate, 2003	0.32
Hospital Beds p.c., 2003	−0.04
Infant Mortality rate, 2003	−0.43
Life Expectancy, 2003	−0.26
Poverty rate, 2000	−0.64
Savings % GDP, 2003	0.03
Unemployment rate, 2006	0.37

3. Go to the StateMaster website (www.statemaster.com) and find two indicators that you would like to correlate. Select one state from each of the five following regions: Northeast, South, Midwest, Mountains and Plains West, and West Coast. Record the values of the two indicators for just these five states and then present them in a scatterplot. Does the relationship seem to be positive or negative? Is this what would be expected?
4. Use the following scatterplot and regression statistics to benchmark whether the United States and Sweden were overachievers or underachievers in terms of their unemployment rates for 2006. What is the overall impact of government size on unemployment? Does this support the conservative or the liberal theory? How do the relative performances of the U.S. and Sweden appear? Is this consistent with the overall relationship? Why or why not?

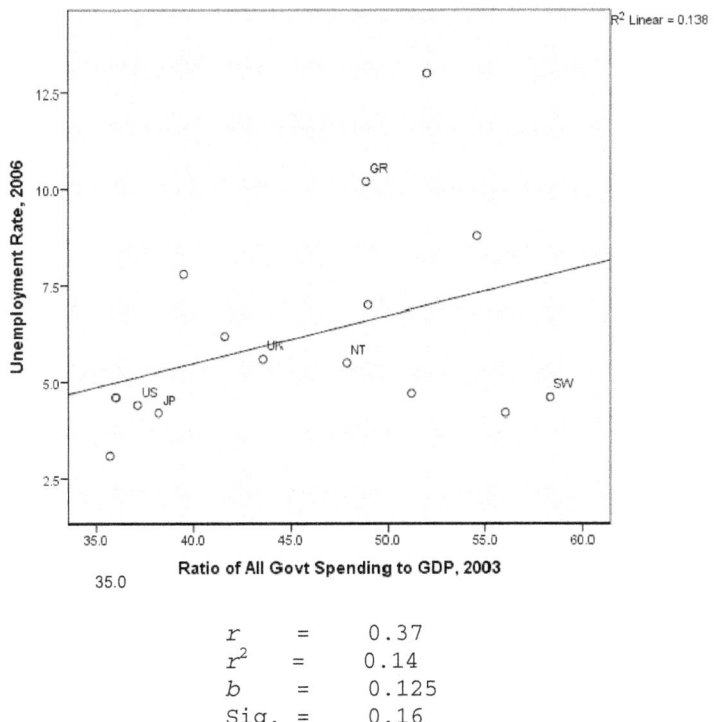

```
r    =    0.37
r²   =    0.14
b    =    0.125
Sig. =    0.16
```

Chapter 12

Multiple Regression and Path Analysis: More Complex Models of the Policy Process

The regression and correlation techniques discussed in Chapter 11 provide a sophisticated means for examining several important aspects of the direct or simple relationship between two variables. They are distinctly limited, however, because they cannot be used to test more complex models. In particular, they do not tell us how several independent variables affect a dependent variable in combination, which certainly is often of analytic interest. **Multiple regression** models the impact of several explanatory variables upon a dependent variable and presents a concise statistical summary of their combined and individual effects. Likewise, an extension of multiple regression also provides valuable results. Neither simple regression nor multiple regression indicate how an explanatory factor indirectly influences a dependent variable through a third item or intervening variable. Yet, some of the statistics generated by multiple regression can be applied in **path analysis** to sort out the direct and indirect effects among a small set of variables in what is termed a **causal model**.

The first section of this chapter describes the basic statistics associated with multiple regression; and Section 12.2 applies multiple regression to provide a more sophisticated analysis of the conservative and liberal hypotheses about the impact of government size on the economic and social performance of developed nations. This is followed by a discussion of the more technical assumptions of multiple regression with emphasis on the problem of **multicollinearity** in Section 12.3. Section 12.4 then provides an overview of the calculation of path coefficients and their use in estimating the direct and indirect effects in a causal model.

12.1 THE BASICS IN MULTIPLE REGRESSION ANALYSIS

Multiple regression extends the logic of simple regression by providing models of the combined impact of a set of independent variables upon a dependent item, when all are at the interval level of measurement. It is a powerful technique because it provides direct estimates, both of the combined impact of the independent variables and of the relative influence exerted by each explanatory factor. In multiple regression, the correlation coefficients **Multiple R** and R^2 measure the strength of the combined impact of the independent variables in terms of the percentage of variance that they explain in the dependent variable. **Unstandardized regression coefficients (b's)** indicate how much change in the dependent variable is produced by an increase of one unit in a specific independent variable when the effects of the other independent variables are controlled. **Standardized regression coefficients (betas)** measure the relative impact of each explanatory factor. Finally, the **statistical significance** of these correlation and regression coefficients can also be calculated.

Although the calculations are mathematically much more complex, multiple regression just extends the principles of bivariate regression to analyses where there are two or more predictor variables and produces a similar equation for calculating a predicted value for Y from a case's values on the independent variables X_1 to X_n.

$$Y = a + b_1 X_1 + b_2 X_2 + \cdots + b_n X_n.$$

Since there are several independent variables, the a and b coefficients no longer directly represent the intercept and slope as they did in the simple two-dimensional plot. However, they convey analogous information.

First, a is the value of Y when all the X's equal 0. Second, the b's represent the amount of change caused in Y by an increase of one unit in X, although in multiple regression this is the change that results when the effects of the other independent variables are taken into account.

Thus, the a and b coefficients can be used to calculate **predicted values for Y** for every case from its scores on the X's (independent variables). Just like estimating how closely the dots cluster around the regression line in simple regression, the **Multiple R and R^2** correlation coefficients then measure how closely the predicted values of Y correspond to the actual or observed values for all the cases in the analysis. The range of Multiple R is from 0, when there is no relationship at all, to 1, when a linear combination of the independent variables in the regression equation exactly predicts the value of the dependent variable for every case. Since R represents the combined impact of several variables, distinctions cannot be made between positive and negative effects. Therefore, it is always positive. R^2, like r^2, is the percentage of variance in Y that is explained or accounted for by the combined impact of all the independent variables taken together.

12.1.1 Statistics Showing the Strength of the Overall Equation

As an example, Table 12.1 presents a multiple regression model of GNP growth for 1980–1989, using four explanatory factors:

(1) Government spending as a percentage of GDP to indicate government size.
(2) The high school enrollment ratio to measure human capital development.
(3) The savings rate to tap supply-side resources.
(4) GDP per capita to depict overall economic resources.

The top third of Table 12.1 gives the statistics for the whole equation. Multiple R and R^2 measure the combined impact of the four explanatory variables, while their significance statistic is also reported. The Multiple R is a very strong 0.72; and R^2 shows that in combination the four independent variables explain just over half (52%) of the differences among the industrialized nations in terms of growth

Table 12.1: Multiple regression explaining economic growth among the developed nations, 1980–1989.

Dependent Variable: GNP GROWTH, 1980–1989

Overall Equation

Multiple R	0.72
Multiple R^2	0.52
F	3.81
Significance	0.027
a	1.40

Separate Effects of Independent Variables	Beta	b	Sig
Govt Spend % GDP, 1980	−0.59	−0.037	0.012
High Sch Enrollment, 1979	0.36	0.023	0.082
Savings % GDP, 1980	0.26	0.035	0.23
GDP p.c., 1980	0.08	0.00003	0.68

Bivariate Association with GNP Growth	r	b	Sig
Govt Spend % GDP, 1980	−0.51	−0.033	0.022
High Sch Enrollment, 1979	0.26	0.016	0.285
Savings % GDP, 1980	0.42	0.056	0.06
GDP p.c., 1980	0.14	0.00005	0.54

rate. The Multiple R is noticeably higher than the strongest simple correlation of −0.51 for the size of the government's budget relative to GDP, as reported in the bottom part of the table. Consequently, the other independent variables obviously exert substantial effects of their own. The F of 3.81 shows that this combined impact is statistically significant at the 0.027 level. Finally, the a of 1.40 represents the analogue of the intercept in a simple regression equation in that it shows the value of growth when all four explanatory items equal zero. While a vital part of the regression equation, this intercept really has no substantive meaning.

12.1.2 Statistics Showing the Independent Impact of Each Explanatory Variable

The next or middle portion of the table then presents the independent influences of the four explanatory factors controlling for the effects of the other predictors. The unstandardized regression coefficients (b's) in the middle column show how much change in the economic growth rate results from a one unit increase in each of these independent variables. Note that these b's are somewhat different than the ones from the simple regressions reported in the bottom or third section of the table on the direct or bivariate association between each of the explanatory variables and economic growth rate. This is because they show the effect after the influence of the other three predictors has been controlled. For example, the initial slope coefficient for savings was 0.056, but once the effects of the other three independent variables are taken into account, the b for savings in the multiple regression equation changes to 0.035.

These **unstandardized** coefficients, however, cannot show the relative influence of the explanatory variables. When an independent variable has a small range of possible values (e.g., 0 to 10) a one unit increase will almost inevitably produce a larger change than does an independent variable having a huge range (e.g., zero to a million) no matter what their comparative explanatory power might be. For example, GDP per capita is measured in much larger units (tens of thousands of dollars) than the other three independent variables (which can only vary between 0 and 100%). Correspondingly, the b for GDP per capita of 0.00003 is several magnitudes smaller than the other b's which range between 0.02 and 0.04.

Thus, statisticians have developed another measure for estimating the relative explanatory influence of the independent variables. These **standardized regression coefficients** (which are also called **beta weights or coefficients**) show the amount of change in the dependent variable produced by an increase in a particular independent variable controlling the effects of the other explanatory factors **when all have the same "standardized" units of measurement**.[1] Because all the independent variables have the same unit of measurement, those that produce the greatest changes in Y (as indicated by having the highest betas) can be considered to have the greatest influence on the

---

[1] Technically, as discussed in Chapter 8, such standard scores or Z scores measure how many standard deviations above or below the mean each case lies.

dependent variable. Thus, the **beta coefficients show the relative impact of the independent variables** and form one of the most important results in multiple regression.

The betas in Table 12.1 show that government size or the ratio of government spending to GDP exerted an extremely strong depressing effect on GNP growth even after the effects of the other independent variables are controlled, as indicated by its beta of -0.59. Once this effect is taken into account, both high school enrollment (beta $= 0.36$) and the savings rate (beta $= 0.26$) had moderate positive effects on growth. Like the strong negative relationship between government size and growth, the finding that more savings leads to higher growth supports the conservative perspective. Still, the moderate impact of the high school enrollment ratio gives liberals a ray of light by showing that human capital has some importance for economic performance. Finally, a nation's economic resource base had no influence whatsoever on its economic performance during the 1980s, as demonstrated by the very low beta of 0.08 for GDP per capita.

The last column in Table 12.1 contains the statistical significance for the independent effect that each of the four explanatory variables had upon economic growth during the 1980s, which applies to both beta and b. As would certainly be expected given its strong impact, the government/GDP ratio is highly significant at the 0.012 level. Yet, because of the small number of cases (see the section on the "Assumptions of Multiple Regression"), even the moderate influences exerted by the high school enrollment (sig $= 0.082$) and the savings rate (sig $= 0.23$) do not meet the normal standards for statistical significance.

12.2 USING MULTIPLE REGRESSION TO TEST THE CONSERVATIVE AND LIBERAL HYPOTHESES ABOUT THE EFFECTS OF GOVERNMENT ACTIVISM

In Chapter 11, when we applied simple regression and correlation to test the competing conservative and liberal hypotheses about the effects of large and liberal government, many of the conclusions could be only tentative or partial because of the suspicion that the direct or simple correlation of government size with specific economic and social indicators might be changed if the effects of other factors were taken into consideration. Multiple regression allows such more sophisticated examination of the effects of a set of variables. This section, hence, applies multiple regression to sort out the relative influence of several variables in testing the conservative and liberal hypotheses about the social and economic consequences that flow from having a large or small government.

12.2.1 Testing the Conservative Theory of Economic Performance

The simple regressions reported in Chapter 11, in general, supported both the conservative contention that countries with larger governments will have worse economic performance and the liberal prediction that nations with larger governments will experience better social outcomes. Yet, these results could only be considered preliminary because the effects of additional explanatory variables, such as indicators of national wealth or human capital, might well modify the simple or direct correlation of government size to economic performance and social outcomes.

For the 1980s, at least, the regression explanation for economic growth in Table 12.1 that was discussed in the previous section provided strong support for the conservative theory about the deleterious economic consequence of big government. Government size had a strongly negative impact on economic growth for that decade even after the other potential influences on economic performance are taken into account. Moreover, while the liberals were right in saying that human capital helps economic performance, this relationship was only moderate and did very little, if anything, to counteract the pronounced tendency for large governments to depress economic growth rates.

Similar findings emerge from the analysis in Table 12.2 which replicates this regression model for the 1990–2004 period with the one difference that change in the size of government is used as the indicator of government role since the analysis in Chapter 11 indicated that this facet of government role, rather than sheer size, was the prime factor affecting economic dynamism in the 1990s. The relationships for the 1990s are a little weaker than for the preceding decade. For

Table 12.2: Multiple regression explaining economic growth among the developed nations, 1990–2004.

Dependent Variable: ECONOMIC GROWTH RATE, 1990–2004

Overall Equation

Multiple R 0.66
Multiple R^2 0.43
Significance 0.061

Separate Effects of Independent Variables	Beta	b	Sig
Change in Govt/GDP Ratio 1990 to 1997	−0.44	−0.059	0.043
GDP per capita, 1990	−0.38	−0.00015	0.093
High School Enroll, 1989	0.30	0.032	0.17
Savings Rate, 1989	0.15	0.034	0.46

example, the Multiple R is 0.66 for the 1990s as opposed to 0.72 for the 1980s; and the betas for government role, savings rate, and high school education are all somewhat lower for 1990–2004 than 1980–1989. Still, the overall results are exactly the same. Countries that expanded their governments had considerably lower rates of growth than those that reduced them, as indicated by the beta of −0.44 for change in the government/GDP ratio; and high school enrollment and savings rate with betas of 0.30 and 0.15, respectively, each had marginally positive effects on growth as well. Thus, the major impact on growth again is the stifling effect of large government, which is only slightly counterbalanced by the positive influence of human capital development.

There is, however, one important difference between the influences on economic growth after 1990 in the developed world, as opposed to the previous decade. For the 1980s, economic resource base was totally unrelated to growth (see Table 12.1). In contrast, the scatterplot in Figure 12.1 shows that GDP per capita for 1990 had a moderate *negative* correlation of −0.36 with economic growth over the succeeding decade. Even when the effects of the other explanatory factors included in the multiple regression in Table 12.2 are taken into

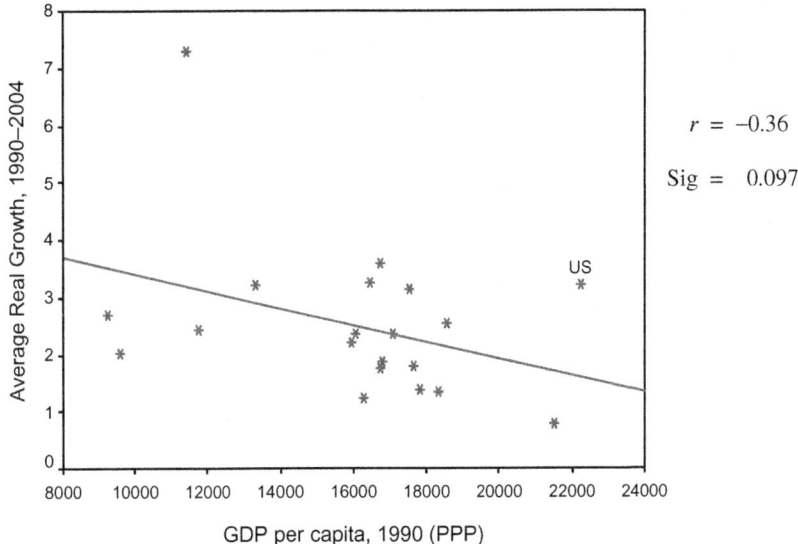

Figure 12.1: Regression line for plot of the relationship between GDP per capita and economic growth for all developed nations, 1990–2004.

account, this relationship remains almost unchanged as indicated by the beta of -0.38.

Rather than suffering a disadvantage from their lesser wealth and resources, therefore, the poorer nations in the developed world had a significant advantage during the 1990s (unlike earlier) that allowed them to catch up to the wealthier members of the group. Evidently, they moved into the phase of industrialization where productivity gains are the greatest (see the S-curve in Figure 1.1 in Chapter 1). The fact that the 1990s were a period of catch-up in the industrialized world, furthermore, makes the strong growth that occurred in the United States all the more impressive because, as the richest and most advanced industrial nation in the world, it would not have been expected to have a particularly stellar economic performance — see how far it is above the regression line in Figure 12.1, for example.

12.2.2 Testing the Liberal Theory of Social Outcomes

Moving on to the liberal hypothesis that big government promotes better social outcomes, a similar picture emerges in that the multivariate

Table 12.3: Multiple regression explaining infant mortality in the developed nations.

Dependent Variable: INFANT MORTALITY RATE, 2003

Overall Equation

Multiple R	0.51
Multiple R^2	0.26
Significance	0.17

Separate Effects of Independent Variables	Beta	b	Sig
Govt Spending % GDP, 2003	−0.36	−0.045	0.156
GDP per capita, 2003	0.27	0.000056	0.28
High School Enroll, 1995	−0.13	−0.029	0.60

Table 12.4: Multiple regression explaining the poverty rate in the developed nations.

Dependent Variable: POVERTY RATE, 2000

Overall Equation

Multiple R	0.80
Multiple R^2	0.64
Significance	0.001

Separate Effects of Independent Variables	Beta	b	Sig
Govt Spending % GDP, 1997	−0.83	−0.36	0.000
GNP per capita, 1999	−0.36	−0.00035	0.04
High School Enroll, 1995	0.22	0.20	0.21

results do nothing to belie the results from the simple regressions in Chapter 11 supporting this theory. Figures 11.4 and 11.5, for example, showed that industrialized nations with larger governments do indeed have better social outcomes in the form of lower rates of infant mortality and poverty. Tables 12.3 and 12.4 present multiple regression results which confirm that controlling for other factors does not change this support for the liberal perspective. In these tables, infant mortality and poverty levels are explained in the regression equations by government size, secondary school enrollment, and GNP per capita.[2] The Multiple R's are a little higher than the simple correlation of these two variables with the government/GDP ratio — 0.51 to −0.45 for infant mortality and 0.80 to −0.71 for poverty. This indicates that GNP per capita and high school enrollment provide some, but fairly limited, additional explanatory power beyond that exercised by government size. Yet, in both tables, government size remains the dominant influence on these social outcomes with any independent effects of the other two explanatory factors being fairly marginal.

12.2.3 More Evidence of the Paradox of Large Government

The results of the simple correlational analysis in Chapter 11 suggested that there might be a paradox associated with big government in that it is good in some ways but bad in others. In particular, larger governments appeared to have better performance than smaller ones in terms of social outcomes but worse in terms of economic dynamism. The more complex statistical analysis based on multiple regression in this chapter does little, if anything, to alter this conclusion. The strong impact of government size on economic and social performance changed little when other explanatory factors were controlled, implying that the paradox of large government really does reflect how the world works today. For politicians, this is almost certainly bad news because it suggests that policies that promote better outcomes in some areas hurt national performance in others, leaving them an unresolvable dilemma about what works. For political scientists, in contrast, this may well be good news because it certainly implies that **policy matters**.

12.3 ASSUMPTIONS OF MULTIPLE REGRESSION

Multiple regression, as might be expected, is subject to the same assumptions underlying linear regression. Thus, all the variables

---

[2] While (as seen in Chapter 11) a quadratic equation provides a significantly better explanation than a linear one of wealth's impact on infant mortality, the linear format is used here to make the results simpler because, even in the quadratic model, GDP's independent influence on inequality is marginal.

included in the analysis must be at the interval level of measurement, meet various technical requirements about the normality of their distribution, and have linear relationships with the dependent variable. The overall equation, in addition, must include the relevant explanatory factors. Multiple regression obviously provides a much better check on spurious relationships than bivariate analysis since more independent variables are included. However, the summary statistics produced by multiple regression cannot directly tell us whether curvilinear relationships exist. Thus, it is sometimes valuable to check simple scatterplots before accepting multiple regression outputs.

Multiple regression adds to the problems about statistical significance when the sample size is small. In addition to the strength of the correlation and the number of cases which influence statistical significance in simple regression, significance in multiple regression is also affected by the number of independent variables. Increasing the number of independent variables decreases the confidence that we can have in any particular estimate, both for the overall Multiple R and for the b's and betas for the separate effects exercised by the independent variables. For example, dropping the weakest independent variable from the equation (GDP per capita) in Table 12.1 above does not change the Multiple R of 0.72, but does lower its significance substantially from 0.027 to 0.011, as is shown in Table 12.5. In addition, dropping GDP per capita makes almost no difference in the independent effects exercised by the three remaining independent variables. Consequently, even fairly strong relationships may not attain statistical significance if there are more than a couple of independent variables, as several examples in this chapter illustrate.

There is one specific danger in multiple regression, though, that does not exist in simple regression. This concerns the relationships among the independent variables. Problems can arise if the independent variables are too highly correlated among themselves. This produces what is technically called **multicollinearity**. If two predictor variables are too highly intertwined, it is impossible to disentangle their separate effects; and the results produced by multiple regression become weird and unrealistic. In such cases, one may get a very high positive beta coefficient (not uncommonly over 1), while the other will have a very low negative beta (not uncommonly under -1).

Table 12.5: Effects of dropping a marginal independent variable from a multiple regression.

A. Initial Results

Dependent Variable: GNP GROWTH, 1980–1989

Overall Equation

Multiple R	0.72
Multiple R^2	0.52
Significance	0.027
a	1.40

Separate Effects of Independent Variables	Beta	b	Sig
Govt Spend % GDP, 1980	−0.59	−0.037	0.012
High Sch Enrollment, 1979	0.36	0.023	0.082
Savings % GDP, 1980	0.26	0.035	0.23
GDP p.c., 1980	0.08	0.00003	0.68

B. Results After Dropping Independent Variable with No Effect

Dependent Variable: GNP GROWTH, 1980–1989

Overall Equation

Multiple R	0.72
Multiple R^2	0.52
Significance	0.011
a	1.40

Separate Effects of Independent Variables	Beta	b	Sig
Govt Spend % GDP, 1980	−0.58	−0.036	0.010
High Sch Enrollment, 1979	0.36	0.023	0.089
Savings % GDP, 1980	0.29	0.038	0.153

When multicollinearity exists, the Multiple R may well be artificially inflated to a value much higher than any of the simple r's between the independent and dependent variables, as well. Usually, multicollinearity does not become a problem unless some of the independent variables have extremely high intercorrelations. When the Multiple R or betas indicate that multicollinearity is present, one of the variables causing it obviously must be removed from the regression equation if the results are to have any validity. Again, these dangers of multicollinearity point to the need to study your results carefully, rather than simply copying down the statistics that are spewed forth by your computer!

For example, there is a very strong correlation of 0.73 between size of government in 1997 and whether or not a nation has a system of "democratic corporatism" which refers to a style of policy-making based on consensual bargaining between government and the major powers in society, such as business, labor, or the church.[3] As a result, there is strong evidence of multicollinearity when both, along with GNP per capita and high school enrollment, are used to explain the number of hospital beds available to the residents of a country. As the multiple regression results in Table 12.6 show, using them

Table 12.6: Multiple regression explaining hospital beds showing evidence of multicollinearity.

Dependent Variable: HOSPITAL BEDS PER 1,000, 1997

Overall Equation

Multiple R	0.81
Multiple R^2	0.66
Significance	0.005

Separate Effects of Independent Variables	Beta	b	Sig
Corporatist Government	1.12	10.19	0.001
Govt Spend % GDP, 1997	−0.78	−0.39	0.009
High School Enroll, 1995	−0.49	−0.53	0.017
GNP p.c., 1999	0.01	0.00001	0.96

Bivariate Association with GNP Growth	r	b	Sig
Corporatist Government	0.51	4.60	0.032
Govt Spend % GNP, 1997	0.08	0.040	0.73
High School Enroll, 1995	−0.04	−0.045	0.85
GNP p.c., 1999	0.48	0.0005	0.029

---

[3] Harold L. Wilensky, *Rich Democracies: Political Economy, Public Policy, and Performance* (Berkeley: University of California Press, 2002), Chapter 2.

both in the equation produces a Multiple R which is considerably higher than any of the simple r's (0.81 to 0.51). The real evidence of multicollinearity is seen in the betas, though. The extremely high positive beta for corporatism of 1.12 coupled with the strongly negative one for the government/GDP ratio of -0.78 is precisely the type of weird result that multicollinearity produces. Furthermore, the huge differences between the r's and betas for the other two independent variables also suggest that multicollinearity is distorting the results in the multiple regression.

12.4 PATH ANALYSIS AND CAUSAL MODELING

So far in this chapter, multiple regression has been used to evaluate the simultaneous impact of a set of explanatory or independent variables upon a single dependent variable. Sometimes, however, it is valuable to explore the relationships among the independent variables themselves in what is termed a **causal model**. Figure 12.2 presents an arrow diagram of a simple causal model involving three variables in a two-stage relationship concerning the impact of government role on economic growth for the developed nations during the 1990s. The guiding theory here is the conservative one that big government undercuts economic efficiency and growth. In particular, as sketched in Figure 12.2, both the absolute size of government in 1990 and the change in government size between 1990 and 1997 would be predicted to have influenced the 1990–1999 economic growth rate; and, in addition, the size of government in 1990 could well have affected changes in government size over the 1990s.

This creates a two-stage model. In the first stage, the initial size of the Government/GDP ratio in 1990 is assumed to influence changes in government size over the 1990s in Path A in the model. At the second stage, both 1990 government size and 1990–1997 change in government size are hypothesized to affect economic growth during the 1990s in Paths B and C, respectively. Paths A, B, and C each represent a **direct influence** of an independent variable upon a dependent one. In addition, the government/GDP ratio exercises an **indirect influence** on growth through its association with change

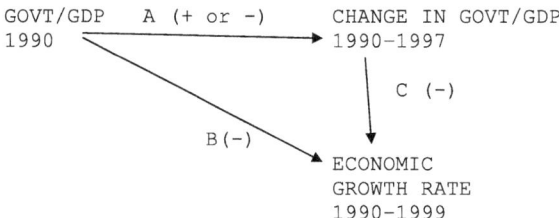

```
Direct Effects
Govt/GDP Ratio on Change in Govt/GDP:      Path A
Govt/GDP Ratio on Economic Growth Rate:    Path B
Change in Govt/GDP on Economic Growth:     Path C


Indirect Effect
Govt/GDP Ratio on Economic Growth:         Via Paths A & C


Hypothesized Relationships
#1   Paths B and C should be negative because of the economically
bad effects normally attributed to big government.

#2   The predicted direction of Path A is indeterminate because
either of two causal dynamics could be at work:
     a) There might be a positive relationships if bigger
        governments in 1990 continued to be spend more
        over the 1990s.
     b) There might also be a negative relationship if bigger
        governments in 1990 faced more severe budget problems
        and, thus, had greater pressure to cut spending.
```

Figure 12.2: Direct and indirect relationships in path model.

in government size, as represented in the figure by a combination of Path A and Path C.

In terms of the actual hypotheses about the direction of these relationships at the bottom of Figure 12.2, the conservative logic that big government undermines economic performance would clearly predict that both Path B and Path C would be negative. The direction of Path A, though, is harder to predict *a priori*. On the one hand, if relative government size in 1990 is taken to represent the pro- or anti-government feelings of the population and the state, larger governments would be more likely to expand than smaller ones — thereby creating a positive relationship. On the other hand, if the largest governments in 1990 suffered from the greatest budget problems, they would then be the ones most likely to restrain spending — thereby creating a negative relationship.

The nature of this ambiguous Path A is important for the overall model. If the relationship is positive, the direct and indirect effects of government size in 1990 on economic growth during the 1990s will be consistent. If government size's impact on change in the government/GDP ratio is positive then its indirect effect on economic performance should be negative too, because the intervening variable is presumed to be negatively related to growth in Path C. That is, if Path A is positive and Path C negative, their product should be negative as well. However, if larger governments in 1990 were forced to restrain spending more than others, this would make Path A negative. In turn, if both Path A and Path C are negative, government size's indirect impact on economic growth will be *positive* and, thus, be in the opposite direction from its presumed direct effect. Thus, its overall impact will be inconsistent in the sense that it consists of both positive and negative effects that must be counterbalancing or contradictory to some extent.

12.4.1 Chained Multiple Regressions and Path Analysis

Multiple regression analysis can be used to construct statistical estimates of the relationships in such a causal model. This is done in a three-step process. First, multiple regressions are calculated for each dependent variable in the model upon all the causally prior variables, creating a chain of linked regressions. Second, the standardized regression (beta) coefficients in these analyses become the **path coefficients** linking the variables in the causal model. Third, these path coefficients are used to compute the direct and indirect effects of any variable on all those causally subsequent to it.

For illustrative purposes, we will construct and interpret a causal model of economic growth during the 1990s explained by the two indicators of government role in Figure 12.2 plus the savings rate which is a factor often emphasized by conservatives in their linkage of big government to bad economic performance. These variables are listed in causal order below in the sense that each one is assumed to be potentially influenced by all the ones before it:

X_1 Ratio of government spending to GDP, 1990
X_2 Change in Govt/GDP Ratio, 1990–1997
X_3 Savings as % of GDP, 1999
X_4 Average Real Economic Growth Rate, 1990–1999

To test the causal model of the relationships among these four variables, three separate regression analyses must be computed:

(1) X_4 on X_1, X_2, and X_3;
(2) X_3 on X_1 and X_2; and
(3) X_2 on X_1.

The results from these three chained regressions are presented in Table 12.7. The first regression in this table provides very strong support for the model being tested. The high Multiple R of 0.77 in the top table under Equation #1 shows that, in combination, the three explanatory variables posited by conservative theory to shape a nation's economic competitiveness and dynamism had a very strong impact on the economic growth rates of the advanced industrial nations during the 1990s. The R^2 shows that the equation explains 59% of the variance in economic growth among the developed nations. This Multiple R, in addition, is well above the highest simple correlation of -0.56 for change in the government/GDP ratio (see the far right of the bottom table under Equation #1), indicating that the other two independent variables added considerable predictive power. Thus, this model is quite powerful in its ability to distinguish the high growth from the low growth nations in the developed world during this decade; and it is also clear that the model needs to include more than one explanatory variable.

Moreover, when we look at the individual effects in the bottom or second little table under Equation #1, all three independent variables have exactly the effects that were predicted by conservatives. Change in the government/GDP ratio had a strongly negative impact as indicated by its beta of -0.60. Thus, nations whose governments grew the least or reduced the most had the best economic growth. Also, as predicted by conservatives, the nations that saved the most had more dynamic

Table 12.7: Chained regressions for the causal model of economic growth rate, 1990–1999.

Equation #1

Dependent Variable: ECONOMIC GROWTH, 1990–1999

Overall Equation

Multiple R	0.77
Multiple R^2	0.59
Significance	0.001

Separate Effects of Independent Variables	Beta	Sig	BIVARIATE r	Sig
Govt/GDP Ratio, 1990	−0.34	0.047	−0.17	0.45
Change in Govt/GDP, 1990–1997	−0.60	0.002	−0.56	0.008
Savings % GDP, 1999	0.41	0.018	0.48	0.029

Equation #2

Dependent Variable: SAVINGS RATE, 1999

Overall Equation

Multiple R	0.14
Multiple R^2	0.02
Significance	0.84

Separate Effects of Independent Variables	Beta	Sig	BIVARIATE r	Sig
Govt/GDP Ratio, 1990	0.01	0.97	0.04	0.85
Change in Govt/GDP, 1990–1997	−0.13	0.59	−0.13	0.56

Equation #3

Dependent Variable: CHANGE IN GOVT/GDP RATIO, 1990–1997

Overall Equation

Multiple R	0.26
Multiple R^2	0.07
Significance	0.27

Separate Effects of Independent Variables	Beta	Sig	BIVARIATE r	Sig
Govt/GDP Ratio, 1990	−0.26	0.27	−0.26	0.27

economies than those that were less frugal, as indicated by a fairly strong positive beta of 0.41. Finally, while we saw in Chapter 11 that government size in 1990 was only marginally associated with economic growth after 1990, once the effects of the other two independent variables are taken into account statistically, the government/GDP ratio did exercise a moderately negative influence, as indicated by its beta of -0.34 which is statistically significant at the 0.047 level.

In fairly sharp contrast, the results from Equations #2 and #3 indicate that the associations among the three explanatory variables for economic growth are quite meager. As shown by the very low Multiple R of 0.14 for Equation #2, the two indicators of government role have almost no impact on the savings rate. Thus, while conservatives are correct that big government hurts and high savings helps economic performance, they are wrong about the linkage among these factors. Evidently, the ill effects of big government are not transmitted through a low savings rate.

As noted in Figure 12.2, there is some ambiguity regarding what to expect about the relationship between government size in 1990 and subsequent change in the government/GDP ratio. *A priori*, we might predict that bigger governments would have more statist philosophies and, thus, would grow more or shrink less than smaller ones. However, this could well be counteracted by the fact that they might be under greater fiscal stress. Actually, Equation #3 found that the correlation between these two variables is -0.26, indicating that for the 1990s the second logic was somewhat stronger than the first. This is especially important because, as discussed above, it means that the impact of government size in 1990 on economic growth will be inconsistent. In particular, its negative direct effect will be offset to some extent by a positive indirect one exercised through the change in the government/GDP ratio as an intervening variable.

The betas from these three regressions can then be used to construct the path model illustrated in Figure 12.3. Note that the number of independent variables increases by one as you move up the causal model. Change in the government/GDP (X_2) only has one independent variable, government size in 1990 (X_1). The savings rate (X_3), in turn, is dependent on both (X_1) and (X_2). Finally, all the other

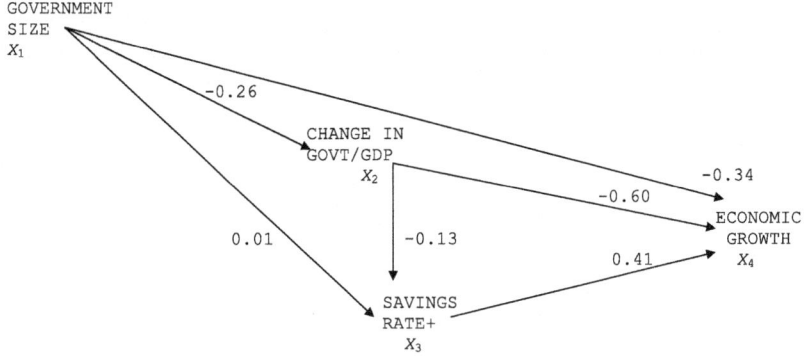

Figure 12.3: Full causal model with path coefficients.

variables are used to explain whether a nation's economic growth (X_4) is high or low.

12.4.2 The Theory of Path Analysis

The theory of path analysis rests on three principal assumptions about the nature of the direct and indirect causal influence that one variable exercises upon another within a causal model, as well as the spurious or noncausal association between them.[4] First, the direct impact (DC for direct causal) of one variable upon another is measured by the path coefficient between them. This is the beta coefficient in the relevant multiple regression.

Second, a variable can have an indirect impact (IC for indirect causal) on another if it is separated from it by one or more intervening variables. This indirect effect is estimated by summing the products of the path coefficients along each indirect path. For example, Figure 12.3 shows that there is one indirect path between X_2 (change in the government/GDP ratio) and X_4 (economic growth) through X_3

---

[4]For an excellent discussion of path models see, Jae-on Kim and Frank J. Kohout, "Special Topics in General Linear Models", pp. 368–397 in Norman H. Nie, C. Hadlai Hull, Jean K. Jenkins, Karin Steinbrenner and Dale H. Bent, *SPSS: Statistical Package for the Social Sciences* (New York: McGraw-Hill, 1975), especially the section on "Path Analysis and Causal Interpretation", pp. 383–397.

(savings rate) whose magnitude is calculated by multiplying P_{23} by P_{34}. Using the path coefficients in Figure 12.3, Table 12.8 calculates this as:

$$IC = P_{23}P_{34} = -0.13 \times 0.41 = -0.05.$$

Similarly but a little more complexly, there are three indirect paths between X_1 (government size) and X_4 (economic growth) through X_2 (change in government/GDP ratio), X_3 (savings rate), and both X_2 and X_3 which equal:

$$IC = P_{12}P_{24} + P_{13}P_{34} + P_{12}P_{23}P_{34}.$$

For our causal model displayed in Figure 12.3:

$$IC = P_{12}P_{24} + P_{13}P_{34} + P_{12}P_{23}P_{34}$$
$$= (-0.26 \times -0.60) + (0.01 \times 0.41) + (-0.26 \times -0.13 \times 0.41)$$
$$= 0.16 - 0.00 + 0.01 = 0.17.$$

Obviously, the more stages in an indirect relationship, the more complex the calculation.

Table 12.8: Calculation of indirect path effects.

Two-Stage Indirect Effects

#1 Change in GOVT/GDP (X_2) on Economic Growth (X_4) Through Savings Rate (X_3)

Path$_{23}$ × Path$_{34}$ = $-0.13 \times 0.41 = -0.05$

#2 Government Size (X_1) on Savings Rate (X_3) Through Change in GOVT/GDP (X_2)

Path$_{12}$ × Path$_{23}$ = $-0.26 \times -0.13 = 0.03$

Three-Stage Indirect Effect

#3 Government Size (X_1) on Economic Growth (X_4) Through Change in GOVT/GDP (X_2) and Savings Rate (X_3)

(Path$_{12}$ × Path$_{24}$) + (Path$_{13}$ × Path$_{34}$) + (Path$_{12}$ × Path$_{23}$ × Path$_{34}$)
$= (-0.26 \times -0.60) + (0.01 \times 0.41) + (-0.26 \times -0.13 \times 0.41)$
$= 0.16 + 0.00 + 0.01 = 0.17$

The third assumption of path analysis requires that the causal model be complete in the sense that only one-way causation exists — that X_2 influences X_4 but not *vice versa* — and that each variable is related to all the ones causally prior to it. If these two conditions hold, then the bivariate correlation between two variables (BA for bivariate association), as measured by the simple correlation coefficient r, can be broken down into three components:

(1) direct causal impact (DC);
(2) indirect causal impact (IC); and
(3) noncausal (NC) or spurious (S) correlation.[5]

If some relationships in the model are left unspecified, either because causal direction cannot be imputed or because weak and/or statistically insignificant relationships are dropped from the model, these omissions will also contribute to the noncausal component, creating what might be called "indeterminate noncausal" or INC association.

The following equations express these relationships:

$$BA = C + NC$$
$$C = DC + IC$$
$$NC = S + INC$$

INC = 0 for models with unidirectional causal order where a complete set of causal sequences is specified.

Thus, for complete unidirectional models, such as the one specified in Figure 12.3:

$$BA = DC + IC + S.$$

For anyone who does not have the intestinal fortitude to keep all the abbreviations used in these equations in their mind, Table 12.9 contains a list of what each means.

---

[5]This is bivariate association not reflecting a true causal relationship that results from the impact of the causal antecedents on both the dependent and independent variables in question.

Table 12.9: Abbreviations used in equations for the relationships in a path model.

BA is the bivariate association between two variables as measured by the correlation coefficient r.

C is the total causal impact of one variable upon another.

DC is the direct causal impact of one variable upon another as measured by their path coefficient, which is the beta coefficient from the multiple regression equation in which the independent variable explains the dependent one.

IC is the indirect causal influence of one variable upon another estimated by the sum of the products of the path coefficients in all the indirect paths between them going through intervening variables.

NC is the noncausal component of the initial bivariate relationship between two variables.

S is the spurious correlation between two variables that results from the effects of causally prior factors on both the dependent and independent variables.

INC is the indeterminate noncausal association resulting from unspecified relationships in the causal model.

Several things, both technical and substantive, should also be noted about causal modeling results. There are two important aspects of these results that are determined by the assumptions in the causal model. First, there can be no indirect effects between two adjacent variables in the causal order (e.g., X_1 and X_2 or X_3 and X_4). Second, the first variable in the causal sequence (X_1) has no spurious association with any of the other variables because there are no causally prior factors specified in the model which can make its bivariate correlations spurious. For example, Table 12.10 below shows that government size in 1990, the first variable in our causal model, has no spurious association at all with any of the other three variables in this path model.

Two other aspects of the results from path analysis are also worth noting. In general (but not always), overall predictive power as measured by Multiple R will decline as one moves further back in the causal order because the theoretical specification is primarily concerned with explaining the first dependent variable in the model. This is certainly true here. In Table 12.7 above which presented the results for the chained regressions, the Multiple R for Equation #1 for economic growth was 0.77, compared to the Multiple R's of 0.14 for Equation #2 and 0.26 for Equation #3. Most of the time as well, the

Table 12.10: Estimates of effects in full causal model.

	Bivariate association BA*	Causal			Noncausal
		Direct DC*	Indirect IC*	Total C*	Spurious S*
RELATIONSHIP					
Economic Growth					
Savings Rate	0.48	0.41	—	0.41	0.07
Change in Govt/GDP	−0.56	−0.60	−0.05	−0.65	0.09
Government Size	−0.17	−0.34	0.17	−0.17	—
Savings Rate					
Change in Govt/GDP	−0.13	−0.13	—	−0.13	0.00
Government Size	0.04	0.01	0.03	0.04	—
Change in Govt/GDP					
Government Size	−0.26	−0.26	—	−0.26	—

*BA = r
DC = beta
IC as computed in Table 12.8
C = DC + IC
S = BA − C

closer an independent variable is to a dependent one in the causal order, the greater will be their spurious association because there are more causally prior control variables affecting their bivariate relationship.

12.4.3 Summarizing the Causal Model for Economic Growth in the 1990s

Table 12.10 presents these calculations for our illustrative causal model of the economic growth rates of the 21 advanced industrial nations during the 1990s. There is one row of data for each of the six relationships in the model: the three independent variables that influence growth, the two that are used to explain the savings rate, and the single influence on the change in the ratio of government spending to GDP.

The first column reports the bivariate association (BA) between a specific independent and dependent variable as measured by the correlation coefficient r. For example, Table 12.7 reported that the change in the GOVT/GDP ratio has correlations of −0.56 with economic growth and -0.13 with the savings rate. The next three columns report the causal impact of an independent variable upon a particular dependent variable. The first is the direct causal (DC) as estimated by beta from the relevant multiple regression in Table 12.7; the second is the indirect causal (IC) as calculated in Table 12.8; and the last is the total causal or C which is simply the sum of the first two. For example, change in the government/GDP ratio has a direct causal impact on economic growth of -0.60 and indirect causal one of -0.05 on growth, creating a total causal effect of -0.65.

Finally, the last column represents the noncausal (NC) association which is the difference between the initial bivariate relationship and the total causal effect or BR − C. Since the causal model is fully specified, there is no indeterminate noncausal (INC), so that this last column also represents spurious (S) correlation. For example, while the savings rate has an r of 0.48 with economic growth, its total causal impact is only 0.41. Thus, the spurious association is:

$$0.48 - 0.41 = 0.07.$$

This is spurious in the sense that it is the component of the original r of 0.48 between savings and economic growth that is artificially created by the effects of the other two explanatory factors upon them. Also, note that government size in 1990 has no spurious association with any of the other three variables. Since path theory tells us that the initial independent variable, in this case the government/GDP ratio in 1990, cannot have any spurious association with any of the other variables in the causal model, a simple way to check your calculations is to see whether BA = C for all its relationships.

Once we have taken the time and trouble to go through what everything means, applying this to interpreting the causal model is fairly simple and short, thank heaven! In terms of the direct effects, Table 12.10 shows that all three explanatory variables influenced the economic growth of the developed nations during the 1990s exactly as conservative theory would predict, with both indicators of government size being negatively related to growth while the savings rate had a positive effect. In contrast, the association among these explanatory variables was quite limited, contradicting the conservative argument that big government would stifle savings and investment.

Perhaps the biggest advantage of causal modeling is that adding indirect effects to an analysis can significantly modify the implications of a single multiple regression about the relative influence of the independent variables. Here, the indirect influence of 0.17 that government size in 1990 exerted on economic growth, primarily through its association with change in the government/GDP ratio over the 1990s, stands out because it is positive in direct contrast the negative direct effect indicated by its beta of −0.34. This occurs, as discussed above, because of the nature of the direct association between government size in 1990 and the subsequent change in government size over the 1990s.

This indirect relationship is substantively important because it explains an anomalous finding in the simple or direct correlations. For the 1990s, unlike the previous 25 years, government size at the beginning of a period did not have a fairly strong negative impact on growth in the subsequent 10 or 15-year period as the correlation between the government/GDP ratio in 1990 and growth during 1990–1999 was only −0.17. Yet, the multiple regression results in Table 12.8 found that a direct causal influence of −0.34 on growth that was counterbalanced by its indirect effect of 0.17. Thus, while the overall negative effect of government size on growth was significantly less in the 1990s than for 1965–1990, it still had a moderate impact in the predicted direction. This change in the nature of its impact evidently occurred because the fiscal strains on the largest governments in the early 1990s forced them to cut spending relative to other nations in direct contrast to their behavior over the previous several decades. This, in turn, reduced the normal association between government size and economic performance and set off the somewhat contradictory inter-relationships among government size in 1990, change in government size from 1990 to 1997, and economic growth during 1990–1999.

Path analysis, therefore, is a valuable application and extension of multiple regression techniques to test not only the relative impact of explanatory variables, but also the indirect effects going through the causal sequences and the inter-relationships among the independent variables. As the preceding example shows, sketching out the more intricate set of relationships in a path model may alter the results significantly and give us a better insight into the dynamics of cause-and-effect that are at work.

EXERCISES

1. Interpret the results of the following multiple regression analysis. First, discuss the theoretical nature of the model being analyzed. What is the dependent variable? What are the independent ones? What would be the conservative, liberal, or resource-base hypotheses about these relationships? Second, use the data from the multiple regression to test this model. How strong is the combined impact of the independent variables? What is the relative influence of each independent variable? How much effect on the dependent variable does a one unit increase in each have? Which effects are statistically significant and which are not? Are the results more consistent with the theories of conservatives or liberals?

   Dependent Variable: UNEMPLOYMENT RATE, 2006

   Overall Equation

Multiple R	0.50
Multiple R^2	0.25
Significance	0.30

Separate Effects of Independent Variables	Beta	b	Sig
Govt Spending % GDP, 2003	0.27	0.089	0.34
GDP per capita, 2003	−0.35	−0.00004	0.20
High School Enroll, 1995	0.05	0.022	0.86

2. From the set of chained regressions below, calculate the estimates for a full causal model (see Table 12.10). Discuss the theoretical model being analyzed. In particular, give short logical hypotheses for each relationship in the model. Does each one reflect the conservative,

liberal, or resource-base perspective about these relationships? Then use the data in the table to evaluate whether each hypothesis is supported and, if it is, how strong the relationship is. Be sure to distinguish between the direct and indirect relationships. Finally, discuss any spurious associations that seems significant. What was the initial or observed correlation? What happened to make it spurious?

CHAINED REGRESSIONS FOR THE CAUSAL MODEL OF INFANT MORTALITY RATE, 2003

Equation #1

Dependent Variable: INFANT MORTALITY, 2003

Overall Equation

Multiple R	0.49
Multiple R^2	0.24
Significance	0.20

Separate Effects of Independent Variables	Beta	Sig	BIVARIATE r	Sig
Govt/GDP Ratio, 2003	−0.34	0.18	−0.43	0.06
GDP p.c., 2003	0.27	0.28	0.21	0.37
High School Enrollment, 2003	−0.11	0.67	−0.14	0.56

Equation #2

Dependent Variable: HIGH SCHOOL ENROLLMENT RATE, 2003

Overall Equation

Multiple R	0.45
Multiple R^2	0.20
Significance	0.15

Separate Effects of Independent Variables	Beta	Sig	BIVARIATE r	Sig
Govt/GDP Ratio, 2003	0.39	0.10	0.04	0.16
GDP p.c., 2003	0.32	0.17	0.22	0.35

Equation #3

Dependent Variable: GOVT/GDP RATIO, 2003

Overall Equation

Multiple R 0.21
Multiple R^2 0.04
Significance   0.38

Separate Effects of Independent Variables	Beta	Sig	BIVARIATE r	Sig
GDP p.c., 2003	−0.21	0.38	−0.21	0.38

Chapter 13

Logistic Regression: Developing More Complete Models of Partisanship

The regression and correlation techniques discussed in Chapters 11 and 12 provide a sophisticated means for examining the relationships among two or more variables that are at the interval level of measurement. Yet, as discussed in Chapters 9 and 10, regression is not really applicable to most of the data in public opinion surveys where the variables are almost exclusively ordinal and nominal. Moreover, while crosstabulation can be used to perform multivariate analysis about the relationships among three or more variables, the results are much more limited than those produced by regression (see Chapter 12).

This creates severe limitations for analyzing public opinion data which, in the past, were sometimes circumvented by "assuming" that ordinal variables approximated the interval level of measurement.[1] Over the past several decades, though, there has been an increasing application of **logistic regression** or **logit** to public opinion (and many other types of) data in political science since categoric data can be modified to fit the requisites for logit which was explicitly designed

---

[1] For example, Warren E. Miller and J. Merrill Shanks, *The New American Voter* (Cambridge: Harvard University Press, 1996) make this argument in one of the most influential analyses of public opinion in the United States.

to explain the probability that something will occur. Indeed, logistic regression is now probably the dominant methodology used in the analysis of public opinion data.

Unfortunately, this technique is so advanced and complicated that it cannot be presented in terms similar to those for the other techniques described in this text. Still, its prevalence in political science makes it almost mandatory to understand for keeping up with the literature in quantitative studies. Furthermore, the similarity of the statistics that it produces to the results of simple and multiple regression should make the interpretation of logistic regression fairly straightforward, even if the calculations and some of the mathematical logic and modeling go far beyond the scope of a basic text.

This chapter, hence, contains an introduction to logistic regression that should allow the reader to interpret the major results produced by the technique and understand the logic underlying the statistics. It begins by sketching three different approaches to relating an independent variable to a dependent one with two categories, which can be conceptualized as explaining the probability that a case has the characteristic denoted by one of the categories of the dependent variable, such as voting for Barack Obama rather than John McCain. In particular, this background section indicates several advantages that logistic regression possesses compared to crosstabulation and simple linear regression in such an analytic situation. The second section then describes the basic statistics in a logistic regression; and the third illustrates the technique further by presenting the results from several more elaborate logit analyses about how political attitudes influence a voter's choice.

13.1 CROSSTABS, SIMPLE REGRESSION, AND LOGIT AS ALTERNATIVES FOR EXPLAINING A DICHOTOMOUS VARIABLE

Logistic regression can be used when the dependent variable has two categories or, to use a technical phrase, is a **dichotomy**. It was developed in medical research, especially epidemiology, where a great deal of research seeks to explain the presence or absence of something, such as a particular disease.[2] This is also often the case with the categoric data from public opinion surveys. If the variable does not naturally have two categories, such as gender (male and female) or being a born again Christian (yes or no), it is often easy to recode it into a dichotomy. For example, presidential vote in 2008, which initially had four categories (see Table 2.1 in Chapter 2), can be recoded and reconceptualized into a dichotomy between McCain voters and Obama voters, with all other categories being considered missing data.

Thus, logistic regression proved to be attractive to political science researchers interested in finding more advanced statistical techniques for analyzing categoric data. As a background for understanding logistic regression, this section compares it to two other statistical techniques for analyzing dichotomous variables, crosstabulation and linear regression. This discussion highlights several advantages of logistic regression, thereby indicating why political scientists have found it to be an attractive methodology.

13.1.1 Crosstabulation: The Standard Approach

A dichotomous dependent variable can easily be crosstabulated with other categoric variables; and, indeed, this was long the standard approach for analyzing such relationships. For example, Table 13.1 contains the crosstabulation of voting for Barack Obama, as opposed

Table 13.1: Crosstabulation of Obama vote by opposition to the Iraq war.

Presidential vote	Iraq war		
	Do not oppose	Oppose	Total
McCain	79.2%	23.8%	45%
Obama	20.8%	76.2%	55%
TOTAL	100.0%	100.0%	100%

Percent comparison, Obama:
76.2% − 20.8% = 55.4% or percentage points
Gamma = 0.85   Approximate Sig. = 0.0004

---

[2] Schuyler W. Huck, *Reading Statistics and Research*, 3rd Edn. (New York: Longman, 2000), p. 590.

to John McCain, by an ordinal variable of whether or not a respondent opposed the Iraq War. Opposition to the Iraq War is given the high value here because, as we shall see, positive relationships make the interpretation of one of the key results from logistic regression much easier to understand.

One would expect a strong positive relationship here; and the table demonstrates that this is certainly the case. Obama received the votes of 76.2% from the people who disapproved the War compared to only 20.8% from those who approved or were neutral toward it, creating a huge percentage comparison of 55.4 percentage points (76.2%–20.8%). Similarly, the correlation coefficient, Gamma, is extremely high at 0.85 and very significant statistically.

13.1.2 Linear Regression: Treating Dichotomies as Probabilities

Dichotomous variables can also be treated as interval-level data. For example, if its two categories are coded zero and one (as they are here for McCain and Obama respectively), a dichotomous dependent variable has a central characteristic that gives linear regression results a substantively appealing and easily understandable interpretation. In such a case, the proportion of cases in the category scored one represents the probability of having the characteristic denoted by that category, in this case casting a ballot in the 2008 presidential election for Barack Obama rather than John McCain.

This property gives the slope or unstandardized regression coefficient b an important substantive meaning. The dependent variable, as just noted, can be conceptualized as the probability that a particular respondent voted for Obama (as opposed to McCain). The slope coefficient measures how much this changes when the independent variable increases by one unit. When the independent variable is also a dichotomy coded zero and one as it is here (one for disapproving the Iraq War and zero for approving or being neutral toward it), this interpretation becomes especially attractive. In such a case, b represents the increased probability of having the trait denoted by the dependent variable (e.g., voting for Obama) that results from having

Table 13.2: Regression statistics for relationship between Obama vote and disapproval of Iraq war.

$$Y = 0.70 + 0.554X$$
$$r = 0.54$$
$$r^2 = 0.29$$
$$b = 0.554$$
$$\text{Sig.} = 0.0004$$

the characteristic denoted by the independent variable (e.g., opposing the War).[3] In short, b is equivalent to the percentage comparison.

As an illustration, Table 13.2 presents the regression results for Obama vote explained by disapproval of the Iraq War. The relationship is a strong one, as shown by the r of 0.54 and r^2 (or predictive power) of 0.29. The slope coefficient equals 0.554, which tells us that the probability that an opponent of the Iraq War voted for Obama is 55.4% or percentage points higher than that of someone who did not disapprove it. Going back to the crosstab in Table 13.1, this is exactly the same as the percentage comparison for Obama. In addition, comparing the Gamma of 0.85 and the r of 0.54 highlights the fact that Gamma tends to be higher than r for the same relationship.

13.1.3 Logistic Regression: A Technique More Explicitly Tailored for Explaining Probabilities

The special nature of dichotomous variables allows linear regression to be used, which can be quite advantageous. A key factor here is the ability to conceptualize such variables in terms of probabilities. Introducing the idea of interpreting these results in terms of probabilities, however, points to some disadvantages of linear regression for modeling such a relationship. In contrast to linear regression, logistic regression has been much more explicitly developed to analyze probabilities. This subsection, hence, discusses three advantages of logistic regression over linear regression. The first two are technical; and there is little argument

---

[3]R. Darcy and Richard C. Rohrs, *A Guide to Quantitative History* (Westport, CT: Praeger, 1995), pp. 211–219.

over their validity. The third concerns how user friendly the results are; and here there may be more disagreement.

The first problem with using linear regression to model a dichotomy is that the probability of an action, in this case voting for Obama rather than McCain, can only vary between zero and one. A linear regression equation, however, often predicts values that are below zero or above one. In contrast, when the variables are transformed into a function based on their **natural logarithm or log to the base e**, the resulting logistic regression equation rectifies this problem because it will produce a set of predicted values that fall within the valid range of zero to one.

The second criticism of linear regression that is relevant here is that its linear or straight-line projects do not necessarily provide the best fit or model for many relationships. In many instances, the relationship follows the logistic pattern in which a given change in the independent variable produces a bigger change in the dependent variable in the middle of its distribution rather than at its extremes. For example, this is clearly the case for the relationship between Obama vote and the seven-category indicator of ideological self-identification in Table 13.3. Here, by far the largest difference in the percentages of Obama vote along the bottom row among the categories of liberals and conservatives occur in the middle of the table between slightly liberal and conservative rather than at the extremes. Advocates of logistic regression argue that this model is more appropriate for many of the relationships that social scientists seek to model than is linear regression.[4] This, of course, is an empirical question for each analysis that you do.

The third argument for logistic regression is that it provides a measure of the impact of one or more independent variables that is easier to understand than the correlation and regression coefficients in linear regression because it represents a concept with which most people are familiar — the odds that something will occur. For example, in medical research the odds that someone will be cured of a specific disease by various possible treatments is obviously of central concern.

---

[4] Janet Buttolph Johnson and H.T. Reynolds, *Political Science Research Methods*, 5th Edn. (Washington, DC: CQ Press, 2005), pp. 431–433.

Table 13.3: Crosstabulation of Obama vote by conservative ideology.

Presidential vote	Ideology							Total
	Very liberal	Liberal	Slightly liberal	Moderate	Slightly conservative	Conservative	Very conservative	
McCain	1%	5%	18%	37%	56%	89%	90%	46%
Obama	99%	95%	82%	63%	44%	11%	10%	54%
TOTAL	100%	100%	100%	100%	100%	100%	100%	100%

More prosaically, devotees of horse racing know that the amount of money that they can win by betting on a horse depends on the pre-race odds that the horse will win. The odds of something occurring are simply the ratio of the number or proportion of times that it should occur to the number or proportion of times that it should not. As an example, let us go back to the crosstab of Obama vote by opposition to the Iraq War in Table 13.1. Among the opponents of the War, 76.2% voted for Obama, while 23.8% voted for McCain. The odds that somebody who disapproved the War would vote for Obama can, thus, be easily calculated as the ratio of these percentages:

Odds of Iraq War = 76.2%/23.8% = 3.20 to 1.
Opponent Voting
for Obama

Thus, as would certainly be expected, the odds that an opponent of the War would have voted for Obama are considerably higher than a ratio of one to one. Conversely, the odds of a non-opponent voting for Obama would be expected to be well under one to one; and this, indeed, turns out to be the case since Obama got only 20.8% of the votes in this group:

Odds of Iraq War = 20.8%/79.2% = 0.263 to 1.
Non-opponent Voting
for Obama

A measure of association based on the **Odds Ratio** or **OR** between two categories in a dichotomous independent variable can thus be used to describe the impact of the independent variable on the dependent one. This can be computed according to the following formula:

$$\text{OR} = \frac{P(\text{yes})/P(\text{no}) \text{ for } A}{P(\text{yes})/P(\text{no}) \text{ for } B}.$$

Where:

OR is the Odds Ratio;
P is the Proportion or Probability of cases in a given category;
A and B are the two categories for the Independent Variable;
"Yes" represents the presence and "No" the absence of the characteristic defined by the two categories of the Dependent Variable.

For the example of Obama vote and opposition to the War in Iraq:

A represents opponents of the War in Iraq;
B represents non-opponents of the War.

Yes represents Obama voters,
No represents McCain voters.

Therefore, the Odds Ratio (OR) for the impact of disapproval of the War on Obama vote is:

$$\text{OR} = \frac{P(\text{yes})/P(\text{no}) \text{ for } A}{P(\text{yes})/P(\text{no}) \text{ for } B}$$

$$\text{OR} = \frac{79.2\%/20.8\%}{23.8\%/76.2\%} = 3.20/0.263 = 12.17.$$

This tells us that the odds that an opponent of the War voted for Obama in 2008 was just over 12 times (12.17 to be exact) greater than for somebody who did not oppose it.

If the independent variable has no effect whatsoever, this Odds Ratio or OR will be one because the odds in the two columns of the crosstab will be exactly the same. The more that the OR departs from one, then, the greater is the impact of the independent variable. As a measure of association, therefore, the Odds Ratio possesses the decided advantage that it is expressed in units that make substantive sense, especially to medical researchers and horse race handicappers. Conversely, it does not possess the standardized range of zero to one of most correlation coefficients, such as r or Gamma. Whether or not this is a disadvantage probably depends upon the eye of the beholder!

13.2 LOGISTIC REGRESSION: THE BASIC RESULTS

This section provides an overview of the results in a simple logistic regression with one independent variable. In particular, the logistic regression of Obama vote on the two-category indicator of opposition to the Iraq War is described in some detail. This example represents the simplest application of logistic regression to the relationship between two dichotomous variables. This is advantageous because several complex calculations in logistic regression can be related to the simple data in the original crosstab. It also suggests, though, that such an advanced technique as logit should only be applied in more complex analytic situations because it really does not tell us much more than can be gleaned from a simple crosstabulation and its associated statistics.

13.2.1 The Logistic Regression Equation

Logistic regression is similar to linear regression in that the best model describing the relationship between two variables is calculated and in that statistics are produced measuring the shape, strength, and statistical significance of the association between the two items. However, because Y is modeled as being a logistic function of X, their relationship cannot be stated in terms of a simple equation, such as:

$$Y = a + bX.$$

Rather, either the left or the right side of the equation must be expressed in logistic terms whose meaning is not so readily apparent.

As in linear regression, logistic regression requires that the variables in the analysis meet certain criteria. The dependent variable must be a dichotomy coded zero and one; and several types of independent variables can be used. First, interval variables (e.g., age and income) and natural dichotomies (e.g., gender) can be directly entered into the explanatory equation. Second, categoric variables can be included in logit with either of the following formats. The variable itself may be divided into a dichotomy; or it may be broken up into two or more dummy variables. For example, attitudes about tax cuts can be divided into support and opposition, creating a dichotomy; and attitudes about abortion can be used to create two dummy variables denoting pro-choice and pro-life positions with people holding intermediate views being treated as the "baseline" group.

In logistic regression, the dependent variable is conceptualized as the odds that it will equal one. For the illustrative analysis presented here, this is the odds that a respondent will vote for Barack Obama. To create a logistic function, the dependent variable is transformed so that it becomes the **natural logarithm or log to the base e (which equals approximately 2.7182) of the odds that a respondent voted for Obama**. Indeed, the term logit refers to the natural logarithm of odds or **log odds**.[5] The log of these odds is a linear function of the value of the independent variable, in this case whether someone disapproved or did not disapprove of the Iraq War:

$$\text{Log of Odds of Voting for Obama} = a + bX.$$

Where:

Log of the Odds or LOGIT is the natural log of the Odds that a respondent voted for Obama rather than McCain;
X is opposition to the Iraq War which is coded one for opponents and zero for people who did not disapprove of the War.

Table 13.4 presents the results of this logistic regression. In some ways, these results parallel those in a linear regression. There is a regression equation with two constants, which defines the shape of the relationship between X and Y; and a variety of statistics indicate the strength and statistical significance of the association. There are very substantial differences as well, however. First, since the constants a and b are used to explain the logarithm of the dependent variable, their substantive interpretation is quite opaque, to say the least! However, b is used to calculate the Odds Ratio, which is substantively meaningful. Second, while measures of the strength of association, such as r in simple regression or beta in multiple regression, are generally the key result in linear regressions; there is much less emphasis upon them in

---
[5] Alfred Demaris, *Logit Modeling: Practical Applications* (Newbury Park, CA: Sage, 1992), p. 2.

Table 13.4: Logit results for the relationship between Obama vote and opposition to Iraq war.

A. Overall Model

a	−1.338
b	2.50
Odds Ratio	12.19
−2 Log Likelihood	1,661.5
G (Chi Square)	470.8
Sig.	0.0004
Pseudo R^2	0.22

B. Effects of Independent Variable(s)

b	2.50
Standard Error	0.127
t	19.65
Sig.	0.0004
Odds Ratio	12.19

logit analyses, where the statistical significance of coefficients is usually the most important factor.[6]

The top half of Table 13.4 contains statistics concerning the entire equation. The two basic coefficients are a which is −1.338 and b which is 2.50. Given the nature of the dependent variable (the natural logarithm of the odds that someone voted for Obama rather than McCain), it is hard to attribute any substantive meaning to either statistic. However, the direction or sign of b is important and substantively meaningful. The b's or logistic regression coefficients are similar to the b's in multiple regression in that they are either positive or negative, depending upon whether the characteristic denoted by the independent variable is associated with voting for or against Barack Obama. We would certainly expect that opponents of the Iraq War would look much more favorably on Obama than on McCain; and, as predicted, b is indeed positive.

Furthermore, b can be used to calculate the **Odds Ratio** that a respondent was an Obama voter rather than a McCain supporter. In

---

[6]For introductory overviews of logistic regression see Huck, *op. cit.*, pp. 590–601; Johnson and Reynolds, *op. cit.*, pp. 429–448. For more technical explanations, see Alan Agresti, *Categorical Data Analysis* (New York: John Wiley, 1990); *Ibid*.

particular, the Odds Ratio (OR) as defined in the previous section equals **the value of e raised to the *b* power**:

$$OR = e^b.$$

Where:

OR is the Odds Ratio;
e is the natural base logarithm or approximately 2.7182;
b is the value of the regression coefficient in a logistic regression.

For the logistic regression of Obama vote on opposition to the Iraq War in Table 13.4, the value of b is 2.50. When e is raised to this power, the Odds Ratio turns out to be a high 12.19, which differs only minusculely due to rounding errors from the Odds Ratio of 12.17 that was calculated from the crosstab in Table 13.1 in the last section. Raising a strange number, like e, to a power defined by the value of the slope coefficient may seem more than a little intimidating. Yet, this is a fairly common function in mathematics. In fact, many calculators will directly calculate this for you. Substantively, this shows that the odds of someone who opposed the War in Iraq voting for Obama were 12.19 times higher than the odds that someone who did not oppose the war would support him. Certainly, this indicates that an extremely strong relationship exists between a person's position on the War and their vote for president. This interpretation also shows the advantage of having a dichotomous independent variable. Technically, the Odds Ratio measures the change in odds of having the characteristic denoted by the dependent variable (e.g., being an Obama voter) that is produced by a one-unit increase in the independent variable. When the independent variable has only two categories that are coded one and zero for the presence and absence of something (e.g., those who disapproved of the Iraq War), the Odds Ratio simply refers to the impact of having the characteristic denoted by the independent variable.

Many logit analyses are primarily concerned with the statistical significance of the relationships that they are modeling. This represents the philosophy of experimental design (see Chapter 4) which asks whether or not the independent variable produces a significant effect.

This is the prevalent research orientation in medical research which pioneered the utilization of logistic regression. Indeed, millions if not billions of dollars for pharmaceutical companies ride on clinical trials of whether a new drug has a significantly different effect from a placebo.

For the overall equation, the statistical significance is based on the **Log Likelihood (LL)** which represents the combined deviation of cases from the predictions of the logistic equation. This is somewhat similar to the squared deviations from the regression line in linear regression which are unexplained by the explanatory equation. Thus, the smaller the LL is, the better is the statistical explanation that a logistic regression provides. By itself, the LL is meaningless for estimating the strength or significance of a relationship. However, again like the "unexplained sum of squares" around a linear regression line, the LL after a variable has been entered into the analysis (LL_C) can be compared to the one before (LL_O) to give an estimate of the improvement in prediction provided by that variable.

The LL is usually not reported directly. Rather, most analyses give the quantity of ($-2 \times LL$) for two reasons. First, the LL is a negative number; and second and far more importantly, $-2LL$ is the value that enters into the calculation of statistical significance with the test statistic G:

$G = -2 \times (LL_O - LL_C)$,
G has a Chi Square distribution.

Where:

LL_O is the **original model** in which only the constant (a) has been entered;
LL_C is the LL for the **complete model** after one or more independent variables have been entered into the logistic regression equation.

For the data in Table 13.4, -2 LL is 1,661.5; and G or Chi Square is 470.84. Such a large Chi Square is statistically significant at the 0.0004 level. Thus, the association between opposition to the Iraq War and Obama vote is very highly significant statistically.

As political scientists increasingly used logistic regression, they became more interested in measuring the overall predictive power of the equations than the medical researchers with their logic of experimental design had been because of the importance of this in the "statistical approach" (see Chapter 4 for the difference between these two methodological orientations). Thus, equivalents to Multiple R in linear regression were developed. While these coefficients are expressed as R^2's, they do not really have the same precise meaning in terms of proportion of explained variance as does R^2 in linear regression. Indeed, there is no consensus among statisticians about what, if anything, constitutes an overall correlation coefficient in logistic regression.[7]

Table 13.4 reports one such estimate that is called **Pseudo R^2**. This Pseudo R^2 is based on a **proportionate reduction or error** in the relationship that is produced by the independent variable or variables. This, in turn, is measured by the standardized difference between the Original and Complete LLs:

$$\text{Pseudo } R^2 = (LL_O - LL_C)/LL_O.$$

Where:

LL_O is the **original model** in which only the constant (a) has been entered;

LL_C is the LL for the **complete model** after one or more independent variables have been entered into the logistic regression equation.

For the impact of opposition to the War in Iraq on Obama vote, Pseudo R^2 is 0.22 which indicates a strong relationship since its square root is 0.47.

The bottom half of Table 13.4 presents the **statistics associated with the regression coefficient** b. Like linear regression, different techniques are used to estimate the statistical significance of the overall equation and the regression coefficient b; and the statistical significance of b is calculated from the ratio of b to its Standard Error. Here, b is 2.50 with a Standard Error of 0.127, which is statistically significant at the 0.0004 level. Finally, as described above, the Odds Ratio of 12.19 is computed by raising e to the 2.50 (value of b) power.

---

[7] Johnson and Reynolds, *op. cit.*

13.2.2 Using Percentages and Probabilities to Describe a Logistic Relationship

One advantage of logistic regression is that some of its results can be presented in "user friendly" terms, such as percentages and probabilities, despite the very advanced nature of its calculations and many of its statistics. This subsection describes a supplement to the basic logit statistics whose substantive meaning is very easy to understand. It shows the calculations for determining the probability that someone with a specific value on the independent variable (e.g., opposing the Iraq War) will have the characteristic measured by the dependent variable (e.g., voting for Barack Obama).

The logistic regression equation can be rewritten so that Y is the probability that a case will have the characteristic coded one for the dependent variable. For this analysis, this is the probability that someone would have voted for Barack Obama. This is a very comprehensible figure. However, because the regression is based on a logistic function, this means that the right or the explanatory side of the equation must be expressed in logistic terms.[8] Indeed, to most of us, this equation might well look horrific at first glance:

$$\text{Probability } Y = 1 = e^{(a+bX)}/1 + e^{(a+bX)}.$$

Fortunately, especially when X is a dichotomy as it is in our illustrative analysis, this formula is quite easy to apply, at least if you have a calculator that will raise e to a given power!

For the example that we are using here, the independent variable has only two values, coded one for opponents of the Iraq War and zero for non opponents. Consequently, only two probabilities can be calculated, one for opponents and one for non-opponents. To compute the probability that an opponent or non-opponent of the War voted for Barack Obama, all that needs to be done is to substitute the values of X, a, and b into the formula for the Probability of Y:

---

[8] Johnson and Reynolds, *op. cit.* provide an excellent explanation of how to translate the Y as Log Odds equation into the Y = probability one.

Probability that a NonOpponent of the War Voted for Obama:

When $X = 0$
$a = -1.338$
$b = 2.50$
Probability $(Y = 1) = e^{(a+bX)}/1 + e^{(a+bX)}$
Probability $(Y = 1) = e^{(-1.338+(2.50\times 0))}/1 + e^{(-1.338+(2.50\times 0))}$
Probability $(Y = 1) = e^{(-1.338)}/1 + e^{(-1.338)}$
$= 0.2637/1.2637$
$= 20.9\%.$

For those who did not oppose the Iraq War, $X = 0$; so that $e^{(a+bX)}$ reduces to e^a or $e^{-1.338}$ because bX must equal zero. Raising e to the -1.338th power is 0.2637. The last step is to divide this quantity by one plus itself, which shows that the probability that a non-opponent of the War would vote for Obama in 2008 was 0.209 or 20.9%.

Similarly, when X equals one, the value of $(a + bX)$ is $(a + b)$ or $(-1.338 + 2.50 = 1.162)$. Raising e to the 1.162 power equals 3.196; and dividing 3.196 by 4.196 shows that the probability of an opponent of the War voting for Obama was 76.2%.

Probability that a War Opponent Voted for Obama

When $X = 1$
$a = -1.338$
$b = 2.50$
Probability $(Y = 1) = e^{(a+bX)}/1 + e^{(a+bX)}$
Probability $(Y = 1) = e^{(-1.338+(2.50\times 1))}/1 + e^{(-1.338+(2.50\times 1))}$
Probability $(Y = 1) = e^{(-1.338+2.50)}/1 + e^{(-1.338+2.50)}$
Probability $(Y = 1) = e^{(1.162)}/1 + e^{(1.162)}$
$= 3.196/4.196$
$= 76.2\%.$

Substantively, this provides another measure indicating a very strong degree of association between these two variables since opponents of the War were almost four times as likely as non-opponents to vote for Obama (76.2% to 20.9%). Methodologically, with very slight rounding errors, these probabilities correspond almost exactly to the percentages for Obama vote broken down by position on the war in Iraq in Table 13.1 (76.2% for opponents of the War and 20.8% for non-opponents). This should give you confidence that the complex logistic regression equations actually produce the quantities that statisticians claim. It also shows that the logistic regression may not add very much to the results of a simple crosstabulation of two dichotomous variables. However, as we shall see in the next section, these probability calculations can be very valuable in charting the relative influence of several explanatory variables.

13.3 MORE COMPLEX LOGIT RESULTS: CREATING MODELS OF HOW ISSUES SHAPE VOTING

Logistic regression is particularly valuable for more complex analyses. As we saw in the last section, many of its user-friendly statistics do not really tell us much more than far simpler methods of presentation when there is only one independent variable, especially if it is a dichotomy. When the independent variable is an interval one or when there are two or more independent variables, however, such statistics cannot be replicated from simple crosstabs. This section, hence, describes more elaborate logits to demonstrate the utility of the technique. The first subsection presents a logistic regression of how several political issues explain presidential vote in combination; and the second shows several types of results when all the independent variables either do not have positive relationships with the dependent variable or are not dichotomies.

13.3.1 Multivariate Logits

The simple two-variable logistic regression presented in the last section provided strong empirical support for the hypothesis that people who opposed the Iraq War would be much more likely to vote for Barack Obama than those who did not. The War, though, was just one of numerous issues that affected voters' evaluations of the presidential candidates. Here, we shall illustrate multivariate logistic regression by adding indicators of attitudes about cultural (abortion) and economic (government services and spending) issues to national security (the War

Table 13.5: Logistic regression explaining Obama vote by positions on the Iraq war, abortion, and government services.

Dependent Variable: Voted for Barack Obama (versus John McCain)

Overall Equation

−2 Log Likelihood	647.026
Chi Square	268.402
Significance	0.0004
a	−2.23
Pseudo R^2	0.30

Separate Effects of Independent Variables	b	St. Er	t	Sig.	Adjusted Odds Ratio
Anti-Iraq War	2.26	0.215	10.47	0.0004	9.53
Pro-Choice on Abortion	1.06	0.205	5.17	0.0004	2.89
Want More Government Services	0.96	0.202	4.76	0.0004	2.62

in Iraq) to see how they shaped the voting decision in 2008. To make the results easier to understand at this stage, attitudes about abortion and government services were recoded into dichotomies with the liberal positions (pro-choice and more government services) coded as one, while all other values were coded as zero. Table 13.5 presents the results from this multivariate logit. These statistics parallel those for the bivariate analyses, but there are some key differences as well.

Similarly to the difference between multiple and simple regression, the statistics for the overall equation measure the impact of several independent variables. The Pseudo R^2 and −2 multiplied by the LL (−2 LL) in the top part of the table both indicate that the two new independent variables contributed significantly more explanatory power to the logistic equation than just a respondent's position on Iraq which was analyzed in Table 13.4. The Pseudo R^2 increased from 0.22 to 0.30; and the −2 LL (which measures the equivalent of unexplained variance) dropped considerably from 1,661.5 to 647.0. Furthermore, this multivariate relationship was very highly significant statistically at the 0.004 level with a Chi Square of 268.4. In contrast, unlike the logit results in Table 13.4 for the impact of just opposition to the Iraq War on Obama vote, there cannot be an Odds Ratio for the overall equation in multivariate logistic regression because the effects of several separate independent variables are lumped together.

The supposition that several of the independent variables exercised significant influence on Obama vote, even after the effects of the others are statistically controlled, receives strong confirmation from the statistics on the individual effects of the three predictors in the bottom half of Table 13.5. There are several important substantive and methodological points to make about these coefficients for the independent variables. First, opposition to the Iraq War, a pro-choice position on abortion, and support for more government services should all make people more, not less, likely to vote for Barack Obama. As predicted, these three b's were positive. Second, all the explanatory factors clearly exercised substantial influence on voting independently of the others, since their b's were highly significant statistically at the 0.0004 level.

Third, the Odds Ratios for the independent variables are now called **Adjusted Odds Ratios** (AOR's) because they represent the independent effect of one explanatory variable after the other two have been controlled or adjusted. For example, in the direct logistic relationship between opposing the Iraq War and voting for Obama, the value of b was 2.50 which produced an Odds Ratio of 12.19 (see Table 13.4). Once the effects of feelings about abortion and government services are taken into account, though, the influence of opposition to the War on voting slips a little, as it has a b of 2.26 and an AOR of 9.53. It is not surprising that adding indicators of economic and cultural liberalism would reduce the impact of liberalism about national security on Obama vote. What might be surprising, though, is that the Odds Ratio remains so high, indicating that the overlap between it and the effects of the other two explanatory variables must have been fairly limited. The AOR's also indicate that being pro-choice and advocating an expansive government had similar and much less pronounced effects on presidential vote than opposition to the Iraq War did, as their AOR's were 2.89 and 2.62, respectively.

As with the AORs, the probabilities that voters with various combinations of characteristics defined by the three independent variables would cast their ballots for Barack Obama cannot be computed from simple crosstab tables. Thus, the multivariate logit results give us valuable and insightful information. The formula for calculating the probability that a respondent voted for Obama looks rather intimidating at first (or perhaps even second) glance:

Probability $Y = 1$ (Obama vote)
$$= e^{(a+b_1 X_1 + b_2 X_2 + b_3 X_3)} / 1 + e^{(a+b_1 X_1 + b_2 X_2 + b_3 X_3)}.$$

Yet, the fact that X equals either zero or one for all three independent variables means that we can get the power to which to raise e by simply adding the regression coefficients that we already have:

$$a = -2.23,$$
$$b_1 = 2.26 \text{ (oppose Iraq War)},$$
$$b_2 = 1.06 \text{ (pro-choice on abortion)},$$
$$b_3 = 0.96 \text{ (want more government services)}.$$

For example, for someone who had no liberal attitudes, $a + b_1 X_1 + b_2 X_2 + b_3 X_3$ would reduce to just a or -2.23 because all three X's are zero. Similarly, for someone who was liberal on all three issues:

$$a + b_1 X_1 + b_2 X_2 + b_3 X_3 = a + b_1 + b_2 + b_3$$
$$= -2.23 + 2.26 + 1.06 + 0.96 = 2.05.$$

Table 13.6 reports these calculations, as well as similar ones for other combinations of political attitudes, and then shows how these figures can be plugged into the overall equation for computing the probability that someone voted for Obama in the bottom half of the table. These results again underline the importance of issues for voting in contemporary America. For example, someone who did not take the liberal position on any of these three items had only a 9.7% probability of voting for Obama. Conversely, someone who was liberal on all three was almost certain (88.6%) to support him on election day. These probabilities, furthermore, show the much greater importance of views on the Iraq War, as compared to those about abortion and government services, in determining vote. Someone who was liberal on Iraq but not on the other two issues had a 50.6% probability of voting for the Democratic candidate in 2008. In stark contrast, people

Table 13.6: The probabilities that people with different combinations of the independent variables would vote for Barack Obama in 2008.

Values of Coefficients Used in Calculations

$a = -2.23$
$b_1 = 2.26$ (anti-Iraq War)
$b_2 = 1.06$ (pro-choice on abortion)
$b_3 = 0.96$ (want more government services)

Formula for Calculating Probabilities

Probability $Y = 1$ (Obama vote)
$= e^{(a+b_1X_1+b_2X_2+b_3X_3)}/1 + e^{(a+b_1X_1+b_2X_2+b_3X_3)}$

Value of $(a + b_1X_1 + b_2X_2 + b_3X_3)$

No Liberal positions: $-2.23 + 0 + 0 + 0 = -2.23$
Liberal on all three: $-2.23 + 2.26 + 1.06 + 0.96 = 2.05$
Liberal on just Iraq: $-2.23 + 2.26 + 0 + 0 = 0.03$
Liberal on just abortion: $-2.23 + 0 + 1.06 + 0 = -1.17$
Liberal on just government service: $-2.23 + 0 + 0 + 0.96 = -1.27$
Liberal on Iraq and abortion: $-2.23 + 2.26 + 1.06 + 0 = 1.09$
Liberal on Iraq and government: $-2.23 + 2.26 + 0 + 0.96 = 0.99$
Liberal on abort and government: $-2.23 + -0 + 1.06 + 0.96 = -0.21$

Probabilities for Different Values of Independent Variables

No Liberal Positions
Probability $Y = 1 = e^{(-2.23)}/1 + e^{(-2.23)}$
$= 0.1075/1.1075 = 9.7\%$

Liberal on All Three Attitudes
Probability $Y = 1 = e^{(2.05)}/1 + e^{(2.05)}$
$= 7.768/8.768 = 88.6\%$

Liberal on just Iraq War
Probability $Y = 1 = e^{(0.03)}/1 + e^{(0.03)}$
$= 1.03/2.03 = 50.6\%$

Liberal on Just Abortion
Probability $Y = 1 = e^{(-1.17)}/1 + e^{(-1.17)}$
$= 0.310/1.310 = 23.7\%$

Liberal on Just Government Services
Probability $Y = 1 = e^{(-1.27)}/1 + e^{(-1.27)}$
$= 0.281/1.281 = 21.9\%$

(*Continued*)

Table 13.6: (*Continued*).

Liberal on Iraq War and Abortion
Probability $Y = 1 = e^{(1.09)}/1 + e^{(1.09)}$
$= 2.974/3.974 = 74.8\%$
Liberal on Iraq War and Government Services
Probability $Y = 1 = e^{(0.99)}/1 + e^{(0.99)}$
$= 2.691/3.691 = 72.9\%$
Liberal on Abortion and Government Services
Probability $Y = 1 = e^{(-0.21)}/1 + e^{(-0.21)}$
$= 0.811/1.811 = 44.8\%$

who were liberal on just one of the other two issues were fairly unlikely (22% to 24%) to support Obama on election day. Similarly, opposition to the War plus a liberal position on one of the other two made a person almost 75% likely to cast her or his ballot for Obama, while being liberal on both abortion and government services but not Iraq resulted in only a 45% probability in voting for him.

13.3.2 The Advantages and Disadvantages of Using Other Types of Variables in Logits

Thus far, the logistic regressions that we have examined have been limited in the independent variables that they included to dichotomies which were coded zero and one and to variables which had a positive association with the dependent variable. This has the advantage of making the b's and AORs directly comparable because all the explanatory items are measured in terms of the same scale. This approach is fairly limiting, however; and very few logits in the professional literature follow this format. In this subsection, hence, logistic regressions with other types of codings will be examined. Working with the three variables in Table 13.5, we shall see what happens when: (1) an explanatory factor has a negative relationship with the dependent variable; (2) an independent variable is not a dichotomy; and (3) the analyst wants to see how several different categories of an item affect the dependent variable.

It is extremely rare in normal political science analysis for variables to be recoded to ensure that all the relationships are positive. We shall

Table 13.7: Logistic regression explaining Obama vote by positions on the Iraq war, abortion, and government services.

Dependent Variable: Voted for Barack Obama (versus John McCain)

Overall Equation

−2 Log Likelihood	647.026
Chi Square	268.402
Significance	0.0004
a	0.21
Pseudo R^2	0.30

Separate Effects of Independent Variables	b	St. Er	t	Sig.	Adjusted Odds Ratio
Pro- or Neutral Iraq War	−2.26	0.215	−10.47	0.0004	0.11
Pro-Choice on Abortion	1.06	0.205	5.17	0.0004	2.89
Want More Government Services	0.96	0.202	4.76	0.0004	2.62

start then by seeing what happens when positions on the Iraq War are reversed with people who support or were neutral toward the War are coded one, while opponents are coded zero. Table 13.7 reports the results when this indicator of views about Iraq is combined with support for abortion and for more government services to explain who voted for Barack Obama. The statistics summarizing the overall equation at the top of the table are exactly the same as they were in Table 13.5 with the exception that the constant a changed because of the negative relationship for position on Iraq. Otherwise, there was no change whatsoever in the combined impact of the three explanatory factors, as indicated by Pseudo R^2, −2 LL, and Chi Square and its statistical significance.

There is obviously a much bigger difference from the initial results in Table 13.5 in the statistics about the individual effects of the independent variables in the bottom half of Table 13.7. Yet even here, changing the direction of the association between attitudes about the Iraq War and presidential vote had only a limited impact. In particular, there was no change whatsoever in any of the statistics about how abortion and government services influenced support for Obama. The b and t for the Iraq War changed from positive to negative, but remained the same in numerical value; and the standard error and statistical significance did not change. The one huge difference is in the AOR. The AOR was 9.53 for opposition to the Iraq War but became a small decimal (0.11) when the direction of the relationship is reversed to negative. This is because the natural log of a negative number is a decimal that gets smaller for lower numbers. Consequently, when both positive and negative relationships are included in a multivariate logistic regression, the AORs cannot be compared to estimate the relative impact of the independent variables.

Many logistic regressions include interval variables among their explanatory items. As an illustration, let us replace the dichotomy of whether someone wanted or did not want more government services in Table 13.7 with a seven-point scale that goes from "provide many fewer services" to "provide many more services".[9] The results for this logit in Table 13.8 indicate that this did produce some marginal changes in the relationships, but there was no essential difference in how these three attitudes influenced presidential vote in 2008. For the overall equation, the finer distinctions that could be made among a respondent's support or opposition to expanding the federal government resulted in a slight increase in the predictive power of the logistic equation. For example, the Pseudo R^2 increased from 0.30 to 0.33; and, correspondingly, the Chi Square increased slightly and the -2 LL decreased slightly.

Unlike simply reversing the direction of Obama vote with views about the Iraq War, using a different metric for one of the independent variables does affect how the other two (positions on the Iraq War and abortion) influenced presidential vote, as their b's, standard errors, t's, and AOR's changed slightly. However, these differences were so small that they were not really substantively meaningful. The big change was in the statistics for government services. Because values on this variable now varied between one and seven instead of zero and one, a one-unit change now had considerably less of an absolute impact on a voter's tendency to support Obama. Consequently, b dropped from 0.96 to 0.43; and the AOR from 2.62 to 1.54. This does not mean that the overall independent influence of attitudes about

---

[9] As discussed in the "Levels of Measurement" section of Chapter 6, this is not technically an interval variable, but it does illustrate these effects quite well.

Table 13.8: Logistic regression explaining Obama vote by positions on the Iraq war, abortion, and government services.

Dependent Variable: Voted for Barack Obama (versus John McCain)

Overall Equation

−2 Log Likelihood	624.458
Chi Square	289.957
Significance	0.0004
a	−1.433
Pseudo R^2	0.33

Separate Effects of Independent Variables	b	St. Er	t	Sig.	Adjusted Odds Ratio
Pro-Iraq War	−2.16	0.219	−9.87	0.0004	0.12
Pro-Choice on Abortion	1.06	0.209	5.06	0.0004	2.87
Want More Government Services (seven-point scale)	0.43	0.068	6.38	0.0004	1.54

the role of government went down, however. Rather, the standard error of b was reduced even more proportionately from 0.202 to 0.068; so that the t test statistic actually went up from 4.76 to 6.83. Finally, the fact that there are now seven categories in this independent variable greatly reduces the meaningfulness of calculating the probability that someone in any particular category would be an Obama voter because it no longer represents the overall impact of the explanatory factor.

All three of the explanatory items used here have a neutral category; so that when they are recoded into dichotomies, the neutral category must be combined with one of the other positions on an issue. For example, neutral and pro-life responses were combined to create a category of opposition to pro-choice on abortion. This can create something of an "apples and oranges" situation. To avoid this problem, the categories of an independent variable are often broken up into several dichotomous **dummy variables** that are coded zero and one. If this is done, at least one category of the original variable must not be included in the dummy variables because it serves as a **baseline** against which the effects of the dummy variables can be compared.

Table 13.9: Logistic regression explaining Obama vote by positions on the Iraq war, abortion, and government services.

Dependent Variable: Voted for Barack Obama (versus John McCain)

Overall Equation

−2 Log Likelihood	624.10
Chi Square	290.30
Significance	0.0004
a	−1.33
Pseudo R^2	0.33

Separate Effects of Independent Variables	b	St. Er	t	Sig.	Adjusted Odds Ratio
Pro-Iraq War	−2.15	0.219	−9.82	0.0004	0.12
Want More Government Services (seven-point scale)	0.43	0.068	6.37	0.0004	1.54
Pro-Choice on Abortion	0.95	0.272	3.50	0.001	2.59
Pro-Life on Abortion	−0.16	0.274	−0.59	0.56	0.88

To illustrate this technique, attitudes about abortion were divided into the two dummy variables of pro-life and pro-choice with the intermediate category of "if a clear need" being used as the baseline. Table 13.9 presents the results of the logistic regression of Obama vote on these two dummy variables, the seven-point scale of government services, and the dummy variable of approval of the Iraq War for which approval and neutral are coded one.

Comparing the results in Tables 13.8 and 13.9 shows that this new way of analyzing abortion had very little impact on the other results. For the overall equation, Pseudo R^2 remained 0.33; and the decrease in −2 LL and increase in Chi Square were minuscule. Similarly, the b's, standard errors, t's, significances, and AORs for attitudes about the Iraq War and government services were almost exactly the same for both treatments of abortion.

One would expect that pro-choice respondents would be more likely to vote for Obama than those in the intermediate category, while pro-lifers should be less likely. This indeed turns out to be the case since b is positive for pro-choice and negative for pro-life. The size of these differences varies substantially, however. People who

Table 13.10: Logistic regression explaining Obama vote by positions on the Iraq war, abortion, and government services.

Dependent Variable: Voted for Barack Obama (versus John McCain)

Overall Equation

−2 Log Likelihood	624.10
Chi Square	290.30
Significance	0.0004
Pseudo R^2	0.33

Separate Effects of Independent Variables	b	St. Er	Sig.
Pro-Iraq War	−2.15	0.219	0.0004
Want More Government Services (seven-point scale)	0.43	0.068	0.0004
Pro-Choice on Abortion	0.95	0.272	0.001
Pro-Life on Abortion	−0.16	0.274	0.56

were pro-choice were much more likely to vote for Obama than those in the intermediate category as indicated by a b of 0.95 and an AOR of 2.59 that were statistically significant at the 0.001 level. In contrast, the lower likelihood of pro-life respondents supporting Obama was nowhere near being statistically significant as its t had a significance level of 0.56.

Finally, three of the four AORs in Table 13.9 do not represent independent variables that are dichotomies with positive relationships with Obama vote, which makes directly comparing them impossible. This implies that reporting these results is not particularly helpful. Indeed, most political science presentations of logistic regressions are somewhat simpler than Table 13.9. For the overall equation, −2 LL, Chi Square, significance level, and Pseudo R^2 are included, as are b, the standard error, and the statistical significance for the individual effects of the explanatory variables. Table 13.10 makes such a presentation for the data in Table 13.9. This has the advantage of highlighting the key results of how strong the combined impact of the independent variables is and of the direction and significance of each one's individual influence.

EXERCISES

1. Discuss the results of the following logistic regression showing the impact of three political attitudes on presidential voting in 2008. What would be the hypotheses about how the independent variables should affect voter choice? How strong and significant is the combined impact of the independent variables? Which specific hypotheses are supported and which are not? Make sure that you include an analysis of the AORs in your discussion.

   Dependent Variable: VOTED FOR BARACK OBAMA (versus JOHN McCAIN)

   Overall Equation

-2 Log Likelihood	734.69
Chi Square	265.87
Significance	0.0004
a	-1.67
Pseudo R^2	0.27

Separate Effects of Independent Variables	b	St. Er	t	Sig.	Adjusted Odds Ratio
Graduated Tax	0.88	0.19	4.68	0.0004	2.40
Universal Health Care	1.82	0.19	9.82	0.0004	6.18
Gay Marriage	1.66	0.20	8.29	0.0004	5.24

2. Using the data in Exercise #1, calculate the probabilities that people with particular combinations of the three attitudes voted for Obama. What do these figures tell us about how these independent variables influenced voting?

Conclusion

Chapter 14

The Joy and Challenge of the Jigsaw Puzzles in Political Research

Our excursion into the world of political science research using quantitative data and methods examined the characteristics of 2,102 American voters and 21 advanced industrial democracies in some detail. Even the fairly basic statistical analyses about the variables in these data sets and the relationships among them that were used to illustrate this text give a good indication of the important and interesting insights that such research can yield, as well as the significant limitations that exist on its findings. In short, quantitative research can provide valuable and vital information about the fundamental questions that political scientists ask. However, while such research can tell us some very important things, it cannot tell us everything.

Let us consider a basic question that this book posed about the political crossroads at which the U.S. seemingly stands today. This asked whether Americans are primarily conservative or liberal on the assumption that knowing the public's ideological predisposition might give us a good idea of where our politics are headed. The answer that we got to this question was either sophisticated and nuanced or confusing and muddled, depending upon one's love or tolerance for ambiguity. Americans are clearly quite conservative on many issues but also quite liberal on others. What this portends for the future of American politics is clearly unclear! Neither of the two dominant ideologies or policy packages appear to fit the bill of popular preference, yet no alternative new public philosophy that is more in line with current citizen attitudes seems to be on the horizon either.

Similarly, the analysis of the advanced industrial nations produced ambiguous results when we examined the arguments of conservatives and liberals about how their philosophies work in the real world. Conservatives contend that smaller government will lead to better economic performance, while liberals argue that bigger government will help produce better social outcomes. Grinding the data through the computer supports both these hypotheses with minor caveats that need not detain us here. This obviously leaves the neutral policy analyst rather confused since what makes one type of desired outcome better seemingly makes another worse. Just as with the public opinion data, liberals and conservatives can both celebrate. However, their debate remains far from resolved.

This concluding chapter seeks to show the contribution that quantitative research can make to political science by situating it within the broader discipline. Section 14.1 briefly discusses both the advantages and disadvantages of the findings developed here about public opinion in the United States and factors affecting the economic and social performance of developed countries for attacking the principal problems posited by the different theoretical approaches or paradigms summarized in Chapter 4. Section 14.2 then reverses this logic and asks what these different approaches might contribute in making the type of quantitative analysis reported in this book more fully responsive to the research questions that seemingly motivate it.

14.1 HOW OUR QUANTITATIVE RESEARCH RELATES TO THE PARADIGMS IN POLITICAL STUDIES

When one considers the full panorama of the paradigms that have dominated the study of politics at one time or another, our endeavors in this book — which would constitute the second type of political behavioralism in Table 4.1 in Chapter 4 — might look rather limited and small. Yet, just because these paradigms have different emphases

The Joy and Challenge of the Jigsaw Puzzles in Political Research 333

PARADIGM	RELATION TO ANALYSES OF PUBLIC OPINION AND NATIONAL ATTRIBUTES
Policy Prescription Machiavelli	Subject matter (citizen attitudes and effects of policies) highly relevant
General Patterns of Govt Montesquieu	Analysis of effects of big government reflects Montesquieu's approach
Historicism Hegel and Marx	Too limited to have much relevance because they only describe situation at one point in time
Formal Institutions I. Normative basis II. Democratization III. Traditional Pol. Sc.	Largely irrelevant to philosophical and legal analysis, though knowledge of citizen attitudes and policy effects might be of some interest
Behavioralism I. Informal politics II. Scientific approach	I. Limited significantly by data availability II. Prime representatives of this approach
Return to Theory I. Economic II. New institutionalism III. Post-modern	I. Could provide test of theoretical predictions II. Could use results, but would add qualitative analysis III. Reject approach as primitive positivism

Figure 14.1: How analyses of public opinion and national attributes relate to the paradigms in studies of politics.

and are directed toward somewhat different research questions, does not mean that they are necessarily antithetical or that they do not overlap in significant ways. In fact, as outlined in Figure 14.1, even the admittedly preliminary results that we have from quantitative research on the U.S. public opinion and the effects of government orientation and policy in the developed world have some relevance for the themes and issues addressed by many of these paradigms.

In particular, quantitative analysis about the behavior of individuals and governments, the principal component of Behavioralism II, would seem especially appropriate for testing many of the economic theories that have been developed as part of Return to Theory I. These models or theories are derived deductively from basic premises about how individuals, interest groups, or governments should act if they apply the economic logic of interest maximization to their political actions. Thus, empirical analysis of these hypothesized relationships should be quite valuable for developing economic theories of politics.

For example, it is widely assumed that entrepreneurs and the wealthy prefer small government, while the poor and the dependent prefer large government. The findings that small governments have been more economically dynamic and that large governments produce better social outcomes, therefore, imply that both sets of citizens are, indeed, correct in their expectations about how the role of government is linked to their specific rational interests.

Yet, our research also shows that the world is far messier and more ambiguous than the neat economic models assumed. The logic in the preceding paragraph would certainly predict that wealth and income should have a very strong impact on ideology and partisanship in the United States and elsewhere in the developed world. Yet, in 2008, there was only a weak association between family income and conservatism among Americans. This certainly suggests that applying simple economic logic to the political realm, while valuable and insightful, does not tell the whole story by a long shot — although the proponents of these theories might retort that such behavioral research has only turned up fairly inconsequential "noise" that really does not challenge the essence of their models.

In theory at least, quantitative research in political science and economics should prove sufficient to test many, if not most, of the hypotheses and propositions in economic theory. This is not true for any of the other paradigms or approaches because they contain elements that are not amenable to quantitative analysis. However, with the caveat that quantitative findings need to be integrated with additional qualitative materials, quantitative behavioral research should be quite valuable to several of these other paradigms. In particular, the logic of relating differences in characteristics of governments to their socioeconomic context and policy outcomes, which formed the core of the analysis in Chapters 11 and 12, is exactly the same as Montesquieu's attempts to find large-scale patterns about political regimes. The current New Institutionalism, moreover, is quite similar in its research agenda as well. Both of these theoretical approaches, therefore, could use statistical results such as those developed in this text, although both would go beyond the "primitive positivism" of relying upon just quantitative data.

The relevance of quantified behavioral analysis to the other approaches included in Figure 14.1 varies considerably. Both public opinion data and aggregate data on political units can give us quite a bit of information on political parties, interest groups, and (to a lesser extent) elites, although the full exploration of such Informal Politics almost inevitably must rely upon qualitative case studies. In addition, policy advice from Machiavelli to Karl Rove should certainly find the subject matters of citizen attitudes and of the effects of policies and strategies highly relevant even if subject to spin-doctoring. In contrast, the type of research represented by this text would be tangential, at best, for the other three paradigms. Political behavior is an alternative subject to Formal Institutions; Historicism with its grand sweep of different eras would probably see such research as exceedingly time bound; and Post-Modernism would certainly decry this approach as reflecting the worst of primitive positivism and limited perspective.

14.2 EXPANDING THE RESPONSE TO THE RESEARCH QUESTIONS MOTIVATING QUANTITATIVE ANALYSIS

The quantitative analysis of politics, in addition, might well benefit from looking to the past and at least considering the relevance of the questions that different paradigms raised for the issues or problems that we consider important are today. This is really the reverse of the point made in Figure 14.1 that even the very limited and preliminary analyses of quantitative behavioralism presented in this book provide findings of at least some relevance for most of the other paradigms in political studies.

This text has been organized around two sets of questions that appear critical for predicting what direction the United States will take from the political and economic crossroads at which it stands as the 21st century opens. First, the questions of whether Americans are conservative or liberal in their political beliefs and what makes them differ in ideological orientations would seem critical factors in determining what direction our nation will take away from the current even balance and gridlock in partisanship. Second, how America's economic and social performance rates internationally and what leads to better outcomes among the developed nations are certainly relevant in deciding whether we should anticipate rising expectations or declining fortunes.

Figure 14.2 presents an overview of how the different paradigms could contribute to the analysis of these issues and questions. The quantitative behavioralism that forms the core of the analysis in this book (Part II of the fifth row in Figure 14.2) can provide a good first approximation of the answers to the basic questions about whether Americans consider themselves conservatives or liberals, about what makes an individual more or less likely to be conservative, about how America's performance in various areas compares to those of other developed nations, and about whether various political strategies produce good or ill results. Yet, as we have seen repeatedly throughout this book, the answers provided by this type of data analysis are far from conclusive. For example, Americans evidently want both conservative and liberal policies; and, moreover, liberal policies seem to work better on some issues and conservative policy on others.

If the quantitative behavioral paradigm cannot answer all our questions, almost every other paradigm in Figure 14.2 can either be a source of some answers or contribute some interesting and vital questions as well. Almost certainly, the path we take from our current political crossroads will be determined by Machiavellian policy advisors for either the Democratic or Republican party who can come up with a policy package that is attractive enough to win it majority support and the domination of national politics for an extended period of time. Perhaps, an inspired policy entrepreneur will be able to make either conservatism or liberalism more attractive or perhaps a new public philosophy will emerge from the public's demand for key aspects of both of our currently competing doctrines.

There is far more to political success than just spin-doctoring, though. Citizens tend to be pragmatic in the sense that they reward parties that are seen as bringing good times and punish the ones associated with hard times. Here, we move to the more theoretical question of what policies work under what conditions. This turns attention to the basic questions raised by Montesquieu about the general patterns of government and policy outcomes. In contemporary

PARADIGM	CONTRIBUTION TO ANALYSES OF PUBLIC OPINION AND NATIONAL ATTRIBUTES
Policy Prescription Machiavelli	Create policy packages that would appeal to important constituencies
General Patterns of Govt Montesquieu	Indicate what types of policies would be effective
Historicism Hegel and Marx	Make theorists sensitive to possible discontinuities between industrial and information ages
Formal Institutions I. Normative basis II. Democratization III. Traditional Pol. Sc.	I. & II. Renewed question of what basic social contract is III. Check whether formal institutions and laws affect policy outcomes
Behavioralism I. Informal politics II. Scientific approach	I. Relation of informal politics to issue & policy effects II. Means of testing policy effectiveness & public desires
Return to Theory I. Economic II. New institutionalism III. Post-modern	I. Good model for formulating policy alternatives and conceptualizing splits in public opinion II. Indicate what types of policies would be effective III. Show need for challenging conventional assumptions

Figure 14.2: What different paradigms could contribute to studies of American ideology and of the economic and social performance of developed nations.

terms, economic theory and the theories associated with the new institutionalism offer differing perspectives on how to attack this question. In addition to their somewhat different subject matters, the former emphasizes deductive theory based on a central explanatory principle, while the latter is more inductive and far more inclusive in the potential explanatory variables, which also suggests the importance of informal politics and other factors that are best studied by qualitative methods.

Several of the other paradigms raise more radical questions for our consideration. Historicism, for example, views societies as moving or evolving through a series of stages with very distinct social, economic, and political relations. Such a transformation may be occurring today in the United States and elsewhere in the developed world as we move from the industrial age to the information age or what Alvin and Heidi Toffler have termed *The Third Wave* (the first two waves being agricultural and industrial societies).[1] If this is so, the disputes between conservatives and liberals over the role of government, which are rooted in the issues of the industrial age, may be becoming somewhat *passé*.

Second, such speculation about fundamental change in the nature of society and government suggests that it might be time to revisit fundamental normative questions about the nature of the "social contract" involved in democracy. After all, conservatives and liberals do not just fight over the role of government because they think that big government produces good or bad results. Rather, their disagreement reflects profound ethical concerns about the nature of the relationship between individuals and their society. Is a large welfare state necessary to ensure the attainment of the conditions posited by such theorists as John Rawls[2] for social justice and equity? Or, does large government constitute a major step on *The Road to Serfdom*,[3] as argued by Friedrich von Hayek?

Finally, post-modern theory accentuates both of these theoretical calls to **move beyond normal science**. Its emphasis on the vital importance of context for understanding and interpreting social phenomena goes beyond the implications of historicism in focusing attention on transformations in basic economic, political, and social relationships. Likewise, its commitment to deconstructing conventional images and assumptions, especially in terms of whether they simply serve as rationales for existing power relationships, underscores the inevitable normative components of political analysis and serves as a call for "transformational politics" to transcend normal science.

14.3 THE JOY AND CHALLENGE OF THE JIGSAW PUZZLES IN POLITICAL RESEARCH

Chapter 4's consideration of the paradigm shifts in the study of politics and of the different approaches to even quantitative analysis implies several reasons for those engaged in political analysis to exercise some

---

[1] Alvin Toffler, *The Third Wave* (New York: Bantam Books, 1981).
[2] John Rawls, *A Theory of Justice* (Cambridge, MA: Belknap Press, 1971).
[3] Friedrich A. von Hayek, *The Road to Serfdom* (Chicago: University of Chicago Press, 1994).

humility about their endeavors. First, at different times the study of politics has centered upon a wide variety of subjects and approaches. There is little reason to declare one subject the holy grail and reject all the others as trivial. Certainly, there is no methodology capable of structuring these very different types of research programs. Second, if the hot topics and methodologies in the study of politics change fairly regularly, the current dominant paradigm may well be *passé* in the not too distant future. More narrowly perhaps, even within the same scholarly tradition, there may be significantly different approaches that each have distinct advantages and disadvantages.

More broadly and theoretically, the history of the development of many of these paradigms follows what the philosopher of science Abraham Kaplan terms the "law of the instrument" — "Give a small boy a hammer, and he will find that everything he encounters needs pounding."[4] More prosaically, each approach started by focusing upon a "hot" political or intellectual subject and then developed an appropriate methodology for treating the issues at hand. Unfortunately, any methodology restricts what can be studied; and sooner or later scholars reject it as inappropriate for the next hot topic. In Figure 14.1, for example, the distinctly odd couple of formal-legal studies and scientific behavioralism both follow this pattern. Such a sequence, therefore, strongly suggests that in doing today's research we should always have an open mind toward what the transformed research agenda of tomorrow might become.

The humility advocated here, however, definitely should not be confused with cynicism or disdain. That no simple research design or even broad scholarly paradigm can tell us everything that we might want to know in the study of politics certainly does not mean that they cannot tell us anything worth knowing. Rather, all these scholarly traditions focused on subjects that people interested in politics found compelling and exciting at some point in time!

In sum, whatever your interests or political loyalties happen to be, political science has some jigsaw puzzles with which you can play.

---

[4]Abraham Kaplan, *The Conduct of Inquiry: Methodology for Behavioral Science* (San Francisco: Chandler Publishing Company, 1964), p. 28.

Different paradigms overlap somewhat in the puzzles that they lay out; so that specific pieces may fit into several different puzzles simultaneously. Just as with real jigsaws, the more challenging the picture, the more pride of workmanship there is upon completion. Unlike the world of jigsaws, the most exciting and compelling questions in the study of politics usually present us with puzzles that have more than a few pieces missing. Rather than leading political scientists to give up in disgust, though, this should just be a spur to more and better research efforts. For example, even our first steps at analysis have implied that both the nature of American public opinion and the relationships among social, economic, and political factors for developed nations are more complex than either conventional conservative or liberal stereotypes. This argues for developing new perspectives on America's political economy that will require both qualitative and quantitative analyses, both normative and empirical concerns, and both simple descriptions of what is and theoretical understanding of why it occurred. It is hard to believe that such a challenge will be dull or boring!

EXERCISES

1. Big government tends to be good for a nation's social outcomes but bad for its economic performance. Discuss how this statistical finding could be used in the following paradigms in political studies: (1) policy prescription, (2) Montesquieu's general patterns of government, and (3) new institutionalism theory.
2. American are conservative on some issues and liberal on others. How would these findings be treated in the following paradigms in political studies: (1) policy prescription, (2) discussions of "social contracts" as the normative basis of government, and (3) postmodernist theory?

Index

Adjusted odds ratio, 319
Aggregate data, 15, 28
Antecedent variable, 228
Arrow diagrams, 59, 60, 68
Assumptions of multiple regression, 272, 276, 281

bar graph, 35–37, 40
Behavioralism, 76, 79, 94, 332, 333, 335, 336, 339
Benchmark, 241, 258, 260, 269
Business cycle, 2, 5

Categoric variable, 17, 138
Causal model, 271, 272, 285, 287–296, 298, 299
Central limit theorem, 182
Chained multiple regressions, 287
Chi Square, 311, 313, 318, 323, 325–328
Codes, 138–140
Coefficient of Determination (r^2), 250
Coefficient of variability, 153
Computer-assisted telephone interviewing, 175
Concepts, 44–48, 51, 57, 68
Conceptualizing political systems, 99
Conditional relationship, 223
Confidence intervals, 171, 193
Conservatives, 3–5, 8, 11, 12, 16, 20–25, 27, 33, 35, 38, 45, 51, 58, 61–63, 65, 69–71, 77, 93, 94, 106, 199, 209, 210, 212–215, 306, 307, 332, 336, 338

Content analysis, 96, 106–108, 111–118
    Focus of analysis, 113
    Form of analysis, 113
    Type of data, 113, 116
    What is coded, 113
    Who does analysis, 113
Contingent conclusions, 64
Continuous variables, 141
Control variable, 219, 220, 222–225, 228–231, 234–236, 238
Correlation, 241–243, 248–251, 253–258, 260, 262, 264, 266–268
Correlation coefficient (Pearson's r), 249–251
Correlation coefficients, 206, 208, 209, 211, 216, 272, 273
    Multiple R, 272–274, 278, 280–285, 288–290, 294, 298–300
    Multiple R^2, 284, 289, 298–300
Correlation matrix, 209, 210, 216, 217, 255, 268
Cross-cutting cleavages, 165
Crosstabulation, 301–303, 307, 309, 317
Crosstabulation tables, 200, 210
    Cells, 201–204
    Marginal, 202–204, 207
Curvilinear relationship, 265

Data array, 23, 28, 29, 31, 32, 34, 40
Deduction, 56, 57, 65

Democrats, 2–4, 9, 12, 13, 20, 21, 40, 43, 55, 60, 62, 108, 109, 111, 114, 210
Dependent variable, 200–202, 205–207, 215, 217, 219, 223, 224, 228, 229, 231, 232, 235, 236, 243, 245, 248, 258, 260–263, 267, 268, 283, 302–304, 306, 308–312, 315, 317, 318, 322, 323, 325–328
Dichotomy, 302–304, 306, 309, 315, 317, 322, 324
Direct causal impact, 293, 294, 296
Distortions, 124, 126, 128
    Bar graphs, 121–123, 125, 128, 142
    Pictographs, 122, 124, 142
Distributions, 15, 28, 145, 146, 148, 151–153, 158–160, 162, 164, 166, 181–183, 187, 188, 193
    Bimodal, 158, 164
    Flat, 158, 162, 166
    In population, 169–178, 181, 182, 188–195
    In sample, 169–182, 188–195
    Normal, 153, 158–160, 164, 166
    Of sample means, 181, 182
    Polarized, 158, 162, 164–166
    Skewed, 149, 151, 152, 158, 162, 164, 166
Dummy variables, 309, 325, 326

Economic performance, 242–246, 248, 251–254, 257, 258, 276, 277, 279, 286, 287, 290
Elite interviews, 95–97, 99
Empirical theory, 53–56, 61, 70, 72
    Five elements, 54
Experimental approach
    Control group, 83–85, 87, 88
    Experimental group, 83–85, 88
    External validity, 85
    Internal validity, 85

Field studies, 96, 103, 104
Formal-legal studies, 76, 78, 79, 339

Frequency table, 22, 23, 36, 39, 40
    Complex full, 22, 23
    Complex partial, 23
    Simple full, 22

Gallup polls, 180
Gamma, 201, 206–209, 211–214, 216–218

Historicism, 76–78, 335, 337, 338
Hypothesis, 57, 60–64, 66–68, 203, 207, 208, 217

Ideology, 5, 11, 15, 19–22, 28, 116
Independent variables, 200–202, 204–208, 215, 223, 228, 232, 233, 235, 243, 245, 250, 251, 260, 262, 263, 268, 271–276, 278, 280, 282–285, 288–290, 295–300, 302, 304–312, 314, 315, 317–319, 322–328
Indirect causal impact, 293
Inferential statistics, 169–171, 181, 182, 187
Intercept (a), 247, 248, 252
Interpretation, 229–233, 235, 236
Intervening variables, 230, 271, 287, 290, 291, 294
Issues, 3,4, 13, 19, 20, 22–28, 39, 40, 317, 320, 322
    Cultural, 3, 20, 25, 26, 28, 40, 317, 319
    Economic, 3, 20, 23, 24, 28, 317, 319
    Security, 3, 20, 22–25, 28, 317, 319

Lambda, 206, 208, 209, 215
Law of the instrument, 339
Levels of Measurement, 121, 137
    Interval, 138, 140–142
    Nominal, 138, 139, 141
    Ordinal, 138–141
    Ratio, 130, 131, 134, 136, 142
Liberals, 3–5, 8, 11, 12, 16, 20–25, 27, 33, 35, 69–71, 77, 94, 106,

114–116, 210, 212, 213, 215, 216, 306, 332, 336, 338
Line graph, 37, 38, 40
Linear regression, 302–306, 309, 310, 313, 314
Linear relationship, 263
Literary Digest poll, 178–180
Log likelihood, 311, 318, 323, 325–328
Logistic regression, 301–306, 309–315, 317, 318, 322–328

Mean, 146–158, 166, 167
Measures of central tendency, 146, 147, 150–152, 166
    Benchmarking, 153, 167
    Summary of variable, 152
Measures of variability, 153, 154
Median, 147–153, 156–158, 165, 166
Median voter, 165
Mode, 150, 151, 158, 164
Multicollinearity, 272, 282–285
Multiple regression, 271–278, 280–282, 284, 285, 287, 291, 294, 296–298
Multivariate logits, 317
Multivariate tables, 219, 220, 224, 233
    Original bivariate table, 235, 236
    Subtables by control groups, 233

Natural logarithm, 306, 310, 311
Nominal data, 206
Normal distribution, 183, 184, 186
Normal science, 73, 80
Normative theory, 70, 71, 338, 340
Null hypothesis, 191, 192
Null relationship, 205, 206

Odds ratio, 307, 308, 310–312, 314, 318, 319, 323, 325, 326
Ordinal data, 206

Paradigms, 69, 72–76, 332–337, 339, 340
Paradox of large government, 257, 281
Partisanship, 19, 20, 22

Path analysis, 271, 285, 287, 291, 293, 294, 297
Path coefficients, 272, 287, 291, 292, 294
Percentage comparison, 201, 204–206, 304, 305
Percentages, 121, 132–135, 143
    Percentage change, 133, 135–137, 143
    Percentage difference, 133, 135
    Percentage point difference, 143
    Simple difference, 132–135
Pie chart, 37, 38
Population parameters, 170, 193
Predicted value for Y, 272
Probabilities, 304, 305, 315, 316, 319, 321, 328
Probability that a sample comes from a population, 189
Proportionate reduction of error, 314
Pseudo R^2, 311, 314, 318, 323–328
Public opinion, 15–17, 20, 22, 26–28, 33, 36, 40
Public opinion data, 301
Public opinion polls, 15

Qualitative analysis, 96, 98–100, 105, 118
Quantitative case studies, 81, 92
Quantitative research, 331–334
Quasi-experimental designs, 81, 84, 86–89, 94
    Pooled, 90
    Time series, 90, 91

Range, 153–157, 166
Reducing relationship, 228, 231–233, 235
Regression, 241
Regression coefficients, 304
    Standardized (beta), 287
    Unstandardized (b), 272, 275
Relationships, 44, 48, 53, 57–60, 63–68, 197, 200, 208, 210, 212, 213
    One stage, 66

Three stage, 56
Two stage, 65, 67
Reliability, 48–50, 53
Removing relationship, 228, 231, 235
Replicating relationship, 223, 224, 226
Republicans, 2, 3, 9, 12, 13, 20, 21, 40, 43, 44, 55, 60, 65, 108, 109, 111, 114, 199, 209, 210
Residuals analysis, 258, 259, 261
Return to theory, 76, 333
Revealing relationship, 223

Sample statistic, 170
Samples, 170–172, 175–182, 190
    Convenience, 173, 177, 178
    Quota, 173, 175, 177, 180
    Random, 171–175, 178, 180–182, 195
    Stratified, 173, 175–177
    Systematic, 173–175, 192
Sampling distribution, 170, 181–183, 188–191
Sampling error, 19, 170, 193
Scatterplot, 241–243, 245, 246, 249, 251
Slope (b), 248, 251, 252
Social performance, 242, 252, 257, 272, 281
Socioeconomic model of voting, 60, 65
Spurious correlation, 294
Spurious relationship, 230
Standard deviation, 153–156
Standard error of (b), 251, 325

Standard error of mean, 190
Statistical significance, 190, 192, 193, 201, 207–209, 243, 250, 251, 266, 267, 272, 276, 282, 311, 313, 314, 323, 324, 327
    F test, 251
    T test, 251
    One-tailed test, 192
    Two-tailed test, 192, 193
Statistical statements, 63, 64
Statisticulation, 126, 127, 129, 131, 136
Summary statistics, 145, 146, 150, 152, 154, 156

Theoretical models, 58, 59, 64, 67, 68
    Antecedent variable, 60
    Dependent variable, 60, 61
    Independent variable, 60, 61
    Invervening variables, 60

Universal statements, 63

Valid percentage, 19, 36
Validity, 48–51, 53, 67, 68
    Construct, 51
    Convergent, 51
    Criterion, 51
    Face, 50, 51, 53
Variance, 153, 154
Voting, 8, 10, 11, 16, 18, 19, 22

Z scores, 183, 185–187, 189, 190

CPSIA information can be obtained
at www.ICGtesting.com
Printed in the USA
LVOW04*1833181115
463165LV00022B/310/P

Augsburg College
Lindell Library
Minneapolis, MN 55454